Stepfamily Life Can Be Hell But It Doesn't Have to Be!

7 Steps to Recreating Family

Annette T. Brandes, Ph.D.

"This is an original, provocative, and practical book, offering guidance and inspiration to couples struggling with the dynamics of the ready-made family. Brandes is an expert who takes us quickly to the bottom line of what is necessary to create a harmonious family that includes children birthed in the previous relationships of one or both partners. I highly recommend it."

BARBARA DE ANGELIS, PH. D.
author of *Secrets About Life Every Woman Should Know*.
Also by De Angelis, *Are You the One for Me?*,
Real Moments, and *Make Love All the Time*

"A MUST READ—will expand your parenting skills and quality of family life. Will bring out one's potential for self-healing. If you are dedicated to growth, this book is essential."

STEPHEN AND ONDREA LEVINE
authors of *Embracing the Beloved: Relationship as a Path of Awakening*.
Also by Stephen Levine, *Healing into Life and Death*,
Who Dies?, and *A Gradual Awakening*

"Annette Brandes brings a wealth of experience and vivid examples to this up-to-date, rich, and practical book. She avoids the old 'stepfamily' terminology and focuses on creative and realistic strategies to help 'new-families' face the difficult issues of 'family recreated by new partnerships'. The richly described process of patiently building caring and stable new-families can be useful to any partners or parents wanting to enrich their lives together."

ALETTA J. HUDGENS, PH. D.
Licensed Marriage and Family Therapist
Licensed Psychologist, St. Paul, Minnesota

Stepfamily Life Can Be Hell But It Doesn't Have to Be!

7 Steps to Recreating Family

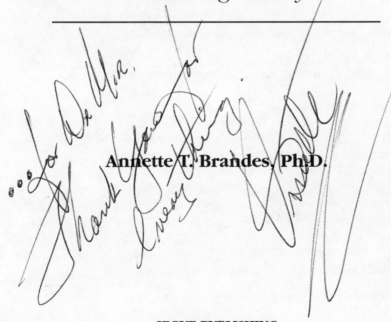

Annette T. Brandes, Ph.D.

SEGUE PUBLISHING
Henderson, Nevada

Portions of this book are derived from real events, but each character is fictional, a composite of numerous case histories and imagination informed by experience. Reference to living persons is not intended and should not be inferred.

Cover and illustrations by Carolyn Johnson
Interior design and typesetting by Sue Knopf
Photography by Elizabeth Edelman

Library of Congress Cataloging-in-Publication Data

Brandes, Annette T.
   Stepfamily life can be hell but it doesn't have to be! : 7 steps to recreating family / Annette T. Brandes. - - 1 st ed.
   p. cm.
   Includes bibliographical references and index.
   LCCN: 99-90414
   ISBN: 0-9671343-3-1

   1. Stepfamilies. 2. Stepparents.
   3. Parenting.   I. Title

HQ759.92.B73 2000   646.7'8
                                  QBI99-623

To Grace and Dick Hegman,

my aunt and uncle

Thank you for being

the unaffected joy and beauty

of a bonded, loving relationship.

Your loving kindness toward each other,

and those around you,

is a source of inspiration

and an example to which I aspire.

I love you.

Contents

Preface ix

Introduction: "A Home Torn by Conflict Is a Madhouse" 1
  About This Book. 2
  How This Book Is Different: Structure Defines Relationships . . . 4
  The Problem: Life in New-Family Can Be Hell 5
  Save Your Marriage: Become Parenting Partners 9
  The Ongoing Challenge: To Change Expectations. 9
  The Goal of This Book. 12

1. Sign-On: "I've Been Hurt Before; Will I be Hurt Again?". . . . 13
  Introduction: What It Means to Sign-On 14
  The Problem: Fear Undermines Ability to Commit. 15
  Save Your Marriage: How to Sign-On. 19
  The Ongoing Challenge: Managing Fear. 24
  Exercise: Clarifying Fear 27

2. Unite: "You Love Those Kids More Than You Love Me!" . . . 35
  Introduction: Divided Loyalties Create Divisions 36
  The Dance: It's Not the Two-Step—It's the Death Spiral 37
  The Problem: Anger Undermines Bonding 41
  Save Your Marriage: How to Unite 44
  The Ongoing Challenge: To Keep the Loving Alive 47
  Exercise: Transforming Anger through Meditation 51
  Exercise: Managing Acute Episodes of Anger 53
  Exercise: The Lovership 55

3. Cooperate: "The Kids Are Running Our Life!" 57
  Introduction: Powerlessness Yields Powerfulness 58
  The Problem: Insolence, Authoritarianism, Chaos 60
  Save Your Marriage: How to Cooperate 65
  The Ongoing Challenge: To Not Alienate the Children. 83
  Exercise: "You Expect Me to What?" 94
  Exercise: Meeting Your Self-Images 96

4. Create: "Your Ex Is Running Our Life!" 97
  Introduction: Possessiveness Causes Power Struggles. 98
  The Problem: Children Caught in the Middle 103
  Save Your Marriage: How to Create 118
  The Ongoing Challenge: To Resist Temptations
    to be Possessive 133

5. Establish: "Who the Hell Am I Here?" 137

    Introduction: Children Resent New-Parent Power 138

    The Problem: Jealousy Leads Partners into Blaming. 142

    Save Your Marriage: Get a Role for the New-parent. 148

    The Ongoing Challenge: To Not Become Overly Powerful . . . 164

6. Solidify: "If I'm So Happy, Why Am I Sad?" 167

    Introduction: Children Resist Becoming New-family. 168

    The Problem: Grief Follows Loss of the Dream. 172

    Save Your Marriage: How to Solidify 175

    The Ongoing Challenge: To Accept Differing Needs
       for Closeness 193

    Exercise: Define New-Family. 199

    Exercise: Define New-Family Expectations 204

7. Support: "I Feel Like Giving Up" 205

    Introduction: New-family Life Doesn't Have to be Hell. 206

    The Problem: Fatigue Leads to Despair 211

    Save Your Marriage: How to Support 212

    The Ongoing Challenge: To Keep Learning, Adjusting
       and Renewing 224

    Exercise: Identifying and Meeting Personal Needs 227

Appendices 229

    Appendix A: Managing Money—Dollar, Dollar,
       Who's Got the Dollar?. 230

    Appendix B: Exercises for Those Still Undecided
       Continued from Chapter One. 238

    Appendix C: Custody and Visitation Alternatives 243

Readings. 246

Acknowledgments 249

About the Author. 252

Index 253

Reader Response Form. 256

Ordering Information 257

Preface

Are you . . .

- Constantly caught between your partner and your kids?

- Often overwhelmed by conflict and chaos?

- Feeling angry most of the time?

- Sick of being cast in the role of "step-monster?"

- Ready to call it quits?

- Ready to pull your hair out?

- Ready to pull your partner's hair out?

- Ready to pull your partner's kid's hair out?

- Unable to find the partner you once loved?

- Not making love anymore?

- Worried because the children seem depressed or unusually combative?

- Concerned because the children's school performance has slipped?

- Uncertain about how best to handle the children's complaints about living out of suitcases and hating visitation?

- Sick of self-help books that don't give you much help?

If you answered yes to any of the above, then this book is for you.

When family is recreated by new partnerships following divorce or the death of a partner, the recreation process is at best difficult. The journey to successful co-leadership in a home is fraught with peril. Picture a couple and their children in a small rowboat on the high seas where heavy wind and turbulent waves threaten their efforts to survive. This imaginative picture is symbolic of many real life situations where the reasons for difficulties are many, and the solutions complicated and demanding. Nevertheless, the waves can be negotiated and the winds of the storm can be calmed.

This book is about the *how* of navigating a difficult and sometimes perilous course. It presents a program that has helped many couples find their way to safe harbor. Their arrival testifies to the triumph of their union and the achievement of family community. When family that is satisfying and fulfilling is the center around which all else in life dances, its members are empowered by security and warmth. Partners in new-family can learn to provide leadership that creates emotionally safe and cooperative environments wherein everyone thrives.

In this book, I share the most significant learning in a fifteen-year professional journey working with individuals in *new-family*. That journey is replete with success and struggle, both professionally and personally. It is one thing to be a successful therapist and another entirely to be a successful *new-parent*. What can seem so clear when looking, as a therapist, across the room at a new-family can be very unclear when gazing, as a new-parent, across the dinner table at children who do not think you have a clue. So, it is out of a struggle that this work was born—the desire to be a good therapist on the one hand, and the recognition, on the other hand, that as a new-parent my flaws were at times a barrier to that which I most desired to achieve. I strove, therefore, to write the book I needed twenty years ago.

At the back of the book there is a form inviting readers to provide feedback about its contents, and to share aspects of their journey they believe may be helpful to others. Some of that information will be included in future editions of this book. All readers are invited to respond.

In the closing paragraph of Chapter Five I write the following:

> The ability to express caring through compassion
> is the greatest power parents can hold. This power
> refuses to strike out, harm, demean, belittle, abuse,
> reject, or shun. Anyone can get angry; anyone can
> express anger angrily. There is no skill required.
> The skill, however, to manager anger, to turn its

> energy away from power that can harm and toward
> compassion, reconciliation, and healing, is the
> nobility inherent in acting from one's Greater Self.
> It is a manifestation of God within.

My belief in the power of caring family, and our ability as human beings to achieve nobility, has driven my work and my efforts. Stable, loving and bonded family is the fertile foundation of a purposeful, sturdy society and the soil from which the trees of individual meaning draw nourishment. People with caring family are not homeless, they are not alone, and they are not adrift on a sea of meaninglessness. In spite of all that has been said about family, and dysfunctional family in particular, there is no greater anchor, no greater wellspring of joy and goodness, than loving family. I wish all new-families success and, indeed, hope that many will be helped by this work.

The Presentation

There are some unique aspects of the written presentation. It will be helpful to know these before beginning. I use *partners* as a singular (this partner or this set of partners) and as a plural (all partners or sets of partners). Every effort is made to clarify which usage is being utilized. There are also times when "they" is used to refer to the singular his or her. This improves readability by eliminating multiple uses of his or her.

I often refer to children and teens collectively as kids. I know kids are young goats—and that some new-parents may think the comparison all too classic—but I use it because in spoken American English we refer to children as kids. Couples in my office talk about his kids, her kids, their kids, and sometimes *those* kids. Kids are seldom spoken of as children. When writing about categories of kids such as teens or young children, I note which group is being referenced.

The reader should note that the titles *new-parent, other-mother* and *other-father* are used interchangeably, depending on the context, to refer to the non-biological parent in the home.

Although this work is written specifically for couples in new-family, counselors and therapists will find it a very helpful resource. The instructional aspects of the presentation can be integrated into a therapeutic treatment plan. Because this book presents the basic building blocks of partnership and family, couples just starting a biological family or those who have young children will also find it useful. The guidance offered can help partners create a foundation upon which functional and cooperative family can be built. It may help partners foresee potentially destructive dilemmas and methods of dealing with many of them.

INTRODUCTION:

A Home Torn
by Conflict Is
a Mad*house*

Introduction

About This Book

One of the fastest growing social phenomena in our society is *new-family*. Individuals create new-family when they become coupled and one or both have children from a previous relationship. These couples may be married or domestic partners; they may be heterosexual couples or same-sex couples. Regardless of how they are categorized, all new-family couples who implement the steps explained in the following chapters will benefit. This is especially so for those whose relationships are suffering because of complications related to the children.

This work was originally undertaken as an answer to requests from clients for a survival guide. In its present form it provides strategies for couples creating new-family. The new-family model is a positive framework for building what has traditionally been known as stepfamily. Unfortunately, a great deal of negativity has become associated with stepfamily, and this negativity works against the implementation of positive parenting roles and healthy interpersonal relationships. It will become clear to the reader familiar with stepfamily how the new-family model differs. This book does not specifically outline those differences.

This book is about ending the war created by complications. It is about the *how* of building parenting partnerships that bring couples to the forefront of leadership in their home. It is about the *how* of creating positive parenting relationships between adults and their non-offspring children. It is about the *how* of accomplishing seven critical tasks that increase the likelihood of the marital relationship not only surviving but thriving. To survive means to endure; to thrive means to enrich the loving sentiments and romance that created the arrangement in the first place. Only about forty percent of couples who begin a new family survive, and few thrive.

As a psychologist I devoted my practice to working almost exclusively with couples and children in new-family. As my practice developed, many of my referrals came from other therapists, and many couples arrived with their relationships in complete disarray and on the verge of disintegration. The reader should take into consideration, therefore, that the viewpoint of this book is informed by experience ministering in the trenches of stepfamily wars. Not all couples will find their relationships in the extensive disarray cited in some of the examples. Nevertheless, they will learn principles that will guide them in recreating family and enhancing the quality of their marriage.

My initial efforts with couples often required the creation of a demilitarized zone so that a peaceful coexistence could be negotiated. Once war has begun, there must be rules for disengagement so that cooperation can be established. Without cooperation, a home remains divided against itself. Anything better or loftier than peaceful coexistence, be it harmony, congenial interdependence or loving kindness, emerges from a base of emotional safety developed in the presence of cooperative exchange. When there is war in a home, there is anger and disregard for the emotional welfare of family members. In order for civility to prevail, anger must be managed and the war must end.

Tragically, new-family arrangements are very unstable. According to the Stepfamily Foundation of New York, sixty percent of stepfamily arrangements end. This high rate of failure is the result of complications associated with integrating children into new relationships. In new-family, biological parents become confused and caught in the middle. New-parents find few, if any, guidelines or guideposts for determining their appropriate role. Children become angry and lonely in a world that seems foreign and hostile. Grief and sadness prevail and turn to anger.

Can this downward spiral of failure that plagues new-family be stopped? It is the premise of this book that it can and that there are basic steps couples can take to improve their chances of creating a satisfactory living together arrangement. These steps create a structure supporting an environment wherein emotionally safe relationships can develop and grow. As couples acquire skills inherent in each step, their relationship is enriched.

How This Book Is Different:
Structure Defines Relationships

This book differs from those that focus on the family traditionally called stepfamily. Stepfamily identity casts family members in negative roles that undermine their positive efforts to build new relationships. The *wicked stepmother, stepmonster* and *stepchild* are examples of negative roles that condition everyone to expect the worst. These and other negatively perpetuated images cause family members to regard the stepfamily as anything but special or unique. They tend, instead, to think of their newly acquired family as the bastard child of a *real family*.

This book presents new ways of thinking about and creating *family—new-family*. It does not refer to new-family as *stepfamily* or *blended family*. This is because new-family is not a step anything. New-family is a very special and unique family unit, but it does not become a big happy sitcom family.

New-family is not a blended family because individuals coming into new-family do not merge into a singular identity resembling that of a biological family—or what will be referred to as *first-family*. Almost everyone with experience in new-family knows that children's resistance to joining in is one reason couples who strive to blend usually encounter serious difficulty. Blending, therefore, is an idealized notion of what couples can accomplish. In *real life,* as you know if you've been in a stepfamily, only partners blend. The partnership, therefore, is where the focus on blending must be placed. It should be noted, however, that there are stepfamily units where a comfortable degree of *we-ness* has been achieved, but it does not happen often enough to reduce the high rate of stepfamily failures. One major reason for those failures is the socially conditioned expectations that put family members out of step before they begin to collectively march toward anything.

In new-family, the expectation is that family members will bond, that they will become emotionally connected or joined. The focus in new-family is on building a structure within which honest and authentic relationships can develop. This book creates a positive framework, a structure on which couples can build new-family. It emphasizes the importance of reducing conflict and the *how* of promoting connections that are the forerunners of bonding.

Conflict is an enemy and most new families experience much of it. The treachery in all conflict is that it destroys love and turns partners against each other. Conflict is, however, a natural and normal outcome when two family units come together under one roof, and this remains so even if one partner does not have children. Conflict must be expected but controlled. It must be kept from spiraling out of control, which it does when there is not well understood, meaningful structure. Structure, in itself, defines relationships. This book teaches couples to build structure.

The Problem:
Life In New-Family Can Be Hell

Yes, life in new-family can be hell, and the reason is simple. Everyone comes with expectations and a vested interest in hanging onto aspects of the past that engendered a sense of security. A birth parent's longstanding, unique tie to his or her children versus a new, fragile tie with the new partner sets up divided loyalty challenges. The children want things one way; the new partner wants them another way. Whose way will prevail? Whom should the birth parent support? Should they support their partner or their children? Because birth parents want to please both their children and their partners, they typically become caught in the middle and, consequently, conflict is a predictable outcome.

In addition, couples tend to want their new-family unit to become *family* in the sense they have either known it in the past or idealize it in the present. They realize rather quickly, however, that this arrangement is not living up to their expectation. "It doesn't feel like family to me" is a common lament. Their hopes

and dreams are dashed. Power struggles reign supreme and trivial matters, such as the direction the toilet paper should come off
the roll, become grist for the mill.

Children are more often than not at the center of struggles, and
sometimes they purposely provoke conflict to gain power. These
provocations hurt and offend new-parents because they challenge
the new-parent's authority. If the new-parent comes forward to
meet the children's challenges, she or he meets a counter-challenge
that escalates conflict. The problems are significantly compounded
if birth parents unconsciously or passively support the children's
challenges, because new-parents are then alone and isolated. The
message is that the new-parent is an outsider.

Once challenges between new-parents and children begin, the
fallout lands in the middle of the partnered relationship.
Consequently, each partner becomes increasingly protective of their
beliefs about the way that things are *supposed* to be done. Partners
who have children in the home tend to protect the children.
Partners who don't have children in the home protect their own
beliefs about how children *ought* to behave. These differing expectations, life-style desires, beliefs about parenting and parenting skills
make it easy for couples to fight over almost everything.

Another source of disappointment is the perception partners
develop about who their partner has become. "What happened
to the person I fell in love with?" they ask. There was a time when
they loved everything about each other, but now they cannot stand
the way the other chews. Once disappointment sets in, it is like
a sore tooth aching more with each bite. Partners' inabilities to
control the course of events within the home, and their solo dis-
united efforts to take control keep them bumping, if not ramming,
into each other.

Children pick up on discord and openly or subtly protect and
support their biological parent. This only makes matters worse
because it creates a situation in which any conflictive incident sets
off a chain reaction of negative responses. This reaction is similar
to what happens when dominos are placed so the first falls into

the second and all others then fall in consecutive order. The dominos tumble until none remain standing. Can this domino effect be stopped? Can couples find their way out of vicious chain reactions or destructive circles? Yes, they can, and it is the *how* of doing so that this book addresses.

Love is Never Enough and Is Sometimes Too Much

Debilitating, destructive conflict does not stop until partners have agreements about how they want things to be. These agreements manage the dominos and eliminate much potential for conflict. When conflict continues unabated, a partnered relationship becomes an emotional boxing match or a living hell. Conflict sours love, and it eventually turns partners against each other—therein lies the reason for the high divorce rate of couples in stepfamily.

Partners must manage conflict before it manages to destroy their relationship. The love they share is powerful and it can be protective, but love alone is incapable of conquering the complexities of new-family. It is one thing to love someone and quite another to live with them and their children. Love can provide partners with the desire to hang in and work through difficulties, but it will not prevent conflict from tearing their relationship apart. Love is the foundation on which parenting partnership is built, but it takes more than love to solve the practical dilemmas created by new-family dynamics.

It is helpful when each partner is willing to examine his or her contribution to the problems. In the presence of conflict, however, partners may be unwilling to risk such vulnerability and, understandably, they may become defensive and blaming. Blaming often surfaces when one partner believes the other is not a loving new-parent. The contention of the blaming partner is that if the spouse would make life more pleasant for the kids who are not her or his offspring, all would be well. In other words, "What's wrong here is that you don't like my kids and you treat them like s&#@!" This is misplaced blame by a couple without solid agreements. The absence of agreements denies them an identity as parenting partners and equal heads-of-household. Agreements build structure. This couple must find common ground if they are going to stabilize their new-family. Until partners present themselves as a *we,* they will live in a madhouse.

Another important quality for partners to acquire is a willingness to not force love on their partner's children. Here again love is not the singular solution to problems. In a relationship with a partner's children love can be *too much.* If a new-parent is too caring, too demonstrative, too quickly it can backfire. Here's why: children and teens do not want too much, too fast, from Mom or Dad's new partner. Kids appreciate being cared about, but if they feel the new-parent's caring pressures them to respond with affection that they do not genuinely feel, they balk. The intention of all balking, in whatever forms it takes, is to keep new-parents at a distance. The foregoing should not be taken to mean that kids do not want to be loved or that love is not important. What children fear is feeling overpowered or smothered.

The new-family is a package deal. One does not join only a partner—one commits to a family group and a new way of life. This new life is about living together and being family but not in the usual sense of family. New-family is different. Given that, it is enormously helpful for partners to educate themselves about the dynamics of new-family. How does new-family work? How is new-family different from traditional biological family? Why don't they work the same? What must couples do differently?

Once couples understand the unique complexities of new-family, they can acquire skills necessary to manage inevitable complications. Knowing how to take charge makes the difference between a failed relationship and a successful one. If partners want to beat the odds they must do two things. One is to learn to be parenting partners. The other is to learn how to continually renew their intimate relationship. Couples may want to recreate family, but it never happens if they lose each other in the process.

Save Your Marriage:
Become Parenting Partners

Partners reduce conflict and take control of their home by learning to manage and lead as co-captains of a team. It sounds simple but it is not easy in the doing. It requires partners to form a parenting partnership and to always be loyal to that partnership. Loyalty means honoring and enforcing mutual agreements about the *how of things* within the home. This means that, first and foremost, partners must work through their differences. It means finding common ground, deciding how to work together and then supporting each other in the doing. This book is about the how of accomplishing these tasks. One of this book's primary purposes is to help partners orient the inner workings of new-family so that their relationship survives those early years. The book focuses on strategies for accomplishing this while ensuring that each partner's unique relationship with birth children is not destroyed in the process.

Focusing on the seven tasks outlined in this book increases a couple's probability of success. Success means that the primary relationship survives, the loving sustains itself, and the new-family unit achieves a comfortable degree of closeness. Success also means that members of the new-family judge it a *meaningful* replacement of their first-family.

The seven tasks are presented in Figure I-1 on the following page. Note that the first letters of each step when put together spell SUCCESS: Sign-On, Unite, Cooperate, Create, Establish, Solidify and Support. These seven tasks, and the means of accomplishing them, shape the contents of seven chapters of this book.

The Ongoing Challenge:
To Change Expectations

Another primary source of conflict is partners' beliefs about what family is *supposed* to be. Couples tend to believe they *must* shape the family into a unit that looks like and feels like a biological family. They *must* present themselves in the world as a *real*

The Escalator to Success

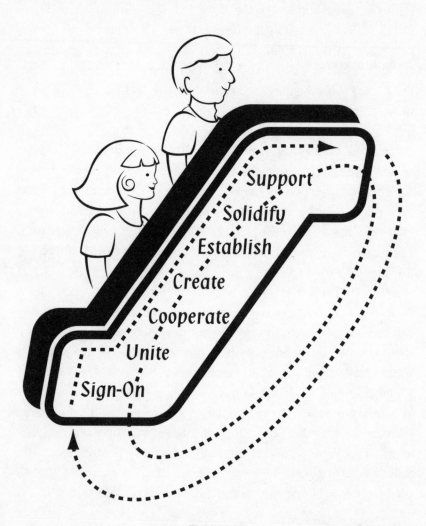

Figure I-1

The seven *steps* are neither sequential nor hierarchical like those on a ladder. They are more like steps on an escalator inasmuch as they are all in motion at the same time. Issues within a step resolve only to arise again at some later point. What goes around comes around. The escalator is always rolling, but as conflict decreases, the ride becomes more comfortable—new-family life SMOOTHES out.

family—something they believe they are not. The family most of us know is a biological unit made up of our mom, dad and siblings (if we have brothers or sisters). This family unit is part of a larger kinship group of blood relations. Blood relationship is largely responsible for biological family having a certain way-of-being and a certain feel about it. This feeling is hard to describe yet easily recognized when experienced. We know "our people" in an intuitive way. This does not mean we necessarily like our relatives but that we know we belong—we *know* when we are an insider.

Since our real and idealized notions about biological family are what remain most vivid in our psyche, it is this sense of family we want to replicate in new-family. Partners want *family,* but *new-family* is not family in the same way that biological family is family. There are remarkable differences. These differences account for conflict's ability to destroy in new-family what it does not destroy in first-family.

Partners fare best when they focus on creating a home where everyone feels welcome and safe rather than on replicating the biological family. Emotional safety is the foundation upon which non-biologically related family members build relationships. It is a prerequisite for those relationships, but it only emerges in a home where new-family members feel accepted. Developing such a base of safety takes time. This is partly because, while partners are attempting to promote such ambiance, they are also defining and setting limits. These limits challenge the children and force partners to work through their differences. If partners are at odds the household is divided.

Changing expectations does not mean throwing out limits, not having rules, or letting everyone have their way—that's chaos. What altering expectation means is allowing a new style of home life to emerge. If partners broaden their notions about what family is, they can build *family-community*. Family-community is different from kinship family, and different from just a collection of individuals under one roof. Family-community is a unit with a unique identity—a unit that has developed a sense of *we-ness*. Each member has an individual and family identity within the home and each feels welcome and accepted. There is support, understanding and compassion. The activities associated with creating family-community unleash a potential for new-family to become something kinder and gentler than the first families from which members derive. When this potential is realized new-parents become *other-mothers* and *other-fathers*.

The Goal of This Book

The goal of this book is to help couples build family and preserve their loving relationships through the difficult days and years of conflict without alienating the children. The chapters that follow are a straightforward rendering of seven tasks successful partners knowingly or unknowingly accomplish. If partners strive to master these tasks, they increase the chances of having a relationship that thrives and a new-family with a comfortable degree of *we-ness*.

It is important for the reader to remember that no book says it all. In that regard, the following passage is presented from Chapter Seven so that the reader is sure to see it in one place or the other.

● ● ●

*If this book suggests doing something
differently than you presently do it, and what
you do works for you, do not change it.
In other words, "If it ain't broke, don't fix it."*

1. SIGN-ON:

"I've Been Hurt Before; Will I Be Hurt Again?"

Sign-On

Introduction:
What it Means to Sign-On

Signing-on in a relationship means one enlists and commits to the journey. Therefore, choosing a partner has something, but not everything, to do with signing-on. It is possible to choose a partner and not sign-on. It is impossible, however, to sign-on without choosing. When a submarine dives to remain submerged for six months, the crew on that submarine has signed-on. When a woman becomes pregnant, with no intention of aborting her fetus, she has enlisted for the journey. When the crew on the space shuttle Challenger lifted off, it was signed-on. When it comes to signing-on there is no tomorrow, only now, right now. One is either on board, or not. We are loyal to our agreement or we are not. And when partners are not *in,* when they have not signed-on, there is no joining, and no genuine union.

Signing-on requires a risky shift. The shift creates a state of mind that at the most basic level says *I'm in.* A state of mind is not something we learn by taking a class. What we can learn are skills that remove or desensitize obstacles that prevent us from sustaining a resolve. One can also learn skills for managing fear. Ultimately, however, signing-on is a leap into uncertainty and the unknown. There are no guarantees. Every submerged submarine is at risk, as is every pregnant woman, as is every astronaut headed for orbit. If our fears control us we are unable to commit to anything except fear. Unmanaged fear robs us of our freedom of choice. It keeps us from risking.

Because we have our most intense and enduring relationship with our fear, signing-on in a relationship that creates new-family is seldom a cakewalk. Our fears are always with us, and it is against their threats that we continually muster emotional defenses.

As individuals we differ in the things we fear. Yet, one common experience is feeling fear when we fall in love. This is especially true for those who have been through painful endings such as divorce, or the unexpected, sudden death of a partner. Painful endings cause a post-trauma conditioning that serves to keep us fearful, on edge and uncertain. Fear is like a vulture of doom; it parks itself on the branches of our hope waiting for the carrion of our dreams.

One painful ending can be all it takes for us to become forever fearful of being hurt again. If fear lurks in the shadows of every new opportunity, it influences our behavior and stifles our ability to open, trust and commit. Over the years, our journey into and out of relationships provides us with either an ever-increasing cache of wisdom, or sensitive, sometimes hardened, emotional edges. These wounded edges represent a mistrust that can make it difficult or impossible to make clear, meaningful and emotionally-safe connections with others.

The fear associated with old wounds that surfaces in new, threatening situations creates an unstable and insecure environment for a growing relationship. Painful remembrances cause us to guard against future injury. Our inner voice says, *I've been hurt before; I'm not going to be hurt again*. That voice represents a resolve to protect our vulnerability and we do so by maintaining emotional distance. Although distance is protective, it separates us from full-emotional participation in a relationship. It makes it impossible to sign-on.

The Problem:
Fear Undermines Ability to Commit

Old pain compromises our ability to sign-on. We might imagine such a predicament as similar to boarding a rowboat for a journey across a large, choppy body of water. Imagine for a moment a rowboat tied to a dock on a large lake. The wind is strong and the waves high. The small boat is tossing to and fro, bobbing up and down. You and your partner, along with the children, must get in this boat and push off into the waves. Your destination is a far distant shore. Your task is to row and navigate in the right direction through rough water: "Can I rely on my partner in rough water? Does my partner know how to row? Is she (or he) strong enough to pull against those waves?" If we can sense the apprehension underlying such questions in this imaginary situation, we can understand the fear gripping many new-partners. Most encounter some amount of apprehension and it is normal to do so.

The couple in Figure 1-1 has not signed-on—they are not in the boat. Their journey does not begin until they get in the boat. Commitment is in the boat, not on the dock.

In real life, apprehension can be helpful if it leads to a conscious reassessment of one's resistance to commitment. A period of conscious reconsideration gives one time to think about elements negatively encroaching on one's situation. Engaging the conscious mind activates reasoning that can prevent emotion from dominating or dictating a decision. Fear gets a hearing but is not allowed to take over.

Apprehension is not helpful, however, if it creates paralysis, which most often occurs when we fear discovering our fear. When we do not want to know what we know, we push fear down. Stuffing fear is an attempt to deny it, but fear is undeniable. It finds ways to be menacing. In relationships, it menaces by provoking a resistance to being too deeply connected. Resistant people avoid intimate situations and encounters. They may provoke fights or become cold to increase distance, and in distance lies emotional safety.

Not honoring fear can cause one to go forward into marriage even when one knows something is amiss. "After all," expressed one woman, "I was at a point where I just couldn't call it off— what would my family think?" Another said, "I know my family wondered if I'd ever make it with anyone. It made me feel so inadequate and flawed. So, although I knew this marriage wasn't the best for me, I went ahead anyway. My fears paralyzed me

Commitment Is Not on the Dock

Figure 1-1

but I didn't realize I was frightened. Consequently, I never got in the boat. I put one foot in but every time something went wrong, I stepped back on the dock. Obviously we never went anywhere and now things are really a mess."

Partners who come into new-family with unrecognized fear, or fear which they recognize but are unwilling to honor, extend little trust. Return for a moment to the image of the boat and the dock. Imagine each partner on the dock with just one foot in the boat. Fear is making it impossible for them to get underway—they cannot commit to the journey. They are unable to extend trust. They are not safe with each other. They are together but going nowhere except, that, is, between the dock and the boat.

Partners want a genuine picture of each other, yet a genuine image is the very thing they fear revealing about themselves. In the early stages of a relationship each person is guarded and uncertain, and each tests the other's devotion. The treachery in the testing game is that neither partner is completely genuine. A mask of calculated behavior hides each partner's genuine nature. What partners see in each other, therefore, are reactions to their own reactions. They want to be pleasing and to provide the other with what they believe the other wants, but it is a guessing game. If fear remains in the driver's seat it is easy to make a mistake because partners will believe they know each other when, in fact, what they have met in each other is fear hidden behind acceptable · behavior. What they see is an illusion. The person with whom they go to bed will not be the one with whom they rise.

How do partners separate fact from fiction, illusion from reality? How can individuals ever become confident enough about themselves and their partners to get in the boat and begin the journey? To the extent that illusion can be shattered, one does so by getting clear about one's fear and the distortions it may be creating. To become clear is to separate one's truth from one's fear based reactions. Clarity is a flashlight that dispels shadows.

Save Your Marriage:
How to Sign-On

Commitment entails many things, among which is a willingness to take a risk—a willingness to be vulnerable, to create change. Signing-on is an agreement, voiced or unvoiced, to join up—to enlist or enroll in an endeavor that from the start is a journey into the unknown. It is a journey into rough, deep water where the howling winds of blustery days can refuse to abate. This journey may lead into dark nights filled with fear and into the pain of stress and bewilderment. Yet, if the sojourners sign-on, row together and stay at the helm, the journey will offer more than just peril. There will be good days, days when the sun shines, days when the wind calms and the waters still. There will be days of peace, laughter, and loving. And, as well, there will be days when everything is just good enough, unremarkable days when life goes on without drama or provocation, and with little stirring.

Karla is a good example of someone who signed-on. During the years before she met David she had established herself as a successful career woman and single mother. She had no idea what lay ahead when she married him. She gave up much hard won independence. Her children resented the remarriage and began to act out. David's children, who were very troubled, were failing in school, experimenting with drugs and generally not making it. His ex was a constant presence in their life. It seemed as though there was no hope, and Karla, a woman who soaked up everyone's feelings, often felt she was coming unglued.

There were many days of despair when it seemed as though ending might be easier than going on. This was especially true when the problems with the children caused conflict between her and David. She loved David dearly and she remembered that being alone as a single parent had its problems too. Growing old alone was not her desire. Karla refused to give up. She did what she needed to do for herself. She took some classes, read some books and found a therapist who could help. She and David went to counseling together. Many of the problems with the children continued, but because of their efforts, she and David were better able to manage them. And, best of all, they preserved their relationship.

The ultimate goal for each partner is to know what it will take to sign-on. What does one need to do to sign-on in the same way the crew of a submarine signs-on? In the way a space shuttle crew signs-on? If you are a woman who has children and you were afraid of childbirth, ask yourself how you managed that fear during the nine months of anticipation. No one is ever partially pregnant; they are in the boat or they are not! There is no halfway. It is the same in relationships. One needs to be wholeheartedly in the relationship. Without total commitment, relationships in one way or another fail. Partners must get in the boat and out into the waters of new-family life with determination to succeed.

Refer to Figure 1-2 and note the difference between it and Figure 1-1. In Figure 1-2 the couple and the children have left the dock behind. They are in the boat rolling on the sea of new-family life. To commit is to get in the boat and to be in pursuit of the shore that lies on the other side of the occasionally stormy sea.

Undermine fear before fear undermines

There are typically three sources of fear associated with new relationships. The first source is a concern about the other person and who he or she is as a human being—Is he stable? Is she honest? Loyal? Sincere? Will he be kind to my kids? A second source is a concern about the extended aspects of a situation and its potential complications—Do I like her children? Can I live with his kids? Can I deal with his ex? The third source is a psychological handcuff to historical baggage—our mistrust, personality traits, disposition and our uncertainties about life, people, and relationships.

One quick means of identifying some of these fears is to imagine signing a pact with your partner that states, "Us at all costs!" It would mean not allowing anything or anyone to stand in the way of your relationship. No cost would be too high. Why wouldn't you, or couldn't you, do that? Make a list of all the rea-

COMMITMENT
Is in the Boat

Figure 1-2

sons you could not, or would not. List every reason, every thought and every reservation that comes to mind, no matter how trivial it may seem.

There are obvious reasons why one would not sign-on at this level, and the safety of one's children would be foremost. Obviously, no one wants to surrender the ability to protect the children. But there can be other reasons as well. The point of the exercise is not to suggest that one should be party to such an agreement, but to unearth reservations being stuffed or over-looked—to get to the emotional bottom line.

Following are reservations others have listed in response to the statement: *I would not join my partner in a pact that said "us at all costs" because:*

- I'm a little afraid of his temper.
- I think she's too controlling with my kids, and she's mean to my oldest daughter.
- I think he drinks too much.
- She has become a lot colder than she was at first.
- If he is that mean to his ex, will he be that mean to me?
- I think she encourages her kids to disrespect their father.
- I don't think he really cares about his kids.
- My former husband passed away and I was left with a large inheritance. He could be after me for my money. He does not accept my children.
- She won't stay out of things that are none of her business.
- I'm surprised he acts like such a baby; sometimes he pouts more than the kids.
- She loses it, starts screaming and has even hit me.
- My kids don't feel welcome in my home when she's there.
- He seems very self-centered. I'm not sure he was there emo-tionally for his first wife or his kids, and I'm not sure he'll really be there for me either.

- She seems only interested in how much money I have and where we'll live. I think she's more interested in my pocketbook than in me.

- I would never surrender my need to protect my children from harm. I'm not done parenting them and I want to be with someone who is supportive.

If we step into a relationship before emotionally committing and then the relationship does not go well, it is enormously difficult to acquire the state of mind necessary to commit. The negative impact of conflict continually erodes confidence and hope. Partners in such a situation face a terrible dilemma because success requires the involvement and devotion of commitment. Consequently, they become paralyzed and stuck.

A book like this one, and exercises like the one above and those at the end of the chapter, can be enormously helpful, but they are not equal to the therapeutic reflection offered by a therapist. Since signing-on in a relationship is necessary if the relationship is going to succeed, it is critical for those struggling with commitment to evaluate all uncertainties and question marks. Because we often need to be challenged to get honest, an emotional journey to inner truth is best accomplished with the help of a licensed therapist, a pastor, rabbi or spiritual advisor who is qualified to take on such a task. This person becomes an illusion breaker or what we might, in fun, call a "ghost buster," because *ghosts* of memory create many of our illusions. It is important to remember, however, that illusions can go both ways: we can idealize a bad situation or devalue a good one. The goal of sessions with a counselor should be to acquire a deeper understanding of one's fears and how they influence one's current reactions. Questions like those that follow should be addressed:

- Is my fear of this situation so overwhelming that I will not be able to sign-on with my partner?

- Am I just over-reacting; is it safe for me to go on?

- Is old stuff haunting me and, if so, is there a way to manage the anxiety it's causing?

- How distorted is my perception?

- Can I keep my fear from undermining my ability to commit?

- Do I need to do some further counseling?

- Do we need to do some counseling together?

- Do the children need some counseling?

Anyone unable to sign-on should seek help no matter what it costs, and it need not cost a lot. In most locations it is possible to find mental health, parish, community or county resources that are not expensive. Do not consider a friend to be a trained, neutral, third party. Friends are never neutral or insightful enough in the way we need someone to be in these matters. That is not because they necessarily tell us what we want to hear, but because they seldom challenge us to dig deeply for the why, what and wherefore of our dilemma.

Partners wishing to do a more in-depth exploration of compatibility may find the book *Are You The One For Me?** by Barbara De Angelis, Ph.D., helpful. It assists couples in creating a compatibility list that is useful for identifying trouble spots they may be overlooking.

The Ongoing Challenge:
Managing Fear

Many couples, though years down the road, have not signed-on. Most often this is because they either did not know how, or did not know how necessary it is. Few couples realize how important it is to sign-on and to have a plan for managing fear across time. In the chapters that follow there is a wealth of information about strengthening bonding and truly signing-on.

Fear without understanding is an enemy whose grip is diffi-

---

* Barbara De Angelis, *Are You the One for Me? Knowing Who's Right & Avoiding Who's Wrong* (New York: Delacorte Press, 1992).

cult to eliminate. People who grapple with fear know just how unrelenting it can be. Because of this, it is better to work toward understanding, taming and managing fear than toward eliminating it. One can learn to control its irrational and paralyzing effects. And we must remember that we would not want to rid ourselves of *all* fear; some is motivating and protective. We should all have a healthy dose of that kind.

Return to the image of the boat at the dock. Imagine that the boat is pointed into the waves. The waves rise and fall, rise and fall. When they are low the water is quite calm; when they are high there is greater turbulence. Fear is like a wave; it comes and goes. It rises and falls and as it does, its intensity increases and decreases. When one is in a boat the goal is to head into the waves, riding them as they rise and fall, and this strategy can also work when one is experiencing waves of fear.

For example, allow the water to represent your fear. Time your breathing to match the waves you are imagining. Exhale as the wave rises and moves toward you; inhale as it falls away. Notice that you are breathing opposite the pattern of the waves. Practice this imagery with your breathing every day even if for just a short time. Then in the future when you feel fear, exhale. Sit down and allow the fear to be the waves. Exhale as the wave rises; inhale as it falls away. These individual efforts at sensing feeling can help one identify fear when it shows up. We cannot deal with fear if we overlook its presence. Every effort we make to recognize its presence helps us gain greater control.

The ideal circumstance is when partners can voice their fear without fear of reprisal from their partner: "I'm afraid I'll be hurt again. I'm afraid you love your kids more than me. I'm afraid you'll leave me. I'm afraid you'll treat me like you treat your ex. I'm afraid you'll be mean to my kids. I'm afraid I can't trust you. I'm afraid to be parental with your kids because I'm afraid you'll get mad at me." The fear that prevents our honesty rides on the back of negative beliefs. These beliefs are our vulnerabilities: "I'm not lovable; I'm not good enough. I'm not pretty enough. I don't earn enough money.

I'm boring. I have poor self-esteem. If they find out who I really am they won't like me. I don't feel safe here. If I speak up I'll get shot down." Because fear arouses a need for psychological or physical protection, we reach for our invisible armor. When we do so, we diminish our capacity for compassionate and intimate union.

Here is an important question for those struggling with fear: *What is the fear that keeps you from telling your partner what it is you fear?* Read that sentence again: What is the fear that keeps you from telling your partner what it is you fear? Find the answer to that question. Once partners are safe enough in each other's presence to talk about their fears, they can silence the noisy internal voice that keeps demanding protection. The need for protection keeps partners from getting in the boat. *Partners must get in the boat. Commitment is in the boat.*

This journey into new-family is more than a journey of heart and soul. It is a journey into fear and toward the achievement of a degree in fear management—call it the FM degree. The journey requires planning, training and support. It requires tenacity, determination and a love that transcends feelings. To feel love is one thing, but *feelings* are unreliable. This journey requires the love inherent in devotion; devotion is that aspect of love that shows up as steadfastness, perseverance and singleness of purpose. Devotion says, *I'm loyal; I'm in—I have signed-on.*

● ● ●

*Tomorrow's happiness is conceived
in the womb of today's risks.
To sign-on is to take a chance.
Sign-on . . .*

Exercise:
Clarifying Fear

The purpose of the following exercises is to help the reader sort out personal fears. There are two sections. The first, *Here We Are— What Do We Do Now?* is for partners ready to work together. The second section is for those who find it impossible to engage the participation of their partner: *Here I Am—What Do I Do Now?*

Individuals not yet in a relationship that will create new-family but considering the possibility, will find special exercises in *Appendix B—Should I Do This Or Not?*

Here We Are—What Do We Do Now?

When a relationship is in a steady course of deterioration, partners need to stop the downward spiral long enough to reevaluate. One strategy historically employed to accomplish this has been separation. Separation, however, tends to eliminate the very issues needing resolution.

A better way to approach the matter is to designate a period of time in which both partners agree to a total commitment. This requires three agreements. One is to not call the relationship into question for the designated period of time. Another is to do everything possible to act as though one is signed-on forever. A third is to work with a counselor.

Partners should start with a period of time on which they can agree: a day, a week, a month, six months. At the end of the appointed time they reassess whether to continue for another agreed upon period or not. Once partners are in counseling they can negotiate their agreements in the presence of their counselor.

A Temporary Enlistment Agreement

Enter below the period of agreed upon time: for example, this week, two weeks, one month, two months, six months, etc.

a) *We have agreed to be signed-on in this relationship for*

_____.

b) *During this time, we will do the following things to reevalu-ate and revive our relationship.* (Make a list of things that you will do as partners. A number of items others have listed follows.)

- We will complete the other exercises presented in this book.
- We will attend counseling every week.
- We will not blame each other.
- We will focus on our relationship.
- We will each take responsibility for enforcing house rules with our children.
- We will spend some time together each week without the children.
- We will talk each day before bed.
- We will make a list of the things bothering us and discuss it with the counselor.

c) *During this time, I will do the following things to analyze my contribution to the problems:* (Each partner should make a separate list. Following are a number of examples.)

- I will finish reading this book.
- I will put the relationship in first place.
- I will attend individual counseling.
- I will not work overtime and I will spend more time at home.
- I will take a more active role with my children.
- I will back off with Sheila's (partner) kids.
- I will quit acting like a jerk at the dinner table.
- I will not make fun of Jeremy's (partner's kid) hair.

Getting Honest Without Getting Angry

If the period of commitment established above is short, partners must move quickly. They may need to find crisis intervention assistance. Counseling is an important step because it helps couples find a way through their difficulties; it helps them envision possibilities they might not imagine on their own. Many couples have saved their relationships because they received professional help at a critical time. Chapter 7 offers many suggestions for finding such help.

Without professional intervention, the odds work against partners in crisis because the level of emotional safety required for addressing issues can be impossible to achieve. One benefit of sitting down with a counselor is that within the safety of that space, problems can be openly aired. Another benefit of using a professional is that if the relationship is going to end, partners need support for closure. There are instances when relationships need to end; however, before arriving at that conclusion, counseling is an important step. No one needs another ending, especially if it is preventable and the issues resolvable. A trained professional can help partners listen to each other and take in things that might otherwise be hard to hear. Things like:

- If you want my support you cannot be as harsh as you are with my children.

- Sometimes I need you to step between your children and me and protect me from their misdirected hostility.

- I'm concerned about your relationship with your daughter; it is almost as though she is your partner.

- I need you to stay out of some things; I can't deal with the kids if I have to fight you every inch of the way.

- Your criticism makes me feel like I've been a bad parent and you overlook how good the children really are. They're just kids—you need to lighten up.

- Your son seems to think he's the man of the house.

- You have to give me room to have my relationship with my children. I've done it a certain way for a long time; I can't do it your way.

- I feel like I'm babysitting your kids. I don't want to be their nanny.

Because so many struggles involve conflicts over the children, it is often possible to find temporary compromises that stabilize the household while further work is done.

Digging Deeper

Answer the following questions by completing the sentence or by circling an appropriate choice. In the parentheses where (p) is indicated, substitute the name of your partner.

- I have been with (p) for_____ months.
- I believe I know (a lot, enough, very little, nothing) about (p).
- I am (totally safe, not totally safe, unsafe) with(p).
- The thing about (p) that makes me most comfortable is:
- The thing about (p) that makes me most uncomfortable is:
- The thing I like best about (p) is:
- The thing I like least about (p) is:
- The thing about (p) that I would like to know more about is:
- The thing about (p) that I would like to change is:
- The thing I like about how (p) parents his or her children is:
- The thing I don't like about how (p) parents his or her children is:
- The thing I like least about (p's) kids is:
- The thing about (p's) kids that I would like to change is:
- The thing I like best about where we live is:
- The thing I like least about where we live is:
- We have talked (a lot, enough, not enough, very little) about how we manage money.

- I have (a clear, not very clear, very unclear) picture of how we will manage money.

- I am (completely satisfied, not completely satisfied, unsatisfied) with our plans about handling money.

- The thing I like best about how we have agreed to handle money is:

- The thing I like least about how we have agreed to handle money is:

- I have (always, never, sometimes) managed money by myself.

- I have (always, never, sometimes) had discretionary money that I spent as I wished without obligation to someone else.

- The thing I like best about myself in this relationship is:

- The thing I like least about myself in this relationship is:

- After completing these questions, write a paragraph about what you discovered or learned. Start it by completing this sentence: I now realize that: _____.

Here I Am—What Do I Do Now?
(Exercises for Those Who Must Address Issues Alone)

Some partners refuse to attend counseling, see a pastor, or do anything that involves the assistance of a third party. If you have such a partner you should find a counselor for yourself. The following exercises will help you prepare.

Can I Change?

On a piece of paper answer the following question either in narrative form or by listing specific items. The assumption to make in answering the question, although it may be an inaccurate one, is that your partner is not going to change in any way. Assume for the sake of the question that you have to make all the changes necessary to endure. List, therefore, only aspects of *your* behavior, not because you are to blame but because, at this point, you are seeking a way to survive in the situation.

How do I have to change to remain in this relationship without being angry or depressed all the time?

Can I Do This?

Carefully review your answers from the exercise above, adding anything else that comes to mind—things you may have over-looked. Then ask yourself, for each item on the list, "Can I do this? Are these changes I can make? Are they changes I am will-ing to make?"

Following are examples of answers given to the question, "How do I have to change" followed in parentheses by answers to the question, "Can I do this?" Actual names are replaced with "my partner."

- *I could stop trying to fix those kids.* (They are such a mess it will be very hard for me because my partner is so totally disinterested in what's happening to them.)

- *I could explain to my partner's son, Michael, what the rules are about my tools.* (I'm not sure that he cares or would lis-ten, or that my wife will support me because it seems that she never does.)

- *I could give up trying to keep the house neat and trying to get those kids to do their share.* (This will drive me nuts! I hate it when the house is a pit and I hate being the one in charge of seeing that it gets cleaned. I can't get those kids to do a thing.)

- *I could stop trying to reason with her ex—stop talking to him.* (He calls me at work so that will be difficult. I guess I'll have to tell him I am not talking to him anymore and to not call me at work. I think I can do that.)

- *I could put a lock on the bedroom door.* (I have to do it for now because I am so afraid, but I can't live like a prisoner in my own home.)

- *I could create some private space, a room where I could escape and close the door, read or work on the computer.* (I can do this if my wife will agree that it is okay for me to have pri-vate space.)

- *I could allow myself to be verbally abused by those kids.* (That's a ridiculous thought. I can't take this abuse any more and I am powerless to stop it. I don't get any support from my partner. If it doesn't stop I have to leave.)

- *I could get away when my wife's kids come over for their visit.* (I can be gone some of the time but I couldn't be gone a whole weekend twice a month. I don't think I can really be around her kids if she doesn't make any changes. I really hate them, and now I hate my partner for not being supportive.)

- *I could quit trying to make us into the kind of family I think we should be.* (I could get some counseling or maybe I could find a support group.)

One interesting thing that can happen is that when one partner changes, the other may begin to change as well, and sometimes the children follow. There are no guarantees, but changes made by any family member do tend to alter the responses of others—change promotes change. An example is when children's behavior has been unbearable because, unbeknownst to the new-parent, the children feel smothered by demands for closeness. The new-parent's insistence that they become "a family" in the way he or she understands family, has created divided loyalties for the children. To cope with conflicted feelings, the children either purposely or unconsciously promote conflict to ensure distance. When the new-parent stops pushing for closeness the pressure comes off and the children relax. Then, lo and behold, everyone feels better, stress goes down and cooperation improves.

2. UNITE:

"You Love Those Kids More Than You Love Me!"

Unite

Introduction:
Divided Loyalties Create Divisions

When couples unite as intimate and devoted partners they acquire a *we* identity—*we* being the united expression of their unique and felt sense of bonding. This *we* identity is not one that robs or overwhelms individual identities. It does not require partners to be in each other's hip pockets. On the contrary, it creates a whole greater than the sum of their individual personalities. This bonding is *true marriage,* not necessarily by law but by commitment, and *true marriage* involves loyalty and devotion to the *we*.

In *The Power of Myth,* Joseph Campbell refers to the ancient image of a wheel to describe marriage. True *marriage* is life at the hub of the wheel rather than on its rim. A marriage on the rim is always one on the way up or the way down. Marriage is devotion to life at the center, an honoring of mutual affection and mutual agreements. Your partner is your bliss. When couples sign-on, their commitment lays the foundation for such a bond, but bonding does not solidify overnight. Bonding is a process, not an event.

One of the most significant barriers to bonding is anger and, in the beginning, the potential for anger is everywhere. One major source of anger is the children: how they behave or misbehave, how they treat their new-parent, what time they arrive, what time they leave, what things they take with them when they leave, or fail to bring back when they return; the fact that they do not do

---

* Joseph Campbell with Bill Moyers; Betty Sue Flower, ed. *The Power of Myth* (New York: Doubleday, 1988), 118.

  Diane K. Osbon, ed. *A Joseph Campbell Companion: Reflections on the Art of Living ,* selected and edited by Diane K. Osbon (New York: Harper Collins Publishers, 1991), 46-55.

their chores and the belief that they are spoiled and running the household. Given the complications, it is easy for couples to suddenly find themselves scowling or screaming at each other across a chasm forged by anger.

One of the treacheries of anger related to the children is that it is very hurtful to birth parents and, therefore, harmful to bonding. Anger about the children is especially difficult to handle because it is so personal, so threatening and its potential so ever-present. Since this anger is hard to resolve it hangs on, and before long partners are emotionally stalked by it. It is like an invisible dragon pouncing from the shadows of every conflict. Every disagreement can end up being about the children, even if initially it had nothing to do with them.

Unresolved anger eventually becomes a bitterness no sweetness pacifies. Forgiving and forgetting lose their power and bitter feelings embed themselves deeply into old wounds that begin to fester anew. Hurt, disappointment and anger bury love, compassion and understanding under an avalanche of resentment. It takes a special kind of staying power to hang on through this kind of pain.

Commitment is a decision; a choice rooted in devotion and nourished by love. Love brings couples into union and it underlies bonding but it does not secure a relationship. A couple's ability to create a satisfying level of emotional safety for themselves and the children keeps them together. In the presence of ongoing hurt, disappointment and anger, emotional safety is unobtainable.

The Dance: It's Not the Two-Step— It's the Death Spiral

When couples come together, they are more tightly tied to their children than to each other. This is normal and to be expected; birth-family ties have been in place longer than the new relationship. And, after all, *blood is thicker than water* (this well-known saying has real meaning in these situations). In order for couples to tighten their bond, birth parents must *loosen* the ties that connect them to their children. To loosen means to relax to a small degree the dependency ties that bind birth parents to their children. It does not mean cutting the children off from connection or turning away from them. To loosen is to let go a tad—it means not holding the children quite so tightly.

What typically happens when partners create new-family is that birth parents become caught between their children and their new partner. Birth parents and their children know what to expect from one another, and therefore there is a pattern of consistency in their interaction. When a new partner enters and wants changes or compromises—not just changes in household rules, but changes in how the other partner parents—it is difficult for birth parents to immediately change well-established patterns. Consequently, birth parents find themselves the target of their partner's anger. Yet, because they are making an effort to please their partner, they also become targets of their children's anger. The birth parent's natural response to this dilemma sets in motion a psychological dance between children and partner.

The dance begins as birth parents move emotionally closer to their partner and slightly away from their children. Because this movement begins the loosening of emotional knots and dependency ties with the children, the children feel the change. No matter how subtle the change, they immediately sense the loss of the *old mom* or *old dad* and in one way or another they express their displeasure. They may withdraw and become sullen or get angry and hostile. They may say such things as, "You don't love us anymore. You never do anything with us anymore. You only listen to him. I hate it here; I'm moving to dad's." They clearly let it be known they are hurt and that they feel left out, neglected or abandoned.

Children's protests frighten birth parents. In response to their fear, birth parents attempt to assuage the children's hurt feelings. In doing so, they move emotionally closer to the children and somewhat away from their partner, who then interprets this distancing as a sacrifice of the relationship to appease the kids. They view their partner as siding with spoiled children who are resistant to

change. When partners express their unhappiness and dissatisfaction they may say, "You love those kids more than you love
me. You baby them; you spoil them. You overprotect them. Your
kids don't respect you. Your kids walk all over you. Your kids run
the show here. We should have never gotten together; you should
be living with your kids. You're really in bed with your kids!"

These accusations from a partner also frighten birth parents.
They do not want to lose their new-partner any more than they
want to lose their children. In response, and again from fear, they
move emotionally away from the children and back toward the
partner. In the same way they attempted to soothe the children's
feelings, they now attempt to soothe their partner's feelings. The
children, of course, feel the shift and begin their protest again.

The dance continues, pushing and pulling birth parents between
children and partner, like a base runner caught between bases.
Eventually, exhausted and dizzy, birth parents want to run away
from everyone.

The following story about Fred and Marge presents an example of a couple caught in the dance. Fred was a generous but
rather controlling individual who liked structure. He wanted things
neat and had a tendency toward regimentation. Since his children knew this they were rather quiet and demure when they
came to visit in his new home. Marge, his new-partner, had three
children who were residents in the home. Marge was quite easygoing with the children. She was not a pushover, by any means,
but in contrast to Fred she was less demanding about details and
definitely less commanding. Where Fred would demand that something be done immediately, Marge would be willing to go with
the flow and to cajole a bit to get the children's cooperation.
Because of Marge's relaxed manner, Fred was able to seize control and impress his will on the children without strong opposi-
tion—even when Marge did not like Fred's demands.

Marge's children felt as if they were strangers in a foreign land.
Doing what had once been a matter of course now led them into
a pile of trouble with Fred. They were sometimes sad and at other

times mad; and they unloaded their feelings on their mother. When Marge tried to talk to Fred about it he became angry, accusing her of not supporting him. Her children, he said, were spoiled and irresponsible. When Marge tried to reorient the children's expectations to the new rules they became angry and raised their voice at her. This was extremely unnerving to Marge because she had never been at odds with her children. She was caught in the middle, and it seemed that no matter what she did either Fred or the children were angry with her.

Eliminating the dance is the major task new-partners must tackle. The dance is a primary source of ongoing anger, preventing bonding and leading to the demise of the relationship and family. Nevertheless, ending the dance must be accomplished gradually. If birth parents loosen ties with their children too quickly, children feel cut off and react by making it very painful for their parent to bond away from them. The result is anger, and once the children are angry or frightened they become resistant, or they may even attempt to drive a wedge into the middle of the coupled relationship. This is what was happening to Marge and Fred.

If the loosening of ties with children occurs too slowly bitterness builds, especially when partners are feeling overrun by each other's children. Moving too slowly delays adjustments that must ultimately occur. It allows territory to be established that is difficult for partners to later reclaim or redistribute. Subsequently, when it is time to make changes, enmity develops creating bitterness akin to a parasite eating up good feelings. It diminishes partners' desire to keep trying, and once they lose their motivation, the end is near.

The emotional shift away from children and toward partner is a process in which timing is everything. The shift needs to proceed with measured caution, like assembling a puzzle. Each piece already in place creates openings into which other pieces can fit. Marge, for example, was able to figure out how to solve the dilemma, how to get herself out of the middle and work out a strategy with Fred and the children that eventually reduced conflict.

How did Marge do this? The following chapters present the

strategies she used. The remainder of this chapter focuses on keeping the loving alive since it is the loving, intimate connection that gives partners the desire and courage to hang on through the hard times. There are many barriers to bonding; almost everything seems to work against it. Yet, when couples build and maintain a solid loving bond, that bond is the glue that holds them together through the tough times.

The Problem:
Anger Undermines Bonding

Angry, aggressive expressions of anger are relationships' greatest enemy. Popular psychology espoused for many years the belief that catharsis was an effective treatment for anger. *Better out than in* was an approach that came into vogue, but it often overlooked the destructive aspects of the expression itself. Therapists had clients pounding pillows with fists and tennis racquets, or punching bags hung in basements or garages. These activities offered good superficial release, but none of the pounding ever made anyone less angry in the long run. What the *pounders* were learning was to express their anger aggressively. Such catharsis can help one temporarily feel better, but aggression and hostility only breed aggression and hostility. Catharsis does not develop control or create compassion or loving-kindness. Another popular approach to confronting anger is to have couples express their anger to each other. The problem, however, is that they express it angrily, leading to resentment that eventually creates more anger. When cutting words slash love in two that love does not always regenerate—regeneration is the purview of earthworms, not earthlings. Remember the childhood taunt? "Sticks and stones may break my bones, but words will never hurt me." Well, it is not true—words hurt, words harm and words destroy. It is easy to get angry. What is not so easy is finding ways to transform anger's negative energy into positive action.

Anger can be thought of as a first-level reaction because when we examine it at deeper levels, it is typically associated with some element of pain. Anger often masks painful feelings such as hurt, disappointment, fear, grief, loneliness, physical agony, despair, hopelessness, jealousy or powerlessness. A helpful effort, therefore, is to get in touch with the feelings behind the reaction. For example, when you are angry ask yourself, "What pain is speaking?"

Those who struggle with anger know how difficult it is to conquer. Anger is a nasty demon once it becomes conditioned as a reaction. Given that, it is often better to approach anger with the same strategy previously discussed for fear. That is, by learning to manage it rather than through efforts aimed at eradicating it— anger can be skillfully managed and moderated.

When we are angry, it is easy to blame it on someone else because the words and actions of others trigger anger. Nevertheless, an angry person is responsible for his or her anger. Our anger *is our anger*. It is a cop-out, and unfair to say, "You made me angry." It is, however, fair to say, "When you did (or said) such and such, I got angry." It is much more effective when solving problems to own the feelings that spawn an angry reaction. For example: I felt hurt when this or that happened; I was disappointed by such and such; I'm jealous of your daughter (son); when this or that happens I react. Own the feeling behind the anger by claiming it; this is *my* hurt, *my* disappointment, *my* jealousy, *my* sadness and *my* pain.

Anyone having a history of problems with anger, including those who may excuse it as just a bad temper, should seek help. A full discussion of how to manage anger is beyond the scope of this book, but a suggestion follows. In addition, the **Suggested Readings** section at the back of the book lists a few resources others have found helpful. The chapters that follow contain many suggestions for keeping partners out of their anger. The most important step in dealing with anger is the first one, admitting the need for help. The second is getting it.

Managing Anger
Because emotion carries a quality of energy, it is possible to subdue the energy of anger and transform it into the energy of another

emotion. The conversion will not last forever, but regular practice can help one learn to moderate anger rather quickly. As one's skill develops, accumulated experience makes one able to sustain a peaceful state for greater lengths of time.

One effective means of developing control over anger is through meditation. Meditation, which trains us to focus our powers of concentration and to slow our emotional reactions, helps us develop the presence of mind required to moderate anger. We learn to use our mind to turn down the intensity of our emotion, to transform angry energy into the energy of peacefulness and calm. We acquire this level of control by making friends with our anger, acknowledging its existence and sitting with it. As long as we treat anger as an enemy we force ourselves to deny that it is ours; it then belongs to the other person. We become defensive: "I'm not angry; you're the angry one!"

When we befriend our anger we can talk to it, we can negotiate with it, we can learn to moderate it and we can be proud for taking control of ourselves. To be in harmony and at peace with those we love can bring great joy.

Meditation exercises are presented at the end of the chapter, but one problem with any exercise is that we are not apt to embrace a discipline requiring serious contemplation when we are in the throes of new love. The heat of romance is more fun, exciting, titillating and novel. Let's face it, it's a rush! Why would we want to interfere with the delicious, juicy joy of new love? One answer could be that we want to go into a new relationship with our eyes wide open. Love can make us do stupid things. To embrace a relationship in consciousness we must awaken to its realities. "Truth waits for eyes unclouded by longing."* Truth saves us from our illusions.

---

* Ram Dass on April 22, 1993, in Minneapolis, MN.

Save Your Marriage:
How to Unite

Bonding requires partners to focus on two different aspects of their relationship, but these two different, yet inseparable, parts are not always recognized. Figure 2-1 illustrates the two parts. One part will be called the *lovership,* the other the *partnership.*

The lovership is that part of a relationship that holds the romance and intimacy, not just sexual intimacy but, also, emotional and spiritual intimacy. The partnership is that aspect of the relationship from which partners lead and manage the home. The partnership makes decisions about the household and the children (where the mustard is kept, how the dishes get done, which way the toilet paper comes off the roll, what the house rules are for the children.) These decisions, as well as many others about routine day-to-day matters, belong to the partnership.

The lovership brings couples into union, but when that union fails it is because the conflict in day-to-day matters has destroyed it. It falls victim to a wedge driven between partners by *the dance* and by anger. Anger diminishes expressions of loving-kindness and when anger reigns, partners spend less time together. Those very things that brought them together, the fun and the loving, cease to exist; then it is not fun any more.

Therefore, in addition to acquiring skills for managing anger, partners must also find ways to continually nurture and renew their loving. Loving relationships need constant care. It is true that intimacy and romance change their form over time, but they do not by themselves dry up and die. Romance dies from neglect. Couples can renew their love and remain interested in their romance, but the effort must be similar to that of caring for a lovely, green plant that needs regular care and special attention in the presence of extreme conditions.

The pop-psychology literature has led many to believe that the ability to experience intimacy is a quality acquired in childhood. Some writers have led their readers to believe that intimacy is unattainable if one grew up, for example, in a dysfunctional family,

Two Major Elements of a Relationship

- Ex Partners
- The Court
- Outside Influences

THE LOVERSHIP/ THE PARTNERSHIP

Figure 2-1

or as the child of an alcoholic. Intimacy is not, however, an acquired aspect of personality. Intimacy, like excitement or happiness, is an experience of circumstances. In relationships intimacy is an experience partners share when they feel close and safe. Intimacy requires the heart's presence, which is why it is possible to have sex without being intimate. Couples should strive to create an environment of emotional safety for it is within that space that expressions of love and affection dance.

Say You're Going to a Movie—Go to a Motel Instead

To have a healthy, satisfying lovership couples must spend time together—time wherein opportunities for intimacy can emerge. One way to do this is by having a weekly date—call it date night. It is a night for a babysitter, or possibly it can be arranged on the night the children are away from the home visiting their other birth parent. Whatever the arrangements, date night must occur on a weekly basis. This means that it happens even when children who reside elsewhere are visiting. Do not postpone going out because the children are coming for the weekend. Make appropriate babysitting arrangements.

The lovership requires time, money and devotion. It must be scheduled and budgeted. It is amazing how many partners resist setting aside the financial resources necessary to nurture their loving. There can be endless reasons for doing so: the kids need new clothes or new boots, the payment on the boat is overdue, the TV needs repair, the car needs new tires, vacation is coming, and so on and so on. The list could be endless.

Some partners resume dating by committing a small amount of money for weekly outings—enough to cover a movie and popcorn. On a weekly basis that amount may not seem like much, but over the course of a month the sum affects the household budget. Finding the extra may be difficult, but as partners come to value weekly date time, they see it as an essential expenditure rather than a luxury. Time together need not be expensive. Many enjoyable activities cost very little and the biggest enjoyment of the evening should come from just being together, not from the amount spent.

Planning, scheduling and preparing for time together is a major responsibility. Who should do it? Sometimes one partner feels burdened by having to do all the planning and resents the responsibility for always being the one to make it happen. One way to prevent this is for partners to take turns handling the arrangements. Designate and clarify periods of time during which one partner or the other assumes responsibility. Trade every other week or month, depending on what works best for the situation. Responsibility for date night includes the selection of possible activities and the offering of choices. It may include picking up tickets, calling the babysitter, informing the children and sundry other chores. By taking turns, each partner is courted, nurtured and appreciated. In a loving relationship each partner is equally important, and this arrangement helps establish and maintain equality.

Remember that the goal of special time together is to nurture the lovership so that the loving remains alive. It is the loving bond that keeps partners in the boat when the water is rough and the heavy winds of conflict blow. Their love is the keel of the relationship and family. Love is the substance of the heart from which compassion can flow. Nothing else will matter if the loving dies —nothing else is strong enough to hold a complicated arrangement of this nature together. What can you do on your next date? Say that you are going to a movie and go to a motel instead.

Rate your lovership: Turn to the exercise, **The Lovership,** found at the end of this chapter.

The Ongoing Challenge:
To Keep the Loving Alive

It is often difficult for partners when they are alone to refrain from talking about the children. The children seem to be ever-present, even when they are not. Issues about the children can become the subject that takes over the relationship. The children become an *it*. *It* can be general child rearing issues. *It* can be something about one of the children that seems overwhelmingly problematic. *It* can be the older children who are living outside the new family. *It* is anything the children do that is the source of contention or conflict between partners.

How do partners keep *it* from consuming their private time when it is difficult to set aside issues that sizzle with feelings? Following are a few suggestions drawn from the successes of other partners:

- Before going out make a list of all the family matters about which you are angry. Leave the list and the angry feelings associated with it at home. You can pick it up and have the feelings back when you return.

- Before leaving home spend some time alone just being quiet and conscious of your breathing. Expel your negative feelings with each exhalation. While you do this, cup your hands in your lap and imagine them holding the loving feelings you have for your partner. Breathe those feelings on the inhalations.

- If you are angry when you leave home, do not talk to each other for the first thirty minutes you are together. Allow the negative feelings to settle and dissipate. One of the greatest cures for anger is delay and holding hands. If partners just hold hands and are quiet, the loving feelings stifled by anger can surface. Sometimes couples spend a whole evening together without talking—that's okay, but always hold hands. It is possible to talk too much, to analyze too much. It leads to paralysis from analysis. There are times when enough said is enough—and sometimes too much.

- Engage in an activity that you know will generate laughter or one that you always enjoy.

- Eat a good meal together but avoid using alcohol.

- Reminisce about the good times.

Compassion

If there is a human quality that is the superglue of bonding, it is compassion. To be compassionate is to hold above all else one's loving feelings for one's partner. We claim our loving feelings by holding on to them and standing in them no matter what.

Those who are compassionate look past their pain and anger to the suffering and pain of loved ones. Those who are compassionate recognize their power to hurt others and, therefore, guard that power lest it hurt someone. Compassion is benevolent and charitable. It seeks to understand; it strives to be kind and gentle. Compassion is the greatest gift lovers can give each other.

Anger sabotages our ability to be compassionate and it creates a need for us to defend ourselves. When we wear a cloak of self-protection it is impossible to attend to a partner's suffering. Our need to defend turns the other person into an enemy. This is why it is so important to recognize that only a small portion of our behavior is about our partner. We turn our partners into screens onto which we project our unresolved anger and pain. This projection causes us to see ourselves in our partner. It is so much easier to disown our faults when we see them in someone else.

In new-family the need for compassion is high because everyone is in pain, especially in the early going. Ask new-family members, "What's your pain?" and there is always an answer. The teen who is acting out and looks angry is sad and hurting. The depressed child is scared and hurting. Dads and moms who seldom see their children only appear untouched by it all; they are lonesome and hurting. Moms and dads whose children are in trouble are sad and hurting. New-parents ignored by their partner's children are disappointed and hurting. New-parents verbally put down or attacked by their partner's children are angry and hurting.

Pain is everywhere because life is full of it. Divorce, death, the upheaval associated with visitation, being party to a custody battle, being a kid who dislikes a new-parent, being a new-parent who dislikes their partner's kids—it's all painful. It is safe to assume that most negative behavior in new-family is an expression of pain.

The ability to be compassionate requires us to put our pain aside long enough to tend to another. This does not mean permanently stuffing or denying it. What it does mean is being noble some of the time. To be noble is to use our courage and maturity to take the high road, to be bigger than our negative feelings. Sometimes a little repression is a good thing, and taking the emotional high road can elevate us into higher realms of understanding.

When there is a consistent expression of compassion between partners, a sense of emotional safety develops. When we are emotionally safe, we risk being vulnerable. We can step away from being self-protective and blaming. Emotional safety makes it possible for partners to meet each other's struggles with gentleness. Emotional safety makes it possible for partners to express remorse and to say, "I'm sorry." The popular cliché that love means never having to say you're sorry is wrong. Love IS the reason for saying, "I'm sorry." Love apologizes, love forgives, and love motivates change. Most of us can handle the absence of tranquility when we feel loved, supported, and appreciated; when we know compassion will seek to understand. Risking vulnerability is something we dare not do when we fear attack or rejection. When children feel safe they talk openly, and they confide. When adults feel safe, they risk being honest. They express their needs and are able to ask for help.

Forgiveness is not a feeling; that is, you do not feel forgiveness. What you feel is the relief that comes from closure, from settling internally the unfinished business of a situation from which the anger results. Forgiveness does not mean you condone bad behavior but that you make a decision to free yourself from responsibility for another person's actions, and from the desire for revenge as well. How another person behaves is about them, and their baggage, and not about something inherent in the one they hurt. When you don't forgive you carry resentment and anger, and in some manner you are emotionally and physically affected by those feelings. Forgiveness says, "Your problems are your problems. I don't understand them and I don't like them, but I release you from my anger." That act frees you from the emotional burden of anger, and with that freedom comes the opportunity for healing. Forgiveness frees you from bitterness anchored in the past, even if that past is as recent as yesterday. There is no gift to self more courageous than one that releases you from your anger, and no gift to others more noble than one that releases them from your anger.

• • •

Love dies in the heat of anger.
Love is renewed in the flames of
intimacy and compassion.
Unite . . .

Exercise:
Transforming Anger through Meditation*

1) Sit in a firm but comfortable chair. Rest your hands gently in your lap and allow your eyes to close. If you find it uncomfortable to close your eyes, focus them on an object about three feet in front of you. Breathe in through your nose and out through your mouth. Follow each inhalation into your body. On each exhalation allow your body to relax just a bit more—keep your back straight and your head up, but with each exhalation settle into the chair. Count ten inhalation/exhalation cycles—then start over again.

2) Notice that as you continue to focus on your breathing you may lose count, your mind will wander and thoughts of one thing or another will intrude. You may think about the grocery list or all the things you have to do yet today. Notice these thoughts but don't be concerned about them. Allow them to come and pass by. Each time you notice that you are no longer mindful of your breathing, return to focusing on it. If you lose count, just start over at 1.

3) After you have done this for a few minutes and are feeling sufficiently relaxed, cup your hands in your lap as though

---

* This is a basic form of meditation that includes imagery. This type of meditation can be found in books by Thich Nhat Hanh, Talku Thondup, Stephen Levine, and John Kabat-Zinn listed in Suggestions for Further Reading.

you were going to hold a ball. Using the power of your imagination allow your anger to flow from you and fill the ball.
Hold the ball while continuing to be mindful of your breathing—breathe in, breathe out.

4) Using your mind's eye, observe the color of the ball. If it
    seems to have no color, then allow it to become the color
    it would be if it had color. Remember, you are working with
    your imagination so you are in control; you can make the
    ball whatever color you wish it to be.*

5) Continue to breathe in an easy, relaxed fashion, in through
    your nose, out through your mouth. Ask yourself what color
    the ball in your hand would be if it held no anger. Again,
    remember that you are working with your imagination. You
    are in control, so allow your imagination to take the lead
    and name the non-angry color.

6) Say to yourself as you breathe in, "I feel my anger." Say to
    yourself as you breathe out, "I breathe out my anger." What
    is important on the in breath is that you experience the feel-
    ing of your anger and on the out breath that you experi-
    ence the feeling of releasing it, letting it go. Keep repeating
    the words as you inhale and exhale.

7) As you continue to do this, allow the image of the ball to
    slowly change from the angry color to the peaceful color it
    would be if it held no anger. Remember you will be dis-
    tracted by your thoughts. Each time you notice the distrac-
    tion just return to your breathing, to repeating the words you
    have chosen, and to observing with your inner eye the color
    of the ball changing.

8) When the ball has become the peaceful color, hold it for a
    few minutes. Allow the peaceful feeling to rest within you.
    You may assist this process by lifting your hands and bring-

---

* Thank you, Jann Frederickson, MSW, MA, faculty member of the Academy of
  Guided Imagery, Mill Valley, CA, for helping teach me the power of imagination.

ing your palms to your chest. Hold them on your chest while you breathe.

9) Finish by turning your hands over and resting them on your thighs. Continue to focus on your breathing and notice your level of relaxation. Each time you do this exercise you will feel less self-conscious and able to become relaxed more quickly.

10) When you are ready, slowly open your eyes and readjust yourself to the room. Sit quietly for a few minutes and be at peace.

11) A variation on this theme is to imagine, instead of a ball that changes color, something that melts, or evaporates. Then allow the anger to melt or evaporate away. Any of these images is fine as long as the intention of the exercise is to transform the energy of anger to the energy of something peaceful—something kinder and gentler. You want to take that peaceful feeling back into yourself and hold it after the exercise.

The supreme challenge is to practice on a regular basis. It requires diligence to set aside time because we are busy people with many responsibilities. But busyness in itself can be a problem inasmuch as it creates stress that intensifies anger. Therefore, finding time to practice is part of the solution because it is the first step in slowing and reducing stress. Set aside thirty minutes a day for practice. Within those thirty minutes use twenty for the exercise and the remainder for either relaxation following the exercise, or for keeping a log of thoughts and feelings that arise during the meditation.

The important thing about a meditation exercise is getting to it. If thirty minutes of practice is an impossibility, is twenty or fifteen minutes possible? What about joining a meditation class? All major cities and suburbs have organizations that sponsor classes for the public. Check around and find out who is offering classes on meditation.

Exercise:
Managing Acute Episodes of Anger

This exercise is a variation of the one above. Use it to gain control when in the throes of intense anger.

1) Remove yourself from the situation as quickly as possible. It is helpful for partners to have prearranged signals to call a time out. Any mutually agreed upon signal will do. Some partners find it useful to use the time out signal used by players in sporting events.

2) Find a place to sit and be alone. Close your eyes and immediately focus on your breathing. Instead of counting inhalations and exhalations, say to yourself, "I feel my anger—I am breathing out my anger." Keep repeating.

3) Continue until your body feels somewhat less tense and you feel less angry. At that point change the words you are repeating to, "I breathe in peace" or "I breathe in calm" (on the inhalation). "I breathe out my anger" (on the exhalation). If the words suggested do not suit you, choose words that do. Use words with which you are comfortable. It is important to experience the feeling of releasing your anger on the out breath.

4) After a few minutes your body will become a bit calmer and you will be able to feel some of the tension in your face, neck and shoulder dissipate. You will have begun to relax, even if only slightly.

5) Change the words again. Repeat, "I am breathing in loving-kindness (peacefulness, calm)—I am breathing out loving-kindness (peacefulness, calm)." Again, use the words that best suit you. Keep repeating until your anger lessens and you can speak without aggression.

6) Once you have relieved yourself of the intensity of your anger, make an appointment with your partner to talk about what happened. This talk should be a calm discussion. Stop if it escalates into anger. Angry discussions accomplish nothing positive and they create more anger.

Exercise:
The Lovership

Following are exercises to help partners evaluate their lovership:

1) The Lovership Analysis

a) When was the last time you went on a date?

b) How many times were you on a date in the last month?

c) Do you have a privacy lock on your bedroom door?

d) How long has it been since you were sexually intimate?

e) What intimacies do you share besides sexual intimacy?

f) How do you show non-sexual affection?

g) Are you comfortable being affectionate in front of the children?

h) How often do you do special things for your partner?

i) What special things do you do?

j) If you never verbally said to your partner, "I love you," how would he or she know that you do? How do you show your love?

k) Do you feel as if you get enough love?

l) Do you feel as if you give enough love?

m) Do you feel satisfied with your lovership?

n) Do you feel there are things missing in your lovership?

2) Rate your lovership

Given your answers above, place an X on the scale representing the strength of your lovership.

1) (Low)_____5_____(High) 10

3) List five things you will do to improve the lovership:

a) _____

b) _____

c) _____

d) _____

e) _____

For example:

- No more excuses; I will be available on date night.

- I will take responsibility for arranging dates when it is my turn.

- I will do something about my anger because it keeps me from wanting to be intimate.

- I will make an effort to understand that our relationship is important. I have been too focused on my work and hobbies.

4) List three things you will ask of your partner:

a) _____

b) _____

c) _____

For example:

- To please not talk about the children when we go out.

- To please not schedule other meetings on date night.

- To not want sex every time we go to bed when you have not been available for conversation during the evening.

- To loosen the ties with the ex; those ties are having a negative effect on us.

- To spend more time with your kids without me. I can't and don't want to always be there. The bitterness keeps me distant.

3. COOPERATE:

"The Kids Are Running Our Life!"

Cooperate

Introduction:
Powerlessness Yields Powerfulness

One partner is always more firm and controlling with the children than the other. The stricter of the two finds the other too easygoing and indulgent. The more lenient one finds the stricter one too harsh and rigid. These differences create friction for many new couples. Within any new household there are strangers, but it is the adults, when functioning as parents, who are most unknown to each other. In their new home partners get a first-hand view of each other as parents and disciplinarians. This is when they discover: "You are not who I thought you were; I don't know if I like you!" It is one thing to know someone as an intimate partner, quite another to know them as the mother or father of their children, or as a new-parent to children who are not their offspring. It is possible to love the one and dislike the other.

Moving a new-family together under one roof upsets all the old rules about who gets what and how they go about getting it. For example, Johnny, an eight-year-old, and his sister who is thirteen, had been alone with Mother for four years. During that time Johnny learned to control his mom by whining (the heavy sigh type) about his emotional pain and dissatisfaction. Mom, who felt responsible for most of Johnny's losses, assuaged his pain, and some of her guilt, by giving in to his demands. Now Mom has a new partner who finds neither Johnny's whining nor his wife's indulgence of it tolerable. The new-parent demands that Johnny behave more maturely. This angers Johnny. The demand also angers Mom because she thinks her spouse is harsh and unkind to Johnny. This struggle creates conflict between Mom and her new partner.

Johnny's sister is also angry at the new-parent because he is unhappy about the length of her phone calls and about her makeup.

Without a word passing between Johnny and Elizabeth they begin resisting and sabotaging the parents' efforts to build a new-family. They dislike their new-parent and they are angry with their mother for letting him be bossy. One powerful way for the children to deal with their anger is to retaliate by resisting parental direction. It perpetuates their mother's unhappiness and it keeps her in the middle.

Johnny and Elizabeth forget their assigned chores or, on occasion, do the opposite of what's expected. For instance, they take food into the TV room onto the new carpet—something definitely forbidden. But eating in the TV room was perfectly acceptable "before what's-his-name came along." They know their mother is being overruled because she devised the old rules. They also intuitively know that because Mother's rules were different, the new rules are vulnerable. Push has come to shove and they know where to effectively shove.

In relationships, power and love become very entwined. When we love someone, we grant them a certain kind and amount of power in our life. We give them certain entitlements. This is normal and not necessarily negative or dysfunctional. What has occurred between Johnny and his mother, however, is not in their best interest because they manipulate each other with emotional threats. Their response to these threats maintains their alliance and excludes others. They are *insiders* with each other and Johnny wants to keep all others as *outsiders*.

Johnny and Elizabeth no longer feel loved by their mother because she has surrendered too much parental power to her new-partner. The children experience this as another loss. Their motivation for retaliation lies underneath their anger in their sense of disorientation, loss and grief. They no longer know how to impress their needs on the family. Many children become depressed when this happens. Some withdraw, others become anxious and cause trouble. Birth parents begin to hear their children exclaim, "I'm going to live with Dad," or Mom, as the case may be. Can Johnny and Elizabeth be helped? Can this new-family find a better balance point?

Johnny and Elizabeth's new-parent is miserable. He had no idea he would be at war with his partner's children. While he was dating their mother he thought the kids liked him and wanted their mom to marry him—they did, but that was before he turned on them with his power. He believes he has no power and that the kids are running the show. This is interesting, is it not? He sees the children as having all the power and they see him as having it. Everyone feels powerless—mom included. Such is the plight in a new home; nobody knows where the power is, yet it seems to be everywhere.

It is painful for adults to feel powerless in their own home or to feel challenged on every matter by children who do not, in the new-parent's estimation, know how to show respect. New-parents can fall victim to a view of themselves as puppets controlled by their partner's kids. Consequently, they experience confusion and some loss of identity. "Who am I here? I am not who I thought I was going to be!" Both men and women who previously had a lot of control in their homes find these situations intolerable:

- What's with these kids! I thought kids were supposed to show respect.

- My kids wouldn't dare behave like this; I'd never put up with this!

- There's an eight-year-old attempting to run the kitchen and it is driving me nuts. I put things where I want them and she rearranges them before I get home from work.

- I lead a successful corporation. My employees are respectful, but at home my wife's fourteen-year-old son tells me how it's going to be. Who the hell does he think he is? Who's paying the bills here?

The Problem:
Insolence, Authoritarianism, Chaos

Because new-parents end up at odds with their partners over the children, they feel powerless. They experience themselves as living with someone who is married to his or her children, and treated as one of the children's roommates. This is not how they imagined life would be. They expected parental status; they expected some deference as an adult and parent, and to certainly have more power than the children.

What typically happens to partners who feel powerless is that they become angry, lonely and depressed. They may throw up both hands and threaten to walk: "Screw you, live with your kids; I'm outta here," is the first sentence of many endings. Or they may withdraw from involvement with their partner's children. Once a new-partner withdraws, life becomes miserable for the mate; he or she ends up having an intimate partner on occasion but a parenting partner never.

We earn respect—we all know that—but the behavior of adults who are usually respectful can regress in tense situations when there is a history of feeling despised and scorned. Most new-parents make innumerable contributions, and some sacrifices, to the welfare of their partner's children. This can make it difficult for them to tolerate contempt. There is a potentially explosive situation in a home when new-parents feel used or ripped off by children who openly resent them.

In a household that works, meaning one that is emotionally safe and where there is civil, polite social interaction, each member of the household has some power to influence the course of events. To be powerless is to be frightened and vulnerable. In the emotionally unsafe household described above, everyone wants to run away—the children to dad's, the new-parent to his former home, and the birth parent to anyplace quiet and peaceful.

One of the mistakes we make in these situations is to believe that the children have too much power. The problem may actually be that the children have too little of the right kind of power. A feeling of powerlessness can cause children to act out in a manner that negatively controls and manipulates the environment. This acting out is an expression of need and their inability to acquire from others (mostly their birth parents) the emotional nurturing that they need. Acting out is an expression of feeling that says, "I'm in pain."

These expressions show up when kids feel the rug has been pulled from under their feet by their parents' divorce or by a new authority figure taking over their lives. Children need, as do adults, to feel they have some power to control their lives; they want to know they are more than just pawns on Mom and Dad's chess-board of life. They need meaningful ways to connect and acquire the emotional goods and support they require.

Granting children power is different from enabling *kid power. Kid power* is too much of the wrong kind of power. When partners abdicate their role and responsibility as parents, children are at risk—having all the wrong kind of power is as bad as having no power at all.

We grant children power by *seeing* their needs, by *hearing* their pain and concerns, by fairly and firmly *leading* them. Doing so grants them an ability to meet their dependency needs. When parents hear the children's need for protection, and command the help and resources necessary to help them, children have the right kind of power.

Parenting requires the creation of boundaries and the courage to keep children within them. Parenting requires leadership and accountability. It also requires the ability to forgive and to reach out with compassion. Parenting can be characterized as the guiding hand that leads children down the road of life, keeping them between the ditches and helping them avoid wrong turns on the road.

In homes where parents claim too little of their power, children interpret the absence of control as an absence of love. At some level they reason, "If you cared about me you would be concerned about how and where I spend my time." These children tend to not trust their parents to take care of them, to protect them, or to see to their best interest. Therefore, they act out for attention and may end up experiencing many treacheries of adult life long before they are out of their teens.

In homes where parents hold too much power, children do not feel trusted and they do not learn to honor trustworthiness as a desirable quality to possess. Children in these situations experience their parents' power as overpowering. They interpret such control as an indication of their lack of worth. When parents are overpowering it works against childrens' internalization of self-esteem, and it encourages the very behavior it is intended to stifle. Lack of self-esteem is at the heart of a great deal of negative, attention getting behavior.

Power in and of itself is not a bad thing. It is not a dirty five-letter word. The appropriate use of power (firmness guided by mature judgment and tempered by self-control) is a necessary, stabilizing element when competing forces require balance. How partners manage power, and the experience of powerlessness, can make the difference between success and failure in the partnership, because power struggles are at the core of all conflict, and conflict in new-family tears the heart of affection to shreds. When conflict reigns, couples are unable to hang onto the cords of their loving connection and children refuse to connect or bond.

Even the youngest children vie for control and can, along with older siblings, become rebellious about why they have to do things differently: "How come we have to do it this way? This isn't the way we used to do it!" Issues that seem very minor can lead to confrontation and argument when each family has functioned differently. For example: Should peanut butter and ketchup be in the cupboard or the refrigerator? Do dirty dishes get stacked in the sink or placed in the dishwasher?

Kid power triumphs when the children know their birth parent is afraid of being abandoned. We tend to think of abandonment as something adults do to children, but it can go the other way also. Children can abandon their parents either emotionally or physically.

If birth parents fear being abandoned by their children while at the same time they are attempting to be the favored parent, the kids gain enormous power. They exercise that power by threatening rejection. Their battle cry is, "Don't tread on me or I'll leave!" Or, "Don't tread on me or I'll no longer be on your side!" If they don't get their way they're gone.

Use your imagination for a moment to create this picture in your mind: it is a scene repeated in many old cowboy movies. An outlaw with a gun is shooting at the sheriff's feet while commanding the sheriff to dance. Does the sheriff have a choice? No, and birth parents who fear their children, or are overly invested emotionally, have no choice either. When fear is in control, threats are similar to those bullets shot at the sheriff's feet. This is kid power in action and in the face of it parents are unable to parent effectively. They are held hostage and the ransom is parental paralysis, whereby authority is surrendered. Such a circumstance may seem extreme but they are not as rare as one might imagine.

These situations are an indication that deep divisions exist between partners, which allow household members the opportunity to divide and conquer. This is a dangerous point because children may become insolent and new-parents unnecessarily authoritarian. The children react to having someone other than their mom or dad taking charge and new-parents react against feeling powerless. Children may get pushy and resistant, or both. New-parents may get loud, pushy or bossy, and some may become tyrannical. In the presence of such circumstances birth parents become exasperated and close out their partner. The household turns cold, nasty, chaotic and inhospitable. There is war. It may be cold war or hot war, but in either case it is hell.

Partners choose to have either a parenting partnership or chaos at the helm of the household. The formation of a parenting partnership requires a decisive choice to end the dance. Partners must choose to join one another in agreements that get birth parents out of the middle and the new-parent out of the stepmonster role. · Some birth parents confuse the choice to join a partner with one of having to choose between their children and their partner. Some new-partners claim that they do not wish to be chosen over and above the children. These are well-intentioned sentiments, but partners must make a choice to either have or not have a parenting partnership. Until there is a parenting team there is no consistency; hence, no stability and no family community. Partners have to draw a circle, label it co-heads of household and step in together. In consort they must lead the household. Their leadership has to support co-parenting and recapture lost power without alienating the children. The partnership must benevolently see to the children's needs. It must foster the children's self-esteem.

Save Your Marriage:
How to Cooperate

A crucial task in all new-families must be to reduce conflict and the negative outcomes of powerlessness. The competition for power must be minimized, and this is the role of cooperation. There is a law in the universe which simply stated is this: the greater the amount of cooperation, the lesser the amount of conflict and the greater the potential for harmony. In the presence of even small amounts of harmony family members have an opportunity to develop feelings of acceptance and safety. When there is cooperation, power's destructive force diminishes because cooperation represents an appropriate sharing of power. In a cooperative environment there is an exchange of assistance and goodwill that fosters mutual and reciprocal respect: You help me with this; I'll help you with that. You give in on this; I'll give on that. You scratch my back; I'll scratch yours.

Once even minimal cooperation emerges, it helps move the new-family toward a higher degree of integration or *we-ness*. In the beginning there are two distinct and competing families in a household. Their emotional connections are very fragile and their new bonds easily shattered by conflict. Because conflict causes biologically related family members to turn back to their blood family loyalties, it diminishes or destroys we-ness. Conflict always reestablishes and reinforces an "us *vs* them" environment. It maintains two distinct families and it keeps them at odds.

Many readers will know of the work of Abraham Maslow and the scale known as Maslow's Hierarchy of Needs. If you are not familiar with the hierarchy, the following explanation will be

---

* Abraham Maslow, *Motivation & Personality* (New York: Harper and Row, 1954).

helpful. Very simply, according to Maslow, some needs are more primary than others. Therefore, unmet needs lower on the hierarchy beg and clamor for attention. That clamoring makes it difficult, if not impossible, to meet needs at higher levels on the ladder. See Figure 3-1.

The first step on the ladder holds our physiological needs; for example, our needs for food and elimination. It is these needs, when unmet, that make it difficult to concentrate on anything else —when hungry we want to eat, when we have to urinate we need a bathroom. Some school systems feed children breakfast because it is difficult to teach hungry children to read. Another example is the sucking need seen in infants. One reason for giving babies imitation nipples is the belief that it will gratify their need to suck. Some theories in psychology suggest that sucking needs unfulfilled in infancy seek fulfillment in other ways at later stages in the life span. For example, the desire to smoke, chew tobacco or eat obsessively may result from unfulfilled sucking needs.

Needs for safety, belonging, love, self-esteem and self-actualization follow physiological needs on the hierarchy. As a point of interest, note that self-esteem comes after love. In Maslow's scheme this explains why those who experience a deficit of love suffer from lack of self-esteem. In other words, self-esteem is viewed as developing on a foundation of love.

The relevance of referring to Maslow's hierarchy is to point out that in new-family the developmental step from safety to belonging is huge. Sustained conflict drives a wedge between safety and belonging, creating a chasm not easily bridged. It is possible to get everyone feeling quite safe and to create some degree of we-ness. However feelings of belonging that have developed in the early going are very fragile and will diminish or disappear in the presence of fighting and power struggles. Conflict breaks down bonding and prevents stability from developing. Review Figure 3-2.

Cooperative actions bridge the chasm between safety and belonging and thereby promote harmony and strengthen bonding. In the presence of harmony, individuals can let their defenses

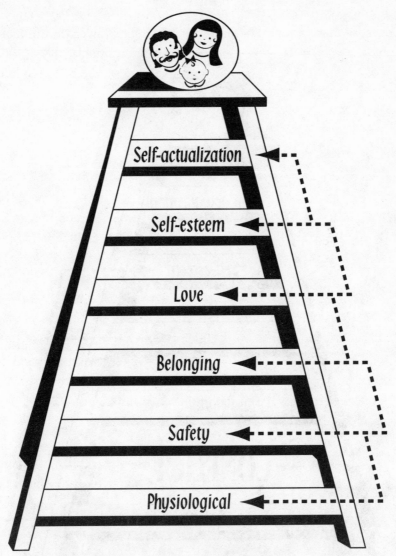

Maslow's Hierarchy of Needs*

Figure 3-1

---

* Maslow, A.H., "Toward a Humanistic Biology," *American Psychologist,* 24 (8): 734-735 (1969).

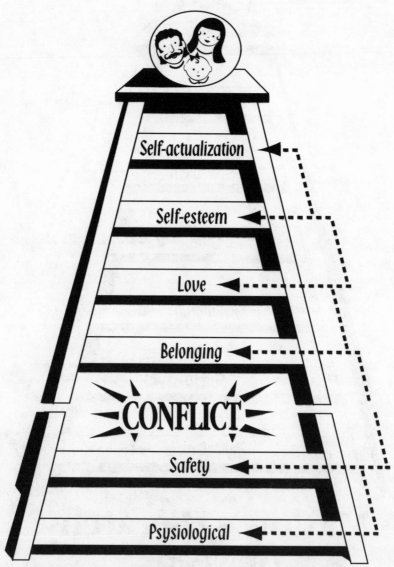

In New-family It's a Huge
Step from Safety to Belonging

Figure 3-2

down and open to emotional connection which is the forerunner of bonding and the backbone of solidarity in family community. Cooperation holds the two sides together. See Figure 3-3.

Partners build a cooperative environment by teaching cooperation. There are three ways to teach cooperation. The first is by example, the second is by example, and the third is, (you guessed it) by example. Teaching by example is the best card couples have in their deck. They cannot teach what they cannot demonstrate in their relationship. Partners must model cooperation for children. They do this by cooperating as partners in the presence of the children and then with the children directly. If children have lived through divorce, chances are they have seen little cooperation.

How much belonging, bonding or *we-ness* will develop because of such an effort is unpredictable. What is predictable is that when there is cooperation there are higher levels of satisfaction than when there is not. In circumstances of sustained satisfaction, bonding has a chance to solidify and thus it becomes less fragile and less pervious to damage from future conflict. Once *we-ness* sustains itself, a new-family can become what the collective intention of the group will allow it to become. However close that is, is close enough.

Cooperate: About What and With Whom?

Cooperation must begin in the partnership and that is where it can be most difficult to achieve. This is interesting because we expect cooperation from children, yet, we can find it difficult to create in the adult partnership. For example, the stricter partner wants things a certain way and the more lenient one wants them another, and unmitigated differences undermine the stability of a household. In order to be successful, partners must learn to manage the complications arising from their disparate desires. Unmanaged, unmediated differences undermine all levels of cooperation and often cause the more lenient partner to feign cooperation by pretending to agree. But silently and passively, the more lenient partner finds ways to sabotage the stricter partner's efforts.

COOPERATION

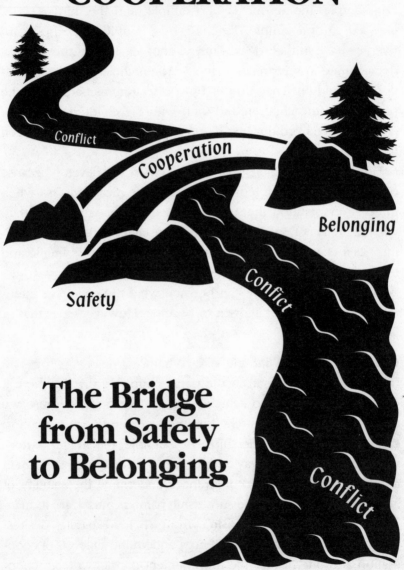

Figure 3-3

Because children are intuitively brilliant, they home in on the contradictions between what the stricter parent says and what the lenient one actually enforces. The children then, in the way that kids will be kids, milk the contradictions. Children, like adults, play the best power cards in their deck, and the best card they hold is the adult couple's lack of unity. Children are seldom sinister, but often clever.

When children act out in the home, resist participation, express desires to run away, withdraw or continually express dissatisfaction, partners should assess whether the problem lies in the parenting partnership. Childrens' problematic behavior can stem, in part, from inconsistencies that result when partners do not have clear, agreed-upon expectations. As we have already learned, partners' inability to co-parent can lie in a judgment made by one or both that the other is too harsh. Hesitancy is then a way of not supporting the harshness. There is a better way; partners can learn to be honest and to discuss their feelings and observations. Most of us know how to get angry or protective, but few of us know how to tell the truth about what doesn't work for us.

A household in chaos is a household divided against itself. In order for a home to not be divided, couples must agree on *how it is going to be* in their home. Their individual preferences should be considered but remain only after both agree that it will become *their way*. They must move from *my style* to *our style*.

It is in the movement from *my way* to *our way* that the *we* of partnership emerges. *We* is a singular voice within the home. Agreeing on *our way* is paramount because partners must support each other with their own children and each other's. What are the rules going to be in *this home?*

Those partners who are birth parents must clarify which expectations they and their children can meet. It is fruitless and harmful to agree to rules and conditions one cannot support, or with which the children will not cooperate. Partners must get honest with each other; they must find consensus.

In new-family no one gets to have things totally his or her way —it is just not possible. Partners without children can find this very exasperating. They expect a birth parent to have more power with the children than she or he actually has. Consequently, the entitlement in parent-child relationships exacerbates a childless partner's sense of powerlessness and alienation. It can leave them feeling left out, overlooked and on the short end of the stick. They assume they are not as special as the children are and, consequently, they resent the children.

Feeling left out and overlooked is not unique to childless partners. Even partners who have children struggle when they see their partner's children getting special treatment. A biological child's unconditional affection from a birth parent can create a mouthful of jealousy that is hard for any adult partner to swallow. This is especially so if the new-partner sees the children getting away with things he or she cannot. It makes the children seem like the golden ones who are above reproach.

It is these observed entitlements that lie at the heart of the protest, *You love those kids more than you love me!* Protesting partners do not object to the children being loved; their objection is to having less power than the children. New-partners want to feel like an equal with their mate and not less than the mate's children. When birth parents grant their children power belonging to the mated partner, the relationship suffers.

United We Stand

To stand united requires agreements each partner can, without hesitation, support. Supporting a rule means not compromising it when the offenders are one's own children or when one's partner is not home. It also means that there is a mutual understanding that when things do not go according to expectation, there are appropriate consequences for the children. Developing trust and being able to surrender some parental control to a new-partner is important, but it does not happen overnight. It is an ongoing, day by day, process. It requires partners to negotiate, adjust, experiment and regroup. When this process of constant reassessment is active there are fewer possibilities for contention and many opportunities to teach cooperation.

If couples are going to be successful as parenting partners they have to talk about their expectations of each other as parents and about their expectations of the children. They must talk about their strategies for building cooperation and what aspect of their personal power each is willing to sacrifice for that goal. They must talk about appropriate consequences for the children and how to carry out those consequences. Partners must be willing to tell each other when they are uncomfortable or dissatisfied with the other's behavior as it relates to the children.

Identifying and negotiating expectations takes time and energy, but the agreements forged reinforce the foundation upon which relationship grows in the same manner that rods of iron reinforce concrete. The absence of mutually acceptable expectations is often the reason couples falter, but the tendency is to blame the children for the problems rather than the relationship. Focus is then placed on the children or on a particular child, rather than on the relationship. A strategy for creating expectations is explained in the exercise at the end of the chapter.

Cooperation results when partners create *united-we-stand* policies for guiding their leadership. A united-we-stand agreement requires discussion and negotiation that results in consensus. Once partners come to terms it is possible to promote cooperation with and amongst the children. But if partners fail to coordinate their efforts they will not gain the children's cooperation. Garnering cooperation requires *trickle-down management*. In other words, cooperation has to be modeled in the parenting partnership so the children can learn through example. Example is the most powerful teacher.

You Scratch My Back, I'll Scratch Yours

One means of teaching cooperation is by using trade-offs. In these exchanges, partners ask for something they need or want in exchange for something the children need or want. This kind of bartering goes on in biological families all the time. Cooperation is a two-way street—I give here; you give there. For instance, Elizabeth wants to spend Saturday afternoon with her friend Jill. She asks permission of her mother, whose response is, "Yes, *but* I need you to cooperate with the planned Saturday agenda and clean your room." Elizabeth mumbles, groans, protests, and then agrees. A deal is struck—Mom gets the room cleaned; Elizabeth gets to go to visit her friend. Cooperation resulted in give on both sides of the equation and a win/win outcome.

Mary, a new-parent, was in a constant tizzy because her husband's daughter, Caitlin, left the bathroom a mess in the mornings. What irked Mary the most was the spilled makeup on the countertop. Mary held a demanding full-time job and was always tired in the evening. Arriving home to Caitlin's mess was becoming more than she could bear, and it was all the more annoying because she drove out of her way to bring Caitlin home from an after-school job. It was a sweet arrangement for Caitlin because she hated the hour-long bus ride home.

Mary decided to stop fighting with Caitlin about the bathroom and to strike a deal with her—a clean bathroom in exchange for the ride home. If the bathroom was clean, Caitlin had her ride the next day. If it was not clean, she rode the bus. Caitlin was incensed that her ride would be dependent on cleaning behind herself in the bathroom and protested to her father, who listened to Caitlin, but supported Mary. He tried to help his daughter understand that everyone in a home has to cooperate to accommodate the many needs that exist. He asked Caitlin to see how she and Mary both benefited from helping each other. In a firm but respectful manner he also reminded Caitlin that her angry response to Mary was unacceptable and that if it happened again there would be consequences. Caitlin's father took a very supportive role that demonstrated cooperation in the parenting partnership and a firm but loving approach to parenting.

Children sometimes take the lead in creating cooperation. Johnny needs to get to the mall to buy a game for his electronic game toy with the money he has saved. The mall is quite far and Johnny knows that his parents are not planning any trips in that direction. Now that there is a new-parent in the house he also knows that whining and sulking will no longer work. In the spirit of two-way cooperation, he asks his mother if there is anything extra he can do to earn a trip to the mall. She tells him yes, that a large stack of laundry needs to be folded and put in the linen closet and doing that chore will earn him a ride. Although Johnny hates to fold sheets and towels, he agrees to do it—another win/win barter.

Sometimes parents feel that, as members of the household, children should not get special privileges or favors in return for chores. That's all fine and good for regular, ongoing chores. However, it should be perfectly permissible for children to exchange an opportunity to do extras for some favor they need from a parent, or to offer barter when extra help is needed from them. It makes them feel like a member of the team and not just a subservient waterboy or watergirl. The demand, "You should do whatever I request of you because you're a kid and I provide for you," is not a fair and cooperative expectation.

Children are to be provided for, and they should receive a lot of things free and clear—just because they exist. Yet, it is certainly acceptable to expect that they be contributing members of the household community. Those expectations, when reasonable and fair, help promote feelings of belonging. Nevertheless, it should also be acceptable for children to expect a favor in return for a favor. Children understand give and take and they know that exchange is the basis of all cooperation. It is one of the first things they learn in school, if not before. When teachers say, "Class, please cooperate," the children know what they mean. Whether or not they do it is another matter, but they do know what is being asked of them.

Just because children know the meaning of cooperation, however, does not mean that new-parents will be any more successful in achieving it than classroom teachers are at times. And this is especially so when partners do not agree about household rules. Therefore, until there is a foundation of cooperation established in a home, new-parents who feel powerless should not be left alone to deal with angry children. Because power is the issue with everyone at this stage, mutual challenges can lead to undesirable reactions on everyone's part. The consequence for new-parents is a heightened sense of impotence that can cause them to use authoritarian tactics to establish their place. Thus, the more authoritarian new-parents become, the more insolent or distant angry children become. A vicious cycle gets set up, and once it is in place trust can be impossible to establish.

New-parents know how easy it can be in challenging circumstances to be harsh, jealous or unkind to children who are not their offspring. And there is, after all, little in our human nature or psychological wiring that prepares us to deal with outsiders in a compassionate, accepting way. One of the insidious rules of nature is "be nasty to outsiders."* Nevertheless, since as human adults we are capable of making informed, rational and compassionate choices, we can muster what it takes to choose the moral high road. We can live the Golden Rule by giving to others what we wish to be given.

Clarifying Partner's Expectations

Partners who can effectively cooperate with each other can teach children what cooperation looks like in a relationship and how they want it to function in their home. Identifying expectations is the first step in defining household ground rules and boundaries. Most conflict that arises in new-family is the result of parenting partners' competing expectations.

Some couples are intuitively astute and simply harmonize with each other's style in an easygoing way, but this is the exception, not the rule. The vast majority of couples struggle to blend differing parenting styles and competing needs for control and order.

When couples articulate their expectations, many interesting and surprising things can happen. First, they may discover how sex-role oriented they are. That is, they tend to expect each other to fit into traditional roles defined by one's sex. For example, women

---

* Lyall Watson, *Dark Nature: A Natural History of Evil* (New York: HarperCollins, 1995) 195-195, 278, and Richard Dawkins, "Genesmanship," chap. 6 in *The Selfish Gene* (Oxford: Oxford University Press, 1976), 88-108.

see to the house; men see to the cars. There is absolutely nothing wrong with this; partners may orient to a division of labor in
any way they choose. What is important is the extent to which
they agree. If they are dissimilar in their views, trouble can result.
For instance, Phil wants the house *spotless* and thinks it is Alice's
job to keep it that way. Alice is, after all, the woman of the house
and only works part time. But Alice does not do spotless and wants
a cleaning person. Alice does not believe that it is the woman's
job alone to keep the house clean. This situation requires negotiation because differences left unresolved will lead to conflict over
this issue.

An important question is the extent to which partners can compromise or redesign life for compatibility within their partnership.
To what extent are they willing to be creative and cooperative in
meeting each other's needs? To what extent are they willing to
model cooperation for the children?

Phil wants Alice to be *mother* to his children but Alice knows
she cannot be. She knows she can do some "mothering" but she
does not want to be identified as mother. Phil's children have a
mother and Alice, being a mother herself, knows the importance
of not intruding on the sacredness of the children's relationship
with their birth mother. Alice needs help explaining this to Phil,
who wants his children to call Alice *mother*.

Phil and Alice need agreements that satisfactorily integrate their
expectations. They are at that delicate point where discussion can
deteriorate into hurt feelings, anger and impasse. Some couples
are able to talk through differences and resolve conflict. Others,
however, need help negotiating compromises. Requiring help is
neither a bad omen nor a sign of impending doom. Asking for
help indicates strength, not weakness. Adults, after all, want things
their way and push meets shove when determined partners cannot reach agreement and are unwilling to seek help.

"I Am Never Enough/I Never Do it Right."

Phil and Alice, like many partners, tend to have only two fights
—his and hers. Alice and Phil fight over many issues, but usually

only about her or his most basic fears. For Phil, it is his belief that no matter what good he does it is never enough, and for Alice, it is the belief that no matter how hard she tries, she never does it right. Phil and Alice have met in an inner critic their worst enemy.

Phil's inner critic repeatedly reminds him that besides not being good enough he is also not important. Phil tries to compensate for his inner critic's harsh judgment by being a perfectionist. He unconsciously believes that doing things perfectly demonstrates his adequacy. By being authoritarian and controlling Phil creates the illusion of having power, and this gives him a sense of importance.

Alice's inner critic sends a somewhat similar message, "You never do it right, and you'll never be able to parent your children correctly." Alice defends herself against her inner critic by overindulging her children in exchange for their dependency. The children's dependency, which looks like devotion, becomes a mask behind which Alice hides her fear of her harsh critic. Her behavior is an attempt to compensate for her negative beliefs about herself.

Both Phil and Alice embrace, as *truth,* something about themselves that is a lie. The lie is their shame—the belief that they are flawed and not good enough. Their fights turn into defensive reactions to their shame because what they *hear* their partner saying is an echo of their own inner voice. The inner critic is not a just judge but an internalized abuser of sorts.

Our personality is the integration of many images, and the inner critic is one that both Phil and Alice carry. In addition, Alice identified these other images: a sad child who felt she never did it right. A somewhat rebellious adolescent who loved to stir up a little fun and sometimes trouble. There was a wise but tired old woman amongst her images, and a mother who felt inadequate and unable to keep up with the demands of motherhood.

Phil and Alice met their self-images by closing their eyes and concentrating for a period each day on the image of a long conference table. During each sitting they would image their self-images seated around this table. They kept a list of all the images imagination created and they noted who was sitting next to whom.

After identifying their major images they placed their inner critic at the head of the conference table. They pretended there was a meeting and that the inner critic was in charge. Alice and Phil began to see the extent to which their inner critic controlled their reactions. In an overly simplistic sense this is what happens internally when the inner critic is in charge of our responses. That voice takes on the executive director role.

Phil and Alice were then instructed to change the table from rectangular to round so there was no head position at the table. What happens to the inner critic when the table changes? What can Alice and Phil do to give their other self-images a stronger voice? Where is their most adequate self and what fear kept him or her from speaking up?

When a demeaning inner critic says, "You are never enough," or "You never do it right," what could the wise or adequate self-images say back? Could it say, "Well, I am not perfect," or "I do make mistakes but mistakes are not failures."? Could it say, "But I am a good person who doesn't want to hurt anyone, and I am eager to work this out."?

As Alice and Phil gave voice to more of their images they became less fearful of their own inadequacy, and thus they were able to be more open and supportive of each other. It is okay to not be perfect, to not always be enough, to not always do it right. Once Phil and Alice accepted that for themselves and each other, it was safe enough for them to expose their vulnerabilities.

How unusual or abnormal is the inner critic struggle of Phil and Alice? It is not at all unusual because most of us have a vulnerability that becomes accentuated in a partnered relationship. There are many reasons for this and not all originate in childhood. Emotional damage and scars can result from failed marriages and the endings of committed relationships. It is possible to make a huge mistake in a decision to marry, and then hang on trying to work it out. In the process one can be grievously wounded. Individuals who have been damaged by a relationship should definitely seek assistance in healing their wounds.

House Rules

The following example lends insight into how complicated matters can be in a new household even before the needs and demands of children are considered. Phil and Alice face an issue they must resolve. If they cannot handle this matter, they will be unable to compromise about many other household ground rules.

Phil wants the children to keep their bedrooms orderly. He wants what Alice considers military inspections once a week. The children who do not meet his standards will forego their allowance. Alice has always allowed the children's bedrooms to be their private space. They could be messy if the children chose to have them that way. Alice thinks Phil is too rigid and he thinks she is a pushover who lets her kids walk all over her. This disagreement has the potential to turn Phil and Alice against each other and provoke chaos. If they cannot find a compromise or if they attempt to force their will on each other, the loser will feel powerless. Consequently, they may knowingly or unknowingly sabotage the rule. Chaos will ensue because the kids will collude with the partner who they know is the weaker. Together they undermine the powerful parent. This is a typical dilemma in new households, and Alice and Phil's conflict points out the importance of being united. What should they do? How can they resolve this dilemma and keep it from turning them against each other? It cannot be both ways. Power is at the heart of their need. How do they keep power from destroying them? What is more important to Phil and Alice—the children's bedrooms or their relationship? If you, the reader, were Phil or Alice, what would you do?

Care must be taken in creating ground rules because it is possible to become too rule-oriented. Then, instead of being heads of household with leadership responsibilities, partners become police. On the other hand, it is also possible to have too few rules. The balance point lies in having as few rules as it takes to assist the smooth flow of interpersonal commerce in the home, but not so few that there is disorder or so many that the climate is stifling and emotionally tense. There is no secret formula for achieving balance. Partners have to feel their way by experimenting with ideas to see what works and what does not. Since trial and error create some ups and downs, it is important to remember that kids forgive inconsistency when parents admit mistakes and when they apologize and demonstrate an effort to be consistent.

Partners have to stay on top of what's happening and constantly assess their progress. They have to consult with each other, negotiate, and be united in purpose and intent. The hardest part is coming to terms—fashioning agreements that create unity.

When Phil's children complain to him about Alice and the house rules, Phil supports his and Alice's agreements in this manner. He says: "These are the agreements Alice and I have made. I know things are different than they used to be, but what we ask is reasonable. I would like you to cooperate with the things Alice asks of you in the same manner you would if I asked you." Succeeding in a manner that creates higher levels of cooperation and integration is dependent on a birth parent's continued efforts to redefine life in the new home for their offspring. That redefinition needs to support partnership agreements. The new-parent cannot redefine home life for their non-offspring children without great struggle and gnashing of teeth, nor is it their responsibility to do so. Reorienting children is most successful when birth parents consistently remind the children that, "This is a new household and there are others to be considered now. We do it differently here than we used to do it. I don't expect you to necessarily like the rules, but I do expect you to cooperate." This responsibility belongs to the birth parent.

Do the ages of children make a difference when it comes to integrating them into a household and garnering their cooperation? Yes and no—age is only one thing that may make a difference. There are many variables contributing to the extent children will cooperate or resist. Younger children do tend to react differently than teenagers, but age alone is no predictor of their ability or desire to connect and bond. Whereas a young child might express displeasure with a birth parent by sitting down between partners, a teen might be impolite, shunning or reclusive.

Money

Money is another matter about which there must be cooperation and agreement. Because feelings of power become attached to money, they trigger many complications. These complications are capable of destroying a relationship overnight.

Because determining the specifics regarding money is of such importance, it is addressed independently in Appendix C. When money issues have an impact on discussions arising in the exercises that follow, turn to Appendix C. The exercise at the end of the chapter is designed to help partners clarify general expectations related to the household.

The Ongoing Challenge:
To Not Alienate the Children

The most important task is for the parenting partnership to assume leadership without alienating the children. This is the challenge. During the transition from the old way to the new way, children need plenty of reassurance of their birth parents' love. Because there are many chances for children to feel left out, they need to be constantly reminded that they count. If life becomes too unpleasant, they find ways to opt out, and this is true even for very young children.

Refer to Figure 3-4. Note the heavier line enclosing birth parent and children and the weaker (dotted) line connecting partners. This represents the bonding pattern when partners first come together. At this point, there is little connection between the new-parent and the partner's children. In real life, adults living for an extended period in situations resembling this circumstance feel powerless and isolated. They experience themselves as outsiders and do not typically feel welcome in their own home. Adults resent feeling they are at the mercy of someone else's children, children who may not like them, acknowledge them, or appreciate their contribution to the economic and emotional welfare of the home.

This arrangement is different from that experienced when the children live with bonded adult partners as is depicted in Figure 3-6.

Figure 3-5 represents the bonding pattern when children feel cut off and betrayed. Note that in this situation all power lies within the partnership. Ties to the children are weak. In real life this would mean the children feel powerless. They are outsiders. They feel unwelcome in this home because of a jarring loss of connection with their birth parent and the unfamiliarity of their surroundings. There is an imbalance of power in figure 3-5, just as there is in 3-4.

Figure 3-6 illustrates the bonding pattern after a couple has established their relationship in the leadership position and retained appropriate, meaningful parental ties with the children. Note that there is a balance of power and a flow and exchange of communication. The children are engaged—there are no outsiders. The line enclosing the couple implies that there is a boundary but it is permeable. The children have access to them and are therefore heard.

Figure 3-6 represents accomplishment of the challenge to balance and bond without severing or alienating the children. The movement from conditions represented in Figure 3-4 to those represented in Figure 3-6 demands constant vigilance of balance. The partnership is the center weight of the family. If cooperation is absent or weak in the partnership, it will be so in the new family.

Children Learn What They Live

It is helpful for partners to be mindful that children are sensitive to the slightest nuance of change that indicates greater emotional distance between them and a birth parent. Whether they have lived through divorce, the death of a parent, or have been an only child with a single parent for many years, they are distance sensitive. Increases in emotional distance are experienced as abandonment.

Children have a right to be possessive of the security they need. Nevertheless, security is not something life guarantees and needing security can be similar to needing a loan from the bank. It can be hardest to get when we need it the most. There are times

BONDING PATTERNS:

In the beginning, couples are more bonded to children than each other.

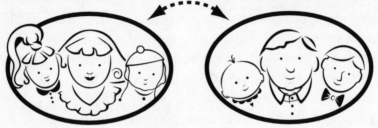

Figure 3-4

When a partnership is too powerful, children are closed off.

Figure 3-5

When a partnership is bonded and children
are connected, there is balance.

Figure 3-6

when kids need to withdraw additional support and reassurance from the family bank, only to find that the family bank is broke, or no longer exists. This is when they feel as if they have fallen into quicksand or that Tyrannosaurus Rex lies in wait around every corner. Children need to know someone is there for them. When they experience their birth parents as absent, they feel there is no place to turn. They feel insecure and vulnerable.

For these reasons birth parents need to keep the needs of the children foremost in their mind, and this is why new-parents need to tread lightly with their power. The notion that children are resilient is true and false. All human beings are quite resilient; the human body is resilient. The adult emotional psyche can take a lot and survive as well. But the psyche of children is vulnerable in all traumatic situations. Yes, children survive, but this does not mean they are resilient. The fact that someone is alive is no measure of resilience. To be resilient is to land on one's feet relatively unscathed following emotional trauma. The degree to which anyone is resilient depends on the state of his or her psychological resources, both internal and external. Children have not yet developed all the emotional resources necessary to get up from an emotional crash, dust themselves off and walk away. Not many adults can do that.

It is more accurate to say that children are fragile rather than resilient. What is most fragile is their sense of *me,* that sense that defines one internally. Kids are trying to figure out not only who they are as individuals but also what kind of person they are: Am I an okay person, a good person? Am I a bad person, a flawed person? Am I likeable? Am I good enough? They translate messages they pick up from their environment into answers about themselves. If they feel loved and safe, they conclude that life is good and they are okay—a good kid, an acceptable person. If they do not feel loved and life is a struggle, they conclude that they are not okay—that they are not good enough or, in some instances, that they are flawed, a bad kid. A child who feels good enough acquires from his or her environment the emotional goods needed for emotional well being. Kids are supposed to have emotional needs; parents are supposed to fill them.

Children's dependency needs make them more vulnerable than adults, because adults are capable of taking care of themselves and their sense of *me* is in place. It may not be the me they wish for in every aspect but they have the ability and freedom to change it or let it be. An adult has the means, to a greater or lesser degree, of acquiring resources. They are no longer dependent on the care of others or the succor of parents to develop a sense of adequacy and mastery, or an honest concept of me.

Each succeeding generation of parents becomes, if they accept the mission, guardians of the self-esteem of the generations that follow. Yet, it is impossible to pass on what one does not have to give. Sometimes one of the positive outcomes of divorce, the loss of a partner or having a problematic child is that help is sought. In the process we empower our sense of *me*. With this new sense of adequacy we become more capable of helping children develop positive beliefs about themselves.

From the foregoing, we can directly glean the value of having a sound parenting partnership in the home. Since many children in new-family come to it through divorce, they have not seen happy, collaborating partners in action. Until they see a cooperative partnership they have no models for creating love in their lives. A couple that comes together and establishes a loving, sound, working-together partnership is teaching the children many important things about love and life. We learn to value and care about things we see our parents cherish. In the presence of loving-kindness, children learn to receive love and express it. They learn to love and to accept love and, best of all, they learn to love themselves.

"My parents never ask; I don't think they care!"

The way to stay in touch with children and not alienate them is to talk to them and interact with them. Get their opinion, hear them by accommodating their reasonable requests or find a therapist, a counselor or spiritual advisor with whom they can talk. Kids are quite good at knowing what they feel on the inside, but getting them to name it or to talk to someone about it can be difficult. We must remember that to understand their feelings, we must ask them to reveal their feelings. Kids seldom volunteer feelings, but when asked privately, they often open up. When children are asked if their mother or father knows how they feel, a common response is, "They never ask!" And sometimes they add, "I don't think they care."

A father said, "I can't figure this kid out; he doesn't talk much. I never know what he's feeling." He admitted, however, that he had never asked. We have a tendency to watch kids and wonder what is going on in their heads—what makes them tick, what makes them act the way they do; but do we think to ask them? This father finally did just that. One day while riding in the car he asked his son what he was feeling and thinking about their new life. A wonderful and painful thing happened for Dad. His son told him. Without anger or blame, the boy revealed how terribly painful and unhappy his life was. He related that without a home life school seemed impossible, homework intolerable, sports lonely and life empty. There were no good times anymore—no movies together, no ski trips, no camping, no real vacations and no fun on the holidays.

The question for Dad was, now that he knew, was he glad he did? He was honest in saying that it might have been easier never knowing. What do we do once we know how painful it is for kids? Is this why we don't ask? By the way, this particular father really did want to know and he went on to make personal sacrifices that significantly improved the quality of his son's life. They both benefited from the improvement in the quality of their bond and more happiness in the boy's life. Dad was no longer able to be so self centered and solely focused on his pleasure. Dad was growing up, learning to make trade-offs, learning to follow through on his responsibilities and learning to appreciate the wonderful qualities in his son. He said he came to see that nothing he was gaining in life was worth gaining at the expense of his son's emotional welfare. He passed up a promotion sought throughout his entire working career to remain active and viable in his son's life. He cried as he told of the bittersweet surrender. He commented on how very strange it was to be feeling such a loss on the one hand while feeling so triumphant on the other. "A job is temporary," he said, " When it is over and you retire who will remember you? A son's admiration is a legacy."

How do you find out what your children are feeling and thinking? Two suggestions follow. Neither of these, however, should be options if you are the least bit angry or intending to have one of those "I'm going to set you straight" talks. These occasions must be congenial, convivial situations where both parent and child are relaxed.

Suggestion 1

Take the children *one at a time* to the fast food restaurant of their choice. Never take two or more if the intent is to have a private chat because the more talkative, verbal kid, the more extroverted of the two, will do all the talking. The quieter one will clam up and say nothing. The fast food setting is casual and does not imply to the child something formal or heavy. Let the child order whatever he or she wants; this is not the time for a discussion about nutrition. Grit your teeth if you have to, but order something you can eat along with them. Sit down and start eating; *do not talk,* just eat. If conversation develops, go with it and let the child lead. If conversation does not develop naturally, ask some casual questions about school, friends, activities, sports, cheerleading or whatever. Let the child tell you things that interest and matter to him or her. Be attentive and involved—exhale and relax as much as possible. Smile and laugh when possible.

After conversation has gone on for a while wait for a lull, that natural period of quiet that eventually occurs in all conversation. Break the silence by taking the lead. Following are some opening lines others have used. Be conversational and friendly with your questions, avoiding a probing tone of voice. If you are feeling those things, it is not the time for this conversation. Express your questions in a loving way:

- "Things have been kind of tough at our house lately; what's it like for you?" Wait for a reply. A follow-up could be, "What's the hardest part?"

- "You've seemed pretty sad lately; are you sad?" Wait for a reply. A follow-up could be, "What's making you the saddest?" If the child answers, "No," you might follow with, "Then why do you seem so sad?" If the response is, "I don't know," you might follow with, "Are you lonely or frightened or _____?"

- "Sabrina, you seem mad all the time; what's happening?"

- "Patrick (age 6), I've noticed you and Billy (age 7, partner's son) have been fighting a lot lately. Do you like Billy?" If the response is, "Yes, he's okay," try, "But what's bugging the two of you that you fight so much?"

- "Seems kind of hard for you with Carol (new partner); can you tell me why?" If the response is, "Not really," try, "I really want to help and it looks pretty painful. There must be something I can do."

- "Melinda (age 13), you seem frightened of Dennis (age 16, partner's son); are you okay? Do you need me to do something?"

- "What are you feeling these days?" Don't ask how are you feeling or the answer will be "Okay." Asking *what* sets up a different kind of answer.

- "How's life?" If the answer is, "It sucks," try, "Can you be more specific? What does sucks mean?" If the child sounds angry you might try, "What are you most angry about?"

Once there is a successful opening, there is no road map to lead you in conversation. Keep foremost in your mind your goal for talking. What is it you want to learn? What is it you want to convey? Does the child seem unhappy, disconnected, depressed, angry, frightened or are you just uncertain about what is inside her or him? Why do you want to know? What will you do with what you learn? You may not have to do anything, but it is wise to know your intention. What if you learn something that requires some action on your part? Are you prepared for that?

Circumstances arise on occasion that demand hasty parental intervention. Parents should watch for significant changes in a child's behavior. There are red flags. For example, if the child is becoming increasingly depressed or socially withdrawn; if he has spoken of suicide or has cut on his body; if she has started using drugs or is getting into trouble with the law. These are times to act. Do not say, "Well, that's the kid's choice," or, "That's the ex's problem." Self-destructive acts are the work of the unconscious mind as it masks or anesthetizes deep pain. Take charge. Stop the child from hurting him or herself. Do not let anyone accuse you of being codependent because you want to stop your child from being a victim of his or her self-destructive behavior. If a parent does not inflate the child's life raft, who will?

It is extremely important to be sincere with children and to not lead them to believe you will help unless you will really do so. Kids are so insightful that they pick up on the slightest bit of insincerity. One can seldom deceive children, they are on to it immediately, but they may never talk about the pain it causes. They just file it in the file drawer labeled, "There is something wrong with me, that's why this important person is lying to me."

If you are willing to help, the following questions may be useful.

- "Is there something I can do to help or make it easier for you?"

- "What would you like me to do that I haven't been doing?"

- "I can't fix what's gone wrong in our lives but I really want to be here for you. I just don't always know how to do that. Can you tell me?"

- "I'm very sorry it has been so hard for you; is there anything that would make it easier?"

This meeting is not a time to attempt to change the child's perception of events that have gotten the two of you to this gathering. Even if you believe the child does not have an accurate view of things, or that the ex has indoctrinated the child, let it go. There is no need to defend or protect yourself or your new partner. And this is not a time to impress upon the child the failings of their other biological parent.

Be there, be present emotionally and hear what the child has to say—*hear the feelings between the words.* What is the child telling you without really saying it in words? Is the child sad, mad, glad or frightened? Try to pick up on what is needed from you. Are there things you would like to say, or could say, that might reassure him or her of your presence? Are there words to let the child know you *hear* her, that you want to help her, that you love him?

It is very hard for parents to see and hear a child's pain and suffering when the parent feels responsible. Their first inclination, therefore, is to want to take the pain away. Painful feelings can be comforted and a child can be assisted in feeling safe in his or her grief, but grief is not assuaged overnight. It is important to be honest about the fact that life is difficult and complicated. Do not sell a child a rose garden unless you can deliver it. Real interpersonal life is not about rose gardens. Offer the child the hope that if everyone pulls together and cooperates, the future in your home can be better. Remind the child that you need her or his cooperation just as she or he needs yours.

Suggestion 2

Another good way to find out what's happening with the children is a variation of the above; again, no siblings should be present. Create a time when you can be with one of the children and some of the child's friends. Perhaps you can chauffeur the ball team, dance line, or neighborhood buddies. Eat with them, watch them, listen to them, observe and listen. It is amazing what you will hear and learn.

This is not as direct and private as Suggestion 1 but it is still informative. Sometimes a child who is quite introverted with adults comes out in a more extroverted fashion around his or her peers. If there are other children in the group who are also in new-family they might indirectly offer some interesting insight. If you want to get the kids discussing the subject of new-family, ask how often they visit their other home, and for how long. Ask them how they like the schedule and they will be off and running, especially if they do not think you are pumping them for anything in particular.

There are also other good opportunities for gathering information. One is a semi-long car ride. Kids will talk when they are along for the ride. And every occasion is enhanced by the inclusion of good food that a child enjoys. Food is a great conversational lubricant.

What do you do with what you learn? Given the challenge of not alienating the children while building new-family, the answer to the question is, do whatever is necessary and reasonable to keep the children feeling secure, safe and loved. Do not emotionally abandon them or become estranged because of changes in your life. Here are suggestions from others who have faced the dilemma:

- Set aside special time for just you and the children and spend time with each of them individually.

- Try to avoid making abrupt changes in how the children have interacted with you. Consistency is very important. Work into changes over time.

- Don't let your partner take over with your children or dictate how you should be with your kids. Do listen, however, to their suggestions. Work together.

- Make sure your kids don't feel that they have become excess baggage that is now in the way.

- Include the kids as much as they want to be included. Don't force inclusion, but don't pass up an opportunity to make them feel welcome and special.

- Ask the childrens' opinions and make their feelings matter in your life.

- Remember, the children have lost a family and the new-family isn't going to fix that loss, even though this change is right for you.

- Keep all your negative thoughts about your ex to yourself and do not permit your new partner to become your ex-partner's basher. It turns the children against your partner. They will resent both of you.

Managing the shift from being more bonded with your children to a bond that balances the needs of both children and new partner is hard work. We tend to hope when we begin a new relationship that it will all just happen, that everything will just fall into place, but it seldom does. Relationships need to be massaged and managed; they need to be nurtured and nourished. Little that is good happens by accident; everything in life has a price. There really is no such thing as a free lunch.* We must work for the good stuff.

• • •

Conflict destroys budding solidarity.
Cooperation is the spirit that nurtures it.
Cooperate . . .

Exercise:
"You Expect Me to What?"

Each partner should write five to ten responses for each statement.

1) Expectations of partners:

- I expect these things of my partner as a partner.

- I expect these things *of myself* as a partner.

2) Expectations of birth parents:

- I expect these things of my partner as a birth parent to his or her children (skip this if your partner does not have children).

- I expect these things of myself as a birth parent.

3) Expectations of new-parents:

- I expect these things of my partner as a parent to my children.

- I expect these things of myself as a parent to my partner's children.

---

* Thank you Milton Friedman for teaching me the economic truth of something we all learn, but may not accept, in kindergarten, if not before. See Milton Friedman, *Free to Choose* (New York: Harcourt Brace Jovanovich, 1980).

Each partner should complete the following tasks:

1) List the most important house rule you want your partner to
    agree to support. (The answer may require a few sentences.)

    _____

    _____

    _____

    _____

2) List five rules with which you want everyone to cooperate
    —including yourself.

    a)

    b)

    c)

    d)

    e)

3) List five specific rules you consider necessary for the children
    (other than those already listed above).

    a)

    b)

    c)

    d)

    e)

Once the recording aspect of the expectations exercise is complete, couples can discuss their similarities and differences. Focus
on one particular area at a time. This is a time to get specific, to
express needs and explore boundaries. What can you say to your
partner in response to what he or she wants that you cannot provide? How much can you compromise to meet your partner? If you
cannot give on particular issues what can you offer on others?

Work together and strive to cooperate by talking, negotiating
and prioritizing. Before implementing decisions, ask the following questions: "What are the most important things to accomplish

right now?" "What's important to focus on today, this week?" It is easy to attempt too much too fast.

This exercise needs to be repeated at various intervals, depending on how quickly goals are accomplished or how often new issues arise.

Exercise:
Meeting Your Self-Images

The following exercise is the one used by Phil and Alice. It is repeated here in a step format for those readers who may wish to use it as a specific learning exercise. It is designed to help individuals develop a better understanding of their self-images.

1) Set aside fifteen to twenty minutes before bedtime. Sit in a comfortable place. Some individuals prop themselves up on their bed. Imagine a long conference table and allow your imagination to fill the places at the table with your various self-images (see page 78). Do not worry that no one will be there; you are working with your imagination, so be creative. You have total control. Work on this for a number of days, until you are satisfied that you have identified your major images. Keep a list or draw a diagram of the table and indicate who is sitting next to whom. If you have a therapist, share your work with her or him.

2) In this step, place your inner critic at the head of the table. Write a brief paragraph about what happens when your inner critic assumes control. What happens to the others around the table when he or she takes over. Note their feelings. Note who is willing to speak and who isn't. Write it down. Do this part of the exercise for a number of days, until you are satisfied that you have explored the feelings of each of the images. It is possible that at any stage of the exercise new self-images will emerge. Make room for them at the table.

3) Change the image of the table from rectangular to round so that there is no head position at the table. Allow everyone

at the table an equal voice in your imagination and permit them to dialog. Continue to allow your imagination to be creative. What happens to the inner critic? How does he or she feel when not at the head of the table? Find the weakest, most frightened image and note how he or she feels. Find the image that represents the strong, adequate part of you and note how she or he feels. Where was this image when the inner critic was at the head of the rectangular table? What would be required to keep the voice of this adequate image in the driver's seat of your life? Find an answer to this question.

4. CREATE:

 **"Your Ex Is Running Our Life!"**

Create

Introduction:
Possessiveness Causes Power Struggles

When a family ends, the cars, furniture, retirement plans and other possessions are divvied up between partners, and although this process is often fraught with struggles, these struggles tend to pale in comparison to those that develop over the children. This is especially true when both parents demand to share the children on equal terms. Yet even when there is little controversy, the legal rights of each parent can cause complications. If partners are also angry and resentful, a war ensues, creating with it a high potential for the children to be emotionally harmed.

Wars between separated birth parents rob children of a peaceful resolution to their uprooted lives. When children are at the center of a tug-of-war, they feel cracked open and defenseless. Divorce uproots them, pulling them from the ground of family. If they then live in the battlefield of their mom and dad's war they experience themselves as homeless, *familyless* refugees. In response to the question, "What does it feel like?" one young boy said, "It feels like my guts are falling out."

Warring between birth parents affects children's attitudes and the demeanor they carry into new-family. Their emotional burdens can create a living nightmare in a new home and for new-parents. In addition, it can create ongoing problems with ex-partners. When new-partners cannot focus on their relationship because one or both is mired in a negative connection with an ex, they are going nowhere. In order to bond in devotion to each other and grow roots in new-family, partners must end wars with ex-partners.

Minimizing negative fallout from custody and visitation agreements is critical for a number of reasons. These arrangements move children into and out of the household, and this movement impacts the stability of the new-family. Because these arrangements keep ex-partners emotionally tied, they greatly influence where the adult energy focuses. If partners are drawn into each other's fights with ex-partners, the energy needed to build a strong bond in their new relationship is drained away. Partners caught up in unresolved anger anchored in the past cannot build a new life with renewed energy. Consequently, negative ties with an ex-partner affect the success or failure of a new relationship.

Anyone associated with a contested custody or visitation matter knows there is no way to prevent children from being affected by the negative fallout. However, ex-partners who are willing to work toward a common good—that good being the emotional health of the children—can minimize the impact.

After divorce, the tendency is for ex-partners to judge each other as inadequate or unsuitable as a parent. Most custody battles are, therefore, about keeping the children away from the bad parent: the ex is too controlling, or too lenient, too much of a friend to the kids or not enough of a disciplinarian. She is too possessive or does not use good judgment. He drinks too much or works too much. She is too religious; he is not religious enough, and on it goes. (The reader may find it interesting that other possessions fueling almost as much passion over ownership are retirement funds and season tickets to sporting events.)

Desiring to prove oneself the better parent, or to deny the children the influence of the ex (the bad parent), leads many couples into civil or family court mediated fights. In this adversarial setting each partner attempts to prove he is the better, and this is most often accomplished by pointing out the weakness and flaws of the other. Even the best and fairest of fights for control of the children can become extremely nasty. There are accusations and counter-accusations, verbal battles over the phone, on doorsteps and sometimes in the presence of the children. Children may be party to adult conversations about their other birth parent, or privy to court documents and proceedings.

Women are sometimes guilty of using their powerful mother attachment to children to coerce them into joining her army. Dad is then the *meanie* who has taken their home and economic security away. He has robbed them of their social status and plunged them into poverty. Since downward mobility is a reality for women and children in most of these situations, and since economic status bestows social status on children at school, it is possible to see how dad becomes the one "destroying their life." Dad, of course, is not always the meanie, nor is he always the selfish one who is ruining the children's lives. A woman's anger can blind her to her responsibility in the downfall of her marriage and what she needs to do to support her children in their love for their father.

Men are sometimes guilty of using their economic power to manipulate the children. They may hire expensive, powerful attorneys to do battle with the ex-wife. Some get into a competitive, conquer-the-mountain mentality that motivates them to throw everything into winning the children. There is nothing wrong with being competitive; a competitive spirit has brought many of them success. Nevertheless, when it comes to one's children and custody, a win/lose attitude is not a sound or healthy one. Enormous pain awaits children when their dad's competitiveness becomes the need to conquer for the sake of conquering, especially if there is no real heartfelt desire to embrace the daily chores of parenting that accompany winning. Some men are not as interested in physical custody as they are in *showing the bitch* or in *putting the bitch in her place*. The tragedy is that once these men win custody they find parenting responsibilities an irritating intrusion. The truth is, of course, that the former wife is not always a bitch, and not always the one who is being selfish or ruining the children. A man's anger can blind him to his role in the downfall of his marriage and what he subsequently needs to do to support his children in their love for their mother.

In the smallest of custody fights, or even when there is no fight, there is still some level of negative or sad energy in the space. Children feel it. It is important to remember that some couples do

separate by mutual agreement and without war, yet even in ami-
cable endings there is still an ending. The kids totally get it! They
know the family is over; they know their life is changing. Children
know their mom and dad are ending because they do not like or
love one another anymore. They may well know the details of
what lies behind the divorce. Nevertheless, their happiness and
the ongoing development of their self-esteem will largely depend
on two factors. One is the manner in which each parent portrays
the integrity and worth of the other to the children. The second
factor, inextricably related to the first, is the amount of positive or
negative energy children experience between their birth parents.

In the long run, the way birth parents represent each other to
their children appears to be as important in the post-divorce adjustment of children as the time-share arrangement in the custody
settlement. If parents are not warring and can speak kindly or
respectfully of each other, the children are more capable of managing even very difficult custody arrangements. If, along with not
warring, parents manage visitation arrangements in a smooth, non-
combative and compassionate fashion, children have the best
opportunity for remaining resilient in the face of negative possibilities. If, however, birth parents get into protracted battles born
of selfish desires to be the favored parent, the potential for emotional damage is high.

Another of the problems for new-family, briefly mentioned
above, is the extent to which new-partners become involved in
battles with their partner's ex, and not only the extent to which
they become involved, but also the extent to which they lead the
charge as well. A new-parent must be cautious to not become
competitive with the new-partner's ex. Cindy, Tom and Vi are an
example. Cindy, Tom's new partner, was well-organized and on
top of things. As a mom she was right in there with her kids,
mothering and sometimes smothering. Vi, Tom's ex, although a
loving mom, was quite different from Cindy. By comparison she
was laid-back and easygoing. Tom's children seldom measured
up to Cindy's standards. Cindy was loathsome of Vi and

exasperated by Tom's children. She thought Vi was an inadequate mother unfit to have physical custody of her children. She kept a journal and recorded everything she considered negligent. She pushed Tom into taking Vi to court to gain custody of the children. The effort led to conflict between Tom and Cindy as the focus of their marriage became the custody battle with Vi. In time, Cindy and Tom were at war over almost everything and it eventually led to the dissolution of their marriage.

It is not only helpful for new-couples, but enormously important for each partner to have clear agreements with the ex. It is important, also, to avoid battles with an ex that get the children caught in the middle. Efforts to rescue children from their other parent can end up being more damaging than their exposure to that parent. Unless there is documented abuse (and in the instances alluded to above abuse is not the issue), children can be harmed more by a war of words than by the inadequacies of either parent. Birth parents should always carefully assess the intent behind any effort to rescue. Later in this chapter, the section **For the Benefit of the Children** offers recommendations relevant to *the best interest* of the children.

On rare occasions a complication in settling custody matters stems from accusations of sexual abuse or concerns that the former partner may not protect the children from being sexually abused by his or her friends. It is an understatement to say that accusations of this nature are serious. Yet false accusations are sometimes used to strengthen the hand of an accuser in a custody fight. For an accuser who is dealing from hate, a false accusation is sometimes as good as a conviction since it can damage or destroy the reputation of the accused. Once suspicion is raised it can be hard to erase. False accusations made knowingly or on dubious evidence yield nothing but evil, destructive outcomes. They subject the children to another type of abuse that is every bit as devastating as sexual abuse.

The majority of custody battles where abuse is an issue are not about sexual abuse but emotional abuse. Emotional abuse is extremely difficult to document because a pattern must be observed and documented across time. Most parents make occasional mistakes that the other parent considers out of bounds or abusive. Losing one's temper with the children or raising one's voice at them is part of the travail of human parenting. These incidents, although unfortunate, may not be part of an abusive pattern. The point is that an angry partner looking to point a finger of blame will more than likely find some past action at which to point.

There is great harm incurred by using the term abuse loosely, or by making false accusations. The negative energy attached to the dislike or hatred that accompanies accusations, and the dramas they create and sustain, open the door to significant emotional trauma for children. The children feel the negative energy, and are forced to live with the pain of the drama.

The Problem:
Children Caught in the Middle

When birth parents are at war, the children feel powerless and caught in the middle. For the most part, children have a sense of fairness and a desire to not hurt either parent. When they are at the center of mom and dad's tug-of-war, it stymies their ability to bond in new-family and to flow with the ups and downs of life. If new-family couples want to create a stable home environment for their children, it is essential that they end any war still in progress with either ex. All turmoil generated by war with former partners is a harmful complication for children, new relationships and new-family.

Figure 4-1 represents the grounding and *rootedness* of children when they have a home. Note that when there is *home* there is a center, a sense of security, familiarity and predictability; a sense of ownership and a connection to neighborhood. A home need not replicate the sitcom ideal of family life to provide these qualities for children.

Figure 4-2 represents what happens to many children once they are uprooted and shuttle on a frequent basis between two house-

When Children Have a Home and Are Rooted

- There is a center
- There is a sense of security
- There is familiarity and predictability
- There is a sense of ownership
- There is a connection to neighborhood.

Figure 4-1

holds. Notice that the center is gone, and that if ex-partners are at war the children must negotiate a battlefield. There is erosion of security because there is no stable ground into which roots can be sunk. There is a loss of familiarity and predictability. The children's sense of ownership is diminished, and the possibility exists for connections with neighborhood to be lessened or lost.

Following are things some kids caught in the middle have said in counseling sessions. Note how the angst and the pain appear to influence their overall attitude about themselves and life. Consider how their despair or anger may affect their integration into a new home.

- I'm totally fed up with both of them. Believe me, I don't want to be at either place. If I had a choice I'd go live with my aunt and uncle in Seattle.

- They pretend that they're in favor of this divorce but they are such phonies. They blame each other and just hate each other now. My dad wants me to hate my mother, my mother wants me to hate my dad. I either fake it or just keep my mouth shut. I hate being with either of them.

- My dad went to court to get us but he didn't really want us. He's never home, and we have to spend all our time with Susan (dad's wife) who is such a rag. None of us like her. If we call our mom it is a big deal. We're not supposed to talk to our mom except when we go and visit. All our dad wants is to keep us from our mom. That's crazy. I hate it and I'm beginning to hate my dad. I miss my mom a lot.

- My mother hates my dad because of his girl friend, who she says broke up our family. She never wants us to see him, and she always works it out so we can't find time to spend with him. My mother isn't fair to dad or to Jerri (dad's girl-friend). But it is no better at my dad's. He thinks mom's crazy and he puts her down all the time. I'm beginning to not like either one of them.

- My parents just rip each other apart. They don't get it. My dad's a totally selfish jerk and my mother's a controlling bitch!

When Children Are Uprooted

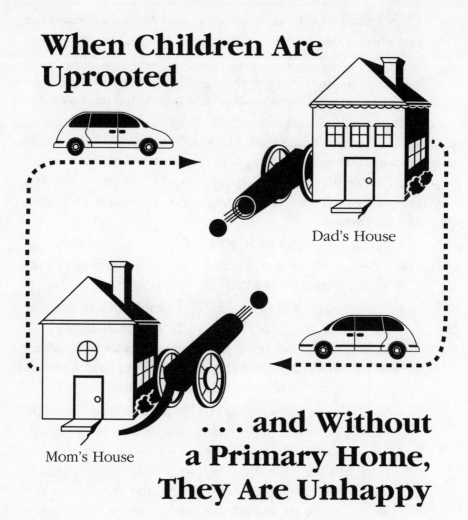

Dad's House

Mom's House

. . . and Without a Primary Home, They Are Unhappy

- No Center
    - The family is in two places
    - The birth parents may be at war
- Erosion of Security
- Loss of Familiarity & Predictability
- A Sense of Ownership is Diminished
- Possible Loss of Connection with Neighborhood

Figure 4-2

How will I ever grow up to be a good person? No matter where I am, it's like a nut house.

- I just go to either place as little as possible, and when I do go home I hang out in my room.

- My mom's new husband hates my dad and is cutting him down all the time. I hate him and I want to go live with my dad, but my dad's wife doesn't like me because my dad and I are close.

- I got so I couldn't stand going back and forth. My parents live 20 miles apart so on the week we were at Mom's, I had to drive myself and my younger brother to school. Because I start earlier than he did he had to wait in the principal's office at his school until his teacher came. Sometimes he didn't get breakfast. Sometimes he'd cry when I made him go in. He's only 7. I know he misses Mom. I felt so sorry for him that sometimes I'd cry after I dropped him off.

  My dad's wife bitched all the time about how much money we kids cost, and about my having a car to drive me and Bud to school. And they were constantly bad-mouthing my mother. It was a pain in the ass, so I stayed away as much as I could but then Bud missed me and he'd cry when I came home and he'd come in and sleep with me.

  My dad is some big deal executive. He's completely tuned out, all he cares about is work, sports and screwing his new wife. You can hear them doing it all the time. I'd turn on the TV so Bud maybe wouldn't hear it. It got so that all I ever did was fight with my dad about what I was supposed to do around the house, and I think I was fighting doubly hard because I was fighting for Bud, too.

  It wasn't any better at my mom's because her new boyfriend was always hanging around. He hates me but he knew I'd fight him if he tried anything. He was mean to Bud, always putting him down for acting like a baby is what he said. My mom wouldn't do anything about it because she

didn't want to upset him or he'd get on her about what a
terrible mother she was.

My mom always says I'm just like my father. How do
you say it? Arrogant and a know-it-all. My dad says I'm just
like my mother, a user and a taker who never says thank
you and doesn't care about anybody.

I don't know why they think you can help. I'm not going
back and as soon as I can get away and get a job I'm going
to take Bud. I love him (breaks down sobbing).

These last words are those of a seventeen-year-old boy who
ran away after a year and a half of fifty-fifty living. When he ran,
he took Bud to his aunt's and left him with a note that said, "Please
don't make him go back."

What is a new beginning for many divorcing adults is a bitter
ending for their children. For children, divorce is the death of the
family of origin. Many divorced couples say, in retrospect, that if
they could have foreseen the pain both they and the children
would face they might have considered otherwise. "Was it worth
it?" they ask. This tormenting question spawns a lot of grief, and
if it is not dealt with it is paralyzing. It prevents those who carry
it from moving on and from parenting in an effective manner.

It cannot be said of divorce that it is always wrong or always
right. Life is just not that simple, and many factors contribute
to an ending. Divorce can bring a refreshed and renewed sense
of life. Children can survive and eventually thrive if the roots
pulled up by divorce find new, rich soil in which to anchor
themselves. This re-rooting of the children must be the primary
task of adults who desire to nurture their children and build
new-family.

Refer to Figure 4-3. This picture represents the situation for children when they are re-rooted and again have a primary home.
There are, of course, consequences for everyone in any re-rooting scenario.

In the book *Second Chances,* Wallerstein and Blakeslee present
the findings of a longitudinal study of families of divorce. They report

Get Children Re-rooted

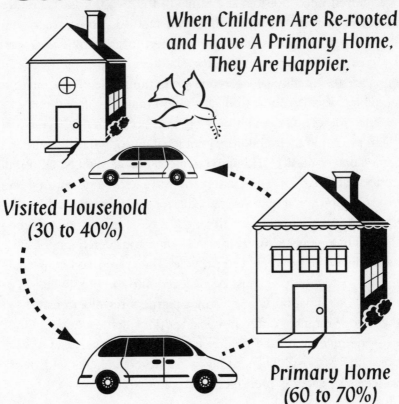

When Children Are Re-rooted and Have A Primary Home, They Are Happier.

Visited Household (30 to 40%)

Primary Home (60 to 70%)

Consequences for the Children

- Restores a sense of center
- Opportunity to grow new roots in fresh soil
- Restores a place of familiarity and predictability
- Restores a place of ownership
- Restores connection with neighborhood

Consequences for Birth Parents

- One parent pays support, but has less time with children
- One parent receives support, but does most of the frontline parenting
- They end the war

Figure 4-3

that by the fifth year after divorce only one-third of the children studied had adjusted, and that well over one-third were worse off.*

Children need not join the ranks of the two-thirds. There are measures that divorcing partners can take to protect their children. These measures assist the children in growing new roots. By creating a primary home for children, former partners can enhance the quality of everyone's emotional life. They make it possible for children to find satisfying home life after divorce.

Since the courts deem it only fair that both parents have equal claim to raising their children, joint legal custody has become the settlement of choice. This arrangement has its pitfalls, as do all custody alternatives. There are many ways to arrange custody and visitation and some options are better for some situations than others. Since every situation is different, it is best for the children when final arrangements favor their needs when considered amongst the alternatives their parents can provide. There are fixed constraints in every situation that must be factored into the possibilities. For example, a situation where former partners travel extensively in their work requires different considerations than one where they live one mile apart and neither travels. A brief overview of various custody possibilities, along with the advantages and disadvantages of each, is presented in Appendix C.

Visitation and Its Effect on New-Family

New-family dynamics are affected by even the most minimal impact of arrangements that keep children moving into and out of the household. Shared physical custody that has children splitting weeks equally between two households can prove to be a new-family's nightmare. When children are present for only a short time, it is almost impossible to develop any consistent parenting relationship with them. It takes the children a day or two to adjust each time they arrive. By days three, four and five they are just getting back in the swing of things. On day six they begin the

---

* Judith S. Wallerstein and Sandra Blakeslee, *Second Chances: Men, Women, and Children a Decade After Divorce* (New York: Ticknor & Fields, 1989), xvii.

emotional shutdown necessary for making the change. On day seven they are emotionally absent and on their way. They repeat the sequence at the other home.

Because new-parents are unable to develop a parenting relationship under these circumstances, they can end up feeling used, like free vending machines programmed to selflessly put out whatever their particular role in the home requires. Women feel like a maid or the nanny (with less respect, however) and men like an ATM machine (also, with less respect). And imagine the coping mechanisms and chameleon quality children develop to play their disparate roles in separate households. The lack of meaning everyone finds in these motel-like settings fuels dissatisfaction and anger. The fallout keeps both partners angry with the children and the ex who seems to have all the power. When children are in and out of a household to such an extent that they cannot grow roots, the new-family's potential for meaningful home life is rather remote. No one bonds.

Another of the ways in which some visitation schedules affect new-family is that it keeps ex-partners emotionally married. If the relationship between ex-partners is positive, with even moderately effective communication and without hostility, their connection is beneficial for the children. If, however, the connection between them is hostile, triangulating or intrusive, there is a lot of impact on new-family. Warring ex-partners need to emotionally divorce and create strong boundaries that keep them from meddling in each other's life.

A lingering emotional attachment between ex-partners also limits their ability to sign-on in their new relationships. When an ex is always leaving messages, always sending lengthy notes with the children, always on the doorstep, it intrudes on the emotional connection in new relationship. New-partners resent the intrusions of a living ghost into their marriage and their life. They feel they are dangling on a thread an ex can jerk whenever he or she chooses. Feeling at the mercy of a partner's old romantic attachment can be aggravating, despairing and lonely.

An inappropriate emotional tie between former partners can also lead children to believe that mom and dad might get back together. It can create for children the illusion that there is still a family with mom and dad. It is grossly unfair to children to maintain such an illusion. The best thing for everyone in a divorced family is to accept that the marriage is over. Painful as that realization may be, it helps bring family members face to face with their grief. Grieving is not a bad thing; it is a necessary thing, a healing thing. It helps finalize an ending. Endings empower beginnings by making possible a life beyond the past. Children caught in the web of their parents' old relationship find it impossible to move through their grief. They become stuck, which thereby impairs their ability and desire to bond in new-family.

How much do ex-partners need to communicate?

There is a need for some communication to transpire between ex-partners, but in many situations it is excessive. In some instances, it is about controlling rather than informing. What information does one parent have that the other really needs? Although that will vary from situation to situation, both parents should know the visitation schedule and the means by which the children are exchanged. Each parent should have medical insurance information and the names of the children's doctors. Each parent should inform the other of any medical emergency. Each parent should have school information. Beyond these basics, former partners must decide what it is they need to know. What they need to know may not account for as much as they would like to know, but boundaries must exist.

Any ex who wants to sabotage the former partner's new marriage possesses powerful weaponry. Those weapons are the children. Meddling takes many forms. One of the more universal is accomplished by negatively influencing the children's attitudes toward the ex's new home and new-partner. Using influence in that manner means using the children and, consequently, con-

demning them to suffer. Often the message intended for the ex
is, "See, the kids don't like you either."

If an ex begins playing this tune it is important not to start
singing along. Do not take the bait—resist reacting. Instead, focus
on your new life. Keep building and strengthening your new marriage and new home. Your best defense against an ex who uses
the children is to not use them back. Be a good parent, trust that
you are, and be there for your children. Let them know that realistic limitations of the divorce prevent you from always being there
in ways you would like to be. Do not be phony, do not permit
the children to feel sorry for you, and do not try to counter the
ex's assaults. Bending over backwards to prove you are not who
the ex says you are does not get past the children. Be the good
person you are and *let your light so shine.* The children will make
their own judgments. If an honest representation of one's self does
not work, nothing else will either.

Recall the story of Cindy and Vi above. One dilemma was created because Vi was seldom home when Tom returned the children from visitation. This meant Tom either had to wait, allow
the children to wait at neighbors' homes, or take the children
back to his home, which was twenty-five miles away. Each time
this happened Cindy became angrier, and her reaction intensi-
fied when Tom came home with the children. Cindy felt totally
jerked around by Vi, and Tom felt caught between two angry,
hostile women. He had never been able to please Vi—part of
the reason he had left—and now he couldn't please his new wife,
either. If he did what Cindy wanted him to do he would leave
the children with neighbors or on the doorstep. It was not, in
her opinion, their problem; it was Vi's problem. But Tom felt that
to dump the kids and run would punish the kids, trapping them
in the middle of a situation they were powerless to resolve. He
refused to punish the children because of their mother's negli-
gence or Cindy's anger. When Vi was over a half-hour late he
returned to his home and took the children to school on Monday
morning. He did not like what Vi was doing, but he refused to

make an issue of it with his children. He loved his kids more than he resented his ex.

If one wants to do the best for one's children in relation to the ex-partner, there are things that can be said to the children to help promote their cooperation. Some examples follow:

- You should cooperate with what your father/mother asks of you in their new home.

- I'd appreciate it if you didn't complain to me about what goes on at your father/mother's place. Those things have to be worked out at that house. Can you talk to your dad (or mom)?

- I am mad at your father/mother but I don't want you to be mad because I am.

- Go and have a good time.

- It is your mother/father's birthday this weekend; let's go shopping so you can take a gift.

- Your father/mother is a good parent (don't say it if you don't believe it).

- You don't have to like mom/dad's new-partner, but you do need to be polite and courteous.

- You don't need to act like I need protection; I'm an adult and can take care of myself.

Why would any parent who is vehemently angry with the former partner offer this type of positive regard to the children? The positive regard is for the children because it helps bolster them; it honors and empowers them to have their own feelings. Attempting to hurt an ex-partner by forcing the children to take on one's negative feelings may ultimately hurt the ex, but it is akin to emotionally skewering the children. Being vested in the best interest of the children requires divorcing partners to rise above their pettiness, to embrace the best of themselves and to sacrifice some selfish ego. Anything parents gain at the expense of the children is not a gain but a loss.

How Much Shuttling Is Too Much?

How much shuttling between moms and dads is too much for children? The answer is, as much as might create the negative side effect of shuttling (explained below) or deny them the sense that they have a *primary home*. One parent said: "But what if creating a primary home for the children means I have to allow my children to live in my ex's home? My ex is a terrible parent." A reality one must accept, and perhaps grieve, is that the children will spend time with an ex who one may judge unacceptable as a parent.

Another reality is that following separation or divorce, the living situation for children is not going to be perfect. And having children live with one parent whose goal is to provide a grounded center for them is better in many instances than constantly shuttling between two households. If the goal is to get the children re-rooted and out of the middle, the task is to accomplish that in spite of whatever unique constraints there may be. What are the sacrifices each birth parent has to make?

Children who shuttle a great deal between two households tend to develop what we will call for the sake of this discussion, *transition syndrome* (TS). TS is an umbrella term used to cover the unhealthy, pathological ways in which children adjust to the lack of stability and to the competing emotional demands of different living environments.

The first criterion of TS is that there be an observable, negative change in the child that occurs after shuttling begins. Often the first observable signs show up at school in declining grades and/or problems with peers or teachers. Problems with performance develop because the children are preoccupied. They become less attentive in the classroom and less capable of meeting expectations. In addition, they become less capable of flowing with the ups and downs of social life and friendships. The nature of childhood and teenage social life is unpredictable, and unpredictability can easily irritate children who are already irritable or depressed. They become extremely sensitive, and events that might have previously been unremarkable now cause them to feel left out and rejected. They may strike out at others or, alternatively, become emotionally numb and withdraw.

Changes also occur at home. Easygoing children may begin talking back; those who were neat and orderly may become messy or unconcerned about their appearance. Perhaps they were talkative and now they are quiet; formerly they went out to play with friends and now they hunker in front of the TV, sullen and preoccupied. They were normal eaters and now they are eating all the time or not at all. They are observably gaining or losing weight. They are more aggressive or more withdrawn. They have begun having nightmares or sleep walking. They always appear tired and are obviously not sleeping well, or they are sleeping all the time.

TS children tend to fall into two broad categories. One group will be called *innies,* the other *outies.* Innies are children who cope with stress by turning inward. They become sullen and moody. They sulk or generally seem sad and unhappy. They become indifferent and disinterested in things that were once of interest to them. Some may appear listless and tired in spite of sleeping more, whereas others just seem quieter and less available. These children can make a parent wonder if there is anyone home in that body.

The danger for innies is that they withdraw from support. Since they don't know what to do with their feelings they hold up as best they can. They become depressed, and eventually their painful feelings lead to more physical sickness than is usual, and sometimes to drug use. Illness can become an all too convenient excuse to stay home from school and withdraw further. In some instances, sickness is used to avoid visitation and the inner turmoil it can create.

- I liked staying home sick, nobody bugged me and I could watch TV. The best was that I didn't have to go to my dad's and be with Betsy the witch. (change of voice, imitating Betsy) "Put your books away, shut off the TV, clean your room, get your chores done, go to bed." (voice changes back) That's all she thinks about. My poor dad, he's such a wimp.

Outies take on the world and everyone around them. They come out to meet their pain and they act on it. They turn it into aggression and become combative. Their school performance typically declines and they may develop behavioral problems in the classroom or on the playground. At home they get along with no one. They challenge everything and everyone. Teenage outies are especially problematic because the power of their aggression makes them deaf to reason and adult influence. They run their own show because neither mom nor dad can any longer influence or control them. Parents become afraid of these children and unwilling to challenge them because the reaction only makes things worse. The following words echo the sentiments of some teenage outies: "To hell with those people; I hate them and neither of them is going to tell me what to do anymore. They have all this advice about how I should live my life but neither of them can get their act together."

The potential for children to become innies or outies is reduced when they can identify one household as the hub of their lives. This is doubly so when they respect the parent with whom they live. The parent is then permitted expectations and can demand accountability. It is easy to see why the parent not living with the children must not sabotage the custodial parent's commitment to teach the children responsibility. When the non-custodial parent is not divisive, the children have the best opportunity for stabilization.

When non-custodial parents have a negative attitude toward the ex, and when ex-partners are continually lambasting each other in front of the children, a high potential develops for the children to take on a split, black-and-white view of reality. This is in part because their birth parents' enmity divides the children's internal experience of reality. Their perception of others may begin to vacillate between an all-good and an all-bad view. This fragmentation is a deep and serious internal conflict that can develop from intense struggles with divided loyalties. When observed, it should be addressed with a therapist, but then all innies and outies should be provided with professional assistance to resolve internal conflicts and to process grief.

It should be noted that some children get on without difficulty visiting households that are very different in value structure. This most often occurs when birth parents are not at war and when the differences between homes are presented in a positive manner. For example, "This is how we do it here, that is how they do it there. One is not necessarily better than the other, just different." When ex-partners remain neutral, or they make *different* interesting but not bad, the children have the best chance of adapting without undue turmoil.

Save Your Marriage:
How to Create

If the goal of birth parents is to see to the best interest of their children, the outcome must be for the children to end up with a stable home. Within this home there needs to be a family-like environment and structure where there are demands for responsible action. Ex-partners need to compromise and make trade-offs which *first and foremost* consider the children's needs for roots, stability, consistency and a home life. We have a tendency to believe that custody and visitation arrangements make little difference in the lives of children, and that kids will be okay, if mom and dad just love them and provide for them. It is not true. Love and physical necessities are not enough. Love has to translate into arrangements that provide for grounding, routine and the reinforcement of qualities that build self-esteem. What children learn when they are continually on the shuttle bus is how to shut off their feelings. They develop personalities they can put on and take off. They learn how to circumvent authority and responsibility, and how to be selfish in the pursuit of survival.

A young girl speaking before a group on the painfulness of her life following her parents' divorce said, "Mom got a house and Dad got a house, and I got nothing." She did not say, ". . . and I lucked out and got two homes." Can we ever really have two *homes* at the same time? It is conceivable that for some children both households are home, but they are the exception rather than the rule. Most often, children who shuttle between households refer to them as "Mom's place" and "Dad's place."

What is *home?* When kids answer that question they produce various responses with a common thread. Some of those responses follow.

- Home is where you can crash.
- It's where I feel safe.
- It's the place where I know who I am; well, most of the time anyway!
- It's where my mother is and where there are good smells, like something baking.
- It's where I keep all my stuffed animals. I put them all on my bed and then at night I talk to them before I go to sleep.
- It's where I can eat when I want to.
- Home is where I can be myself.
- It's where I feel loved.
- It's my favorite place. I have my favorite chair and I like to curl up in it with a warm blanket and veg out in front of the TV.
- It's not mean.
- Home is cozy.
- Home is where my dog lives.
- It's everything! You know, pumpkin pie, ice cream, a mouthy brother, a cuddly cat.
- It's what I get lonesome for.
- Home is where there are no ghosts under the bed.

The common notion expressed in these statements is one of comfort, safety and freedom from having to be anything but *me*. When children say the place they live does not feel like home, it is because they do not experience it as a welcoming, warm and familiar place. They do not feel emotionally safe or comfortable just being who they are without pretense—they must be on guard. They feel like a guest, one who does not have the same rights as a member of the home.

A real home is a place where one has a sense of ownership: *my* toys, *my* room, *my* stuff, *my* closet, *my* drawers, *my* bed, and *our* refrigerator. We all know where home is when we are desperately in need of a bathroom because we have diarrhea. We want to be in the bathroom at *home*. *Home* contains the bed we want to be in when we are sick; *home* is where the person whom we want to care for us lives. *Home* is where there really are no *ghosts* under the bed.

If *home* is more than a residence, more than a place to sleep, more than a place we visit, more than a place where we always have to be on our best behavior, we can see how the transient nature of some children's lives deprives them of a *home*. The home sought by the heart is a place of familiarity, a place where one feels ownership, refuge from the world and abiding comfort.

One young girl said she felt like a human yo-yo shuttling between mom's and dad's on a weekly basis. She reported that what made it most difficult were the different beds and different pillows. It is interesting that that is exactly what many adults dislike about traveling. They miss *their* beds and *their* pillows—some even carry their pillow with them. Children, however, should adjust to anything. What difference should pillows and beds make to kids? Isn't that how some of us tend to feel at times? One might think that children would find the adjustment to different rules the most difficult part of shuttling. Different rules are on the list but often fall behind beds, pillows and even free access to the refrigerator.

Many children respond to a question about where home is by saying they do not know. When asked what they would like if they could make three wishes with the genie's lamp, their typical responses are, "To have my mom and dad quit fighting, to have our family back together, to have a home again," but not necessarily in that order. What divorcing adults may overlook is that while they are moving toward a new life, the children are still looking back on a life lost. The children have lost *their family* and those they love may now be separated into camps that are at odds, if not at war. Divorce, except in extreme circumstances, favors adults, not children.

What do children get from a home that is so important? One practical way to answer that question is to think of the home where you were raised. What did you get that you liked? What didn't you get that you might now wish you had gotten? What did you have to cope with that may have detracted from home really being a home? It is hard to assess what a home might be lacking if one never lived in a setting that didn't feel like home. Yet many of us can remember the strangeness of surroundings, the lack of familiarity we experienced, when we visited our cousins or other relatives. We might remember how self-conscious we became, how we did not know how to ask for a glass of water, or how to tell someone that the toilet had not flushed correctly. Do we remember how discomforting it could be?

Home should feel like the thirst-quenching swallow of our favorite cold drink on a hot day. Home should be a special meal served in bed when we are sick, cool hands on our forehead when it is warm with fever. Home is cookies and milk, pop and chips; it is comfortably slouching in one's favorite spot watching a favored TV show, or playing a favorite video game. Home is a setting for cherished times: a place from where we deserve warm memories.

After separation and divorce it can be hard to create a home for children. Mothers and fathers become part-time parents and they no longer assume complementary roles. All too often they compete and become enemies. After mom and dad acquire new partners children shuttle between two even more disparate worlds. Now, more than just different beds and pillows, there is different everything: different parenting styles, different menus, different chores and different bedtimes—different, different, different. When children regularly shuttle between all those *differents,* and are expected to arrive on the doorstep of the next household adjusted and ready for the next round, they are being pushed into a pit of emotional turmoil. The situation creates the necessity of an unhealthy, dysfunctional adjustment to survive.

Children can become innies and outies for many reasons. Remember that for the behavior to be considered transition syndrome, it must originate after the shuttling begins. When children are innies or outies before a divorce, or develop such a pattern of behavior without shuttling, it is for reasons other than TS. In any case, innies and outies are in serious trouble and sometimes it takes a new-parent to identify the problem and launch an effort to get them help. All the strife of divorce can cause birth parents to become emotionally numb and to overlook the emotional problems besetting their children.

New-parents can see problems birth parents may overlook because they come on the scene with a fresh perspective and a more objective outlook. However, seeing a problem is one thing, helping the children directly, quite another. What a new-parent can do is be compassionate and not demanding of the children, and they can help their partner come to grips with the problems. Troubled children are in need of specialized professional help and the new-parent can play an important supportive role in getting that help.

Given the inner turmoil in the lives of troubled children, it is easy to see why they are terribly problematic for new-parents and new-family. It is almost impossible for new-parents to not tangle with an outie, or not feel shunned and depersonalized by an innie. Imagine an outie who is unresponsive to birth parent direction encountering a new-parent bent on having commanding authority in the home. There are going to be clashes and, more than likely, some very big ones.

It is questionable whether a flaming outie and a new-parent can or should live in the same space since one or both will be hurt. It takes a new-parent who is highly skilled in interpersonal relations and extremely self-secure to manage the inevitable abuse and complications. To do so they must render compassionate, yet firm, care to a soul in pain and ask nothing in return. What they give must be a gift.

Before new-parents assume any role with a troubled child, they should know their partner's expectations and desires. They should also consult with the child's therapist about what their appropriate role can be in the facilitation of healing. It is possible to become too involved and to step in where one is not welcome. The travesty of over-involvement is that it alienates the partner as well as the children.

To live with a partner's troubled children requires a tenacious devotion, and it is difficult for new-partners to be above the fray when consistently a target of the children's hostility. In spite of all they may wish to give, facing conflict and confrontation every day is a terrible way to live. The role demands fortitude and courage—enormous courage.

In addition to clashes with outies, new-parents may clash with innies as well. These clashes, however, have a different emotional tone. Whereas new-parents feel assaulted by outies, they tend to feel non-existent in the presence of innies. Innies shut everybody off and out, but new-parents feel the lockout acutely and take it personally. To a new-parent, therefore, an innie is as disrespectful as an outie, and some new-parents find outies easier to deal with because they are easier to figure out. Innies can seem mysterious, sneaky and underhanded. In truth, both innies and outies are covering for their pain—most are depressed, frightened and lonely.

The Value of Structure and a Primary Home

Children need a home not only because of the comforts it offers but also because of the structure it provides. All children need structure. It reinforces a sense of security and, within its boundaries, they learn responsibility. School, for example, is a form of structure where kids must meet certain requirements and standards. The more stable and consistent the structure of a home, the greater the probability that the children will not always be in contention with what is required of them. It is normal for kids to grouse about their home. This normal whining is different, however, from resentment that exists when there is no home about which to grouse. Sometimes kids need to kick at the foundation of home just to know it is there. They need to know home offers them a particular type of protection and unfailing vigilance. They need to know home is solid, and that appropriate rebellion will not cause it to collapse around them.

The unfortunate aspect of many divorce decrees and custody settlements is that they do not address the need for children to have a *primary home.* The power settlement in custody agreements hinges on mom's and dad's equal claim of the children's time. How the children may fare shuttling through a court-designed obstacle course is seldom considered. In our society children do not have an equal claim on family with their birth parents. The pie splits two ways and the children are not a primary party in the split. The family belongs to mom, dad and the legal jurisdiction in which the family resides. Therefore, kids end up with few, if any, rights and in the end many turn themselves into pretzels to accommodate court decrees.

The most important gift divorcing birth parents can give their children is one solid *home base.* Create for them a home where they keep their treasures, where they can be themselves, where they feel welcome, comfortable and emotionally safe. Both mom and dad have to sacrifice to make this happen. One birth parent will have to take on more of the day-to-day parenting responsibility. The other will have to step back from those responsibilities, but send money and offer emotional support. Neither of these roles is easy.

To create a primary home for children who have been living without one may require the renegotiation of a previous custody/ visitation settlement. That effort can create upheaval and can be filled with risk. Any such decision requires thoughtful consideration. If the damage potential from upheaval could wipe out any benefits to be gained from change, the present arrangement should remain in place. Sometimes it is possible with minimal strife to redesign an agreement better suited to the children. This is particularly so when ex-partners can agree about the importance of one stable, *primary home* for the children.

Love Your Kids More Than You Resent Your Ex

The most ideal living situation for children is to be raised in a family where both birth parents are involved in a concerted and loving effort. Since after divorce this is not possible, the best arrangement is a *primary home* with one devoted parent as the head of household. The *how* of creating a primary home is simple, but not easy. As mentioned above, it may require renegotiating previous agreements, and it definitely requires both birth parents to take on burdensome responsibilities. One must handle the gofer work associated with raising the children while the other takes a supportive but much less direct role. The unfortunate aspect of this is that the parent not directly involved may let go of the children. It takes a great deal of maturity and courage to stay involved with the children when one feels they have little influence.

Parents who pay support tend to feel that it should buy them access and influence. Being caught between one's desire to serve the children's best interest, which means being less directly involved, and one's pain about feeling cut out, is a dilemma of agonizing proportion. Often the response these parents voice is this, "If I step back, is that really good for my kids? Don't they need me?" The answer is nothing short of agonizing. Yes, they need you, but they also need a stable, non-conflictual center for their lives. How can you give them both? How can you support the children in their *primary home,* wherever that is, and still offer them the best of yourself as a birth parent? Can you be in daily touch by telephone? Can you have regular visitation of varying lengths throughout the year? Can you write letters or exchange e-mail? Can you provide them with special benefits?

When former partners are angry with each other, everything relating to the children becomes complicated, and those complications lead to fighting. When children become trapped in the web of their birth parents' fighting, they have a tendency to see one parent as the enemy and the other in need of protection. Mothers are often the ones children protect, but this is not always the case. It can go both ways. Many children feel very sorry for their father, especially if *bad mom* is the one forcing *sad dad* out of the house. If the oldest child is a girl she may be very vulnerable to her father's pain. She may become his protector, and some become dad's surrogate partner, but any one of the children may take on this role. This is something fathers must try to prevent. Out of loneliness they can allow it to happen, but in the long run, it is damaging to the child. It affects the child's ability to eventually bond with a lover from his or her peer group.

The same thing can happen between a mother and one of her sons. The oldest son is particularly vulnerable to stepping in and becoming mother's knight, protector, surrogate partner and man of the house. As it is with father and daughter, this arrangement between mother and son is damaging. Mother will find it difficult to loosen the ties with her son; she may hold him too closely, thereby stifling his development. She may compete with his girlfriends and find it difficult to support his efforts to be in a relationship with an age mate. The son will find it very difficult to allow mother a new lover. He will have trouble letting go of his role with her.

These perils of parent-child relationships occur in non-divorced families as well, but the circumstances that create them are much more apt to occur after separation or divorce. The possibility is so high that it takes effort to prevent them. Mothers and fathers have to take the moral high road and use special precautions to prevent their children from becoming their substitute partners. One way to do this is to not permit the children to become protectors or confidants. Having to fend off the painful emotions of these situations pushes children into maladaptive behavior.

Renegotiating Agreements

How does one renegotiate agreements with the ex? The matter must be met with great sensitivity. One cannot hope to change anything if one cannot encourage the ex-partner to come to the bargaining table. When inviting an ex-partner to renegotiate, know what you want and what you are willing to sacrifice to have it. What will you offer in the barter? One must be willing to make trade-offs and be willing to negotiate on behalf of the children's welfare rather than in pursuit of one's rights.

Any negotiated change to present agreements should result in a signed agreement or legal document. It should identify the children's *primary home*. Beyond that, it should delineate the details of visitation, how the children get to each household and who is to bear the cost of transportation. For many the cost of transportation is not an issue, but if ex-partners live across states, it can be a big one. Whether the document detailing the settlement needs to be a legally enforceable one depends on the quality of the relationship. Do you trust your ex-partner? It is always best in these matters to consult an attorney or a legal service.

One reason children often shuttle between homes is because neither parent wishes to pay support to the other. If each has the children fifty percent of the time, they circumvent the exchange of support moneys. In spite of its financial convenience, this arrangement can be a major barrier to change. Money is a part of most custody battles and often money matters drive custody settlements. There are some parents willing to settle their children into the home of the ex-partner, and even willing to give that ex-partner sole legal custody if it means no longer having to pay support. Unfortunately, neither the legal right of birth parents nor arrangements resulting primarily from financial considerations necessarily serve the best interest of the children.

Couples in the process of divorcing can circumvent much future rigmarole by preventing their initial custody and visitation decree from being vague. Warring partners should never believe they might amenably negotiate details in the future. Warring partners cannot figure anything out without a fight. Leave nothing to chance.

Once agreements are committed to paper and signed, then the important thing is to honor them. Some couples seem to always be in court and to overlook what continually being there does to the children. To benefit the children, stay out of court. Those who pay support, both men and women, must accept this responsibility even when not the parent in the primary home. Those who pay support, but are not the parent in the primary home, have reason to be grateful that someone is doing the day-to-day, front line job of helping raise their children to be responsible citizens. The best possible chance for a stable life emerges for children when divorcing partners make trade-offs in favor of the children.

Following are strategies others have used to begin discussions with an ex about changing custody agreements and visitation:

- I sent my ex a letter telling her about what we learned in your seminar and what can happen to kids that are shut-tlers. I could see this happening in my kids and I was sure she was seeing it too. We were having the children change homes every week. I recommended to her that we keep our 50/50 arrangement but that we split the year differently so the children would have more stability.

- My ex-wife had always wanted to have the children in her home for the school year and have them visit me on week-ends. I had fought her tooth and nail because I just didn't want to turn the kids over to her. I could see, though, that the kids were suffering because of it. I didn't want them full time. With my work it is just impossible. I finally wrote her a letter telling her I would be willing to change our agreement so the kids wouldn't be so uprooted all the time.

- My ex-husband is a very good father but his new wife doesn't like the children very much, and they certainly do not like her. I suggested to him that we meet with a negotiator and change the arrangement. I was very surprised when he actually agreed. We changed the arrangement so that the children are now in my home more than his. They call my place home and they visit their dad. This way he gets to do a lot of fun things with them. I resent that because I do most of what I call the hard parenting, but I can see that the children are doing better since they have a place they feel is really theirs.

- I was given no alternative but to go to court. Unfortunately, my ex just doesn't think all this shuttling back and forth will harm the kids. She doesn't want them full time but she's not going to let me have them either. I am trying through the court to get the children settled in one home or the other for their school year.

- It would take an act of Congress to get my ex to see that the children's needs are as important as his. He's angry with me and because of that he wants to take the children from me. I'd offer to have the children live with him, but I think Kristin, who is 4, still needs as much time as possible with me.

- My ex-wife is a nurse and works shifts. I know it was becoming very difficult for her to have the children as much as she did. I offered to take them more so they could be in my home during school. I could give them rides if they needed and other things as well. I think she really didn't want to give them up because she was afraid she'd lose support money and have to move to a smaller place. I make a good salary, so I offered to keep paying the same amount of support. Afterwards, I was a little resentful about it, but I got over it because I could see I had done the best thing for my kids. Now when they visit her they still have the nice place they had before.

- I wrote my ex a letter and asked him to call you and talk to you about what are the best arrangements for custody from the children's perspective. He did it and I think we have worked out a very good balance for everybody.

For the Benefit of the Children:

There are certain guidelines separating partners can follow to create a home for the children and do what is best for them. Some of these follow.

- Do not fight about or over the children. Accept that after the separation you will have to abide situations that are not ideal. The children are going to spend time with their other parent, someone you may no longer like and who you may think is a lousy parent. Guide your actions knowing that the children love that parent as much as they love you.

- Anchor the children in one home for the school year. Create an arrangement that allows them to leave for school from their primary home and to return to that home after school.

- Establish regular visitation with the parent who is not the head of household in the primary home. Detail all aspects of custody and visitation in writing so that both parents and the children know who is where when. One thing to remember is that as children get into their teens they sometimes want fewer visitations. This is not necessarily because of negative feelings about the parent or other home they visit but because the peer group has become more interesting than mom and dad. That is a very natural course of events. They would just rather be with their friends. Don't take it personally.

- Set up the exchange for the children so they will not witness or meet with fighting. It is important, if there is tension between former partners, to stay off each other's doorstep, and certainly out of each other's homes. It does not damage children to go unescorted to a waiting car in the driveway, if it is a safe area, or to go between cars in a restaurant parking lot. What does damage them is watching their parents fight about them, or listening to either parent lampoon the other. Much of the crying, agony and depression children experience is about the fighting between mom and dad.

- Allow the children some quiet time and emotional distance when they return from the other home. They need time to make the shift. When children first return they can seem disoriented, anxious, angry, upset or withdrawn. Let them be; no questions about how it was at dad's or mom's; no inquiries about what they did or whether they had fun. Asking if they had fun can make it seem as though they are supposed to always have a good time. The long-term outcome of prying is that the children may become unnecessarily protective of the parent from whom they are returning. At any rate, if you don't ask, you may learn later because of what children naturally chatter about.

- If the children come home complaining, do not respond unless you have good evidence that abuse is occurring. Do not phone your ex and demand to know what happened, to scold him or her, to insist that they adhere to the rules of your home, or follow through on discipline from your home. When couples continue to work together amicably after divorce they can establish a lot of consistency. They can support each other while staying out of each other's way. It is difficult but not impossible. Three siblings, twelve, fourteen and fifteen, said in a counseling session, "We've had it. Isn't there a way we can get away from both of them? We sit and watch while they kill each other. It is disgusting and crazy. Will you help us?"

- Do not send elaborate notes with the children to the other home. Keep the children out of the role of postal person. Send formal communication through the mail.

- Do not send the support check with the children.

- Create a procedure for handling emergencies and illness. If the children typically visit even when they are ill, then perhaps a note will suffice, along with any necessary medications. Both mom and dad should have the names and phone numbers of the children's doctors. They should share medical insurance information and ways to reach each other if there is an emergency. If there is illness, the parent who has the children must take responsibility for contacting the other.

- Do not take sides with your children in a dispute they are having with their other parent. If they complain to you, try to help them help themselves. For example, "Have you talked with your father about this? Could you do that? Why not? What if you (offer suggestions)? Does your mother know how you feel? Is there some way you could tell her? You say you can't talk to her; could you write her a note? What if you and your dad saw a counselor together. Do you think that might help?"

  Whenever and however possible, empower the children to deal with the problems of the other home when they are there. A friend's son always came home complaining about life at dad's on the weekends. His mother knew that his dad was a well-meaning person and a sincere parent, so she said to her son, "It is not okay with me that all you do when you come home from your dad's is complain about how it was over there. You need to talk to your father about these things because there is nothing I can do and I am not going to fight your battles with your father." The complaining stopped and the young man eventually returned from dad's a happier child. No one knows if he actually spoke with his father or worked out any of his complaints. His mother never found out if his complaints were legitimate or if they were just what her son thought she wanted to hear. But given her hands-off policy, and following her statement of expectation, the complaining stopped.

- Give your children permission to have a good relationship with their other birth parent. No mom or dad feathers their nest by destroying the children's loving feelings for the other parent. Each parent will secure or destroy their relationship with the children all by themselves. Don't force the children to choose sides.

- Be willing to acknowledge your ex-partner's strengths and the positive things about him or her as a person. Every parent passes on some personal gifts of character to their children. There is good in every parent and almost every parent is good enough. Look again at your ex. That person has good qualities that will affect the children in positive ways. What are those qualities? Some are probably reasons you got together in the first place. See the good in the children and remember they carry fifty percent of that other parent's influence and genes.

- When you and your new-partner attend the children's school or church activities, arrange yourselves in relation to the other family so that the setting is comfortable for the children. Let your relationship with your ex-partner, and the sentiments of your new-partner, determine the distance that should exist between the two groups. Keep tension to a minimum.

- If you and your ex are not on good terms, do not attend school conferences together. Demand that the school provide separate times for both of you. Also have school announcements sent to both households. Schools need to accept that many of their children have two sets of parents.

- Resist all temptations to be selfish and possessive. Do not allow your actions to be motivated by a desire to *get the bitch* (or the "son-of-a-bitch). It only *gets* the kids.

The Ongoing Challenge:
To Resist Temptations to be Possessive

Most birth parents have a natural longing to have their children with them. They want to raise their children, influence their lives and play an important role in their development. The temptation to be possessive often results from the normal adversarial, win-lose atmosphere of divorce court. Divorce settlements are emotionally volatile and it takes mature, adult consciousness to move through them without feeling spiteful or vindictive.

Parents can get into being selfish in three major ways. One is by attempting to deny the children a relationship with their other parent. Another is by dumping all the blame on the ex-partner and belittling or denigrating him or her to the children. And a third is by placing unrealistic, demanding expectations on a new-partner and not protecting her or him from the children's hostility.

The challenge for ex-partners is to resist temptations to be selfish. One way to do this is by ending the war. The fighting does to children exactly what warring ex-partners claim they wish to prevent. Wisdom recognizes that fighting about the children saves the children from nothing. When partners dismantle the family and their children's lives become split between two households, it becomes impossible for a mother to be the mother she intended to become, or for a father to be the father he dreamed of being. It takes courage to realize that after separation one's relationship with the children will change and that it typically becomes less satisfying than one would wish. This is as true for the custodial parent as it is for the non-custodial parent. Everyone's life changes.

Children do not need two involved parents to grow up mentally healthy, content and contributive members of future families and the larger society. What they do need to thrive and develop emotionally is a home that is like the eye of any hurricane swirling around them, a center of peace and quiet, a shelter from the storms of life, a place where they are protected, secure and safe. Home is where there are no ghosts under the bed.

Birth parents have to guard against placing unrealistic expectations on a new-partner. It is selfish and unwise to expect a new-partner to be that person in whose place they stand. A substitute mother is not *the mother;* a substitute father is not *the father.* When new-partners play a role the children will not accept, there is enormous resistance that will work against all efforts at bonding as new-family. What a good new-parent must be is a good *new-*

parent. To expect more than that is unfair to them and the children.

The summation of advice that many couples offer who have been through the trials of custody are these:

- Eliminate potential chances for fighting.

- Stop fighting; get divorced emotionally.

- Have a funeral for all the old issues. Detach and move on.

- Get a life beyond the old family.

- Don't let the sad and angry stories about the ex be the focus of your relationship with your new-partner.

- Don't spend the money you need to educate your children on attorneys' fees.

Create a new home life for yourself and see that the children have one as well. New-family is a beginning that follows an ending. End so you can begin.

• • •

Family dies when the embers
Of love no longer flare,
New family is the Phoenix that
Rises from the ashes.
Create . . .

5. ESTABLISH:

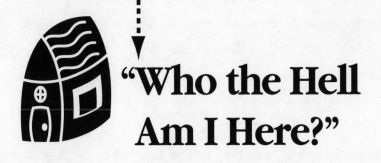

"Who the Hell Am I Here?"

Establish

Introduction
Children Resent New-Parent Power
"Go to Hell! You're Not My Mother."

Knowing how to effectively counter verbal aggression baffles many new-parents. The tempting response is to return rudeness with an insult: *Well, I'm glad I'm not your mother because I wouldn't want you for a kid!* Many new-parents are totally unprepared for the manner in which their partner's children treat them. Although the children's behavior is seldom premeditated, it usually reflects their feeling that the new-parent is an outsider. Even the youngest of the children will let a new-parent know that he does not have the status of a birth parent. Children have unique, permeable boundaries with their birth parents and rigid, more impermeable ones with new-parents.

The moment a new authority figure enters the scene, kids begin sizing them up. The reader may remember how school students treat substitute teachers, testing them to the limits. What kids want to know is just how strict a new authority is going to be. And in new-family it is unsettling and sometimes frightening for children to feel they are at the mercy of someone who comes from outside their circle of familiarity: a stranger, in other words. They wonder:

- Is he going to be mean?
- Is she going to try and be my mother?
- Do I have to do what he says?
- Do I have to like her?
- Will this person hurt me?

For children, it is one thing to like their mom or dad's new friend before the marriage, or before forming the new household.

It is clearly another for them to like this person after he or she claims disciplinary power over them. There are many situations where children are seemingly happy about mom's or dad's new love until the day they become a committed couple through marriage or otherwise. On that fateful day the children can seem to instantly change for the worse. One new-parent said, "I swear, five minutes after the service they became absolute brats."

It is true that children do sometimes change, but they are not the only ones who change in the moment the *I do's* are spoken. New-parents also change inasmuch as their beliefs and notions about who they have just become to the children transform. They now perceive a position of authority with the children that they did not previously hold. Therefore, they regard the children differently and their new perception shapes their expectations—it just appears that the change is only in the children.

New-parents have a tendency to believe that their partnership with a birth parent gives them certain dominion over the partner's children. Without question, every new-parent has a right to be a parent in their home. But the assumption that the new-parent has the right to unquestioned parental authority in the lives of the partner's children is a mistaken one. Such assumptions overlook the children's rights, as well as the children's unique boundaries with their birth parents. The boundary between birth parents and offspring is a boundary founded on intimacy. The boundary between new-parents and children is similar to boundaries between acquaintances or strangers. In the beginning it is more a barrier than a portal. That may change, but initially, the barrier creates a safety zone. When new-parents disregard boundaries, or step over them, children will in one way or another let new-parents know where their authority begins and ends.

A major developmental goal for partners must be to fashion a role for the new-parent that gradually reorients the children's boundaries. The new-parent's role should balance the need for power with the biological parent's ability to be supportive in using that power. In other words, a new-parent cannot be more authoritarian than the children's birth parent will permit. When

new-parents step beyond that point of support there will be reper-
cussions in the partnership. The children's birth parent will become
upset or angry.

New-parents' authority must balance with the children's need
for continuity and emotional safety. New-parents are still strangers
to the children and they must earn their stripes to become more
than that. They do that by establishing a role for themselves that
the children will accept. Children will either quietly resist or become
noisily menacing if new-parents force a role they find unacceptable. There must be mutual respect and regard between new-parents and children facilitated in both directions by the birth parent.

A practical goal for new-parents is to become an equal head-
of-household with the biological parent. Being an equal means
having the same amount of power as the biological parent *within
the domain of the home*. Understanding that the new-parent's role,
at least initially, is an in-the-home role can greatly contribute to
one's success in earning one's place. This is because the children
do not have to guard themselves as diligently against new-parents who know the boundaries and are willing to be patient.

Do No Harm

The moral goal for new-parents is to do no harm. This means
not injuring the children's self-esteem or the biological parent's
relationship with the children. By embracing a moral code that
rises above anger, judgment and attack, the new-parent becomes
a guardian of the good feelings the children have about themselves. This requires one to parent in a manner that is not demeaning or belittling. Because new-parents do not idealize their partner's children, and sometimes do not like them, they can be unduly
critical or harsh, forgetting the powerful negative impact this can
have on a child's psyche.

When new-parents find their partner's children likeable it is a
real bonus for the family. It is not necessary, however, for new-
parents to like their partner's children in order for the household
to function well. What is necessary is that new parents care enough

about the children's welfare to protect them and keep them emotionally safe. They must take a guardian stance. It does not need to be, "I love you, therefore I love your kids," but it must be, "I love you, therefore I will do no harm to your kids."

It is easy enough to understand how and why a new-parent who is shown little respect, shunned, verbally abused or just generally disdained, can lose it. When, in spite of their contributions to the family they are regarded as an outsider, or a second class citizen, they feel used. Facing such circumstances day after day leads to feelings of powerlessness and other strong negative emotions that become difficult to diffuse. This is another reason why it is imperative for partners to agree on house rules and the role the new-parent will assume. Otherwise, the new-parent is continually vulnerable to the emotional impact of depersonalization.

It is also imperative that birth parents not permit their children to harm the new-parent. Children are not always blameless participants, and birth parents are culpable when impolite, abusive, or harmful behavior persists. A birth parent who takes a hands-off stand on relationships between their children and new-partner can be throwing both the children and their partner to the wolves. It is not okay to say to either the kids or the new-partner, "you figure it out." Birth parents must require the children to treat a new-parent with the same regard with which they expect to be treated. Birth parents must see that civility and politeness rule in both directions. *Do unto others as one wishes to be done unto* is a wonderful code for the discourse of human relationships in new-family.

It is not only anger expressed angrily that is harmful to children, but the absence of emotion as well. Both intense anger and cold indifference send messages to children that imply they are not okay, or that *they* are the problem. Shunning is shaming and biological parents must prevent it from happening.

Imagine that hot anger and cold indifference are opposite ends of a seesaw. The way to balance the seesaw is by moving toward its center. Call this area neutral territory. New-parents can func-

tion as leaders in their home from this middle position, being neither too hot nor too cold. Many schoolteachers work effectively
from this position. Teachers seldom like all the children in their
classes—some they tolerate, others they truly dislike, but good
teachers are capable of remaining emotionally neutral toward everyone. Most of us have had at least one teacher who remained stead-
fast in her neutral-emotional role.

Similarly, children seldom like all of their teachers and it is not
necessary for them to do so in order to succeed in class. It is helpful when they find their teachers likeable, but they can and do
learn to relate to those they dislike. This is an ability many of
them can transfer to home and use in developing a living-together
relationship with a new-parent.

New-parents can use teachers as role models for developing
a neutral yet affirming style. By mentally slipping into the role
of teacher, camp counselor, coach, or adult leader of some ilk,
they can learn to rise above the emotion of the moment. From
that place it is easier to be friendly, fair and flexible. When one
is emotionally hooked, it is not so easy. It takes strength to step
back and, at the same time, it takes courage to reach for the
best part of one's self—those parts of heart and mind that elevate us toward understanding and compassion. To live a principled life is a choice not founded on feeling. It is a conscious
decision. New-parents do not need to feel love for their partner's children. They do not need to raise their partner's children. What they need to do is make a choice to be reasonable,
principled, fair and affirming house-parents, and to lead with
integrity and honor.

The Problem:
Jealousy Leads Partners into Blaming

Our identity is a sense of who we are. It is part of our very core
and the stability in our personality expressed across our many roles
(mother, father, attorney, teacher, secretary, machinist, truck driver,
friend, etc.). By the time we become adults we have some clear

ideas about our identity based on knowledge of what we are like. Identity is an internal reference point that unconsciously provides us with a consistent presentation of *me*. Most of us have at one time or another made a statement similar to, "Well, that's me!"

It is possible, however, to encounter circumstances that shake our grounding in the *me*. When this happens we may experience feelings of disorientation, anxiety or unreality. We may question ourselves: "What's going on—who am I here?" We ask because the internal experience of *me* is out of sync with the situation. When this sense of disorientation lingers, panic attacks can occur or inner-earthquakes that cause us to feel we are losing touch or going crazy.

One's sense of identity is particularly vulnerable in new-family, and entitlements often contribute to that vulnerability. *Entitlement,* as used here, refers to the power one person has with another: entitlement is a form of permission. To have entitlement means one has a right to something. For instance, when a teenage girl helps herself to clothing from her mother's closet, without protest from mother, the daughter has entitlement. However, when a new-partner meets with disapproval for likewise taking something belonging to that same person, the new-partner does not have entitlement. These types of exchanges go on in new-family all the time and where entitlements exist, they create jealousy.

To understand how these occurrences shake identity, imagine what happens to partners who feel they have no entitlements when the children appear to have many. These partners experience themselves as being lesser, smaller and/or weaker than the children. "Who am I here?" they ask.

Imagine, however, what happens to the daughter if mom takes some entitlement away from her because mom's new partner does not want the children in the master bedroom. What if he feels it is his private, intimate space and resents coming home to find the children lounged all over his bed watching TV, doing their homework and talking on his telephone. What if he resents that his partner's ten-year-old son goes to bed in his bed. What if he resents that his partner does not insist that her son sleep in his own bed. What if he resents that his wife's son sleeps with her when he travels? What happens when the daughter and son no longer have access to mother's closet or carte blanche access to the master bedroom?

What often happens to children when entitlements change is that they experience it as a loss of love. Because new, more rigid, boundaries create a sense of abandonment, children feel diminished, lesser, smaller and/or weaker and they wonder, *Who am I here?* Since love and entitlements wrap together into the same emotional package, the children may get angry or sad. Changing entitlements requires a new means of understanding and a reframing of the relationship with their birth parent.

Becoming partnered with someone who is also a mother or father is challenging, and dealing with entitlements is a big part of that challenge. One can feel quite secure with a partner and then, *bang!* In a flash one can be uncertain. When women who are new-partners lose a grip on their identity, they come to therapy feeling very powerless and disoriented. *I think I'm going crazy!* is often their opening statement. Emotionally, they are struggling with entitlements that exist between their partner and his birth children. Those entitlements are making the partner feel jealous and vengeful. They want an answer to the question, *Who am I here?*

The sense that one does not count with one's partner, that one is an outsider, or has little if any ability to influence a situation increases the loss of empowerment and self-worth. It leads to valid feelings of jealousy and disappointment. Following are words of new-partners in these situations.

- It feels like he's married to his daughters!
- She doesn't need me; she's married to her son.
- I don't have the same privileges and freedoms in my own home that my partner's children have.

- My partner never gets on her kids, but she's on my back all the time. They can do no wrong and I can do no right!

- Why is it nobody listens to me? When my wife wants advice about her car or something a man might know, she asks her son.

- I have no power here—I feel like the maid who exists to cater to his kids.

- My imaginary picture of our situation is that my wife and I are in the engine of a train. She's in the driver's seat receiving directions from her kids who have the map. They're making the decisions about where we're going. I'm in the tender shoveling coal on the fire so the engine will keep running. I don't know who I am at home anymore. I am a CEO who directs a huge company and comes home to shovel coal. To hell with that, I hate it. I feel very jealous of those kids and it causes me to strike out at them which, of course, only infuriates their mother.

A friend reported that her husband drove his children to school and then picked them up on his return from work. She felt like the life of "their family" transpired during those rides and she was an outsider excluded from the intimacy. She cooked and did the things a mother figure would do, but she did not feel she belonged or counted. She said, "It felt like they had their own private club and I was very jealous that I wasn't included. By the time they got home each day they had arranged our life. You know, I felt like I was just an appendage to my husband's life with his kids because their needs determined so much of it. I mean—who was I anyway?"

When adults feel jealous and like second-class citizens, it handicaps them in bringing forth the best of themselves. It affects their desire to be kind to the children. It denies the adults their sense of adulthood and a sense of certainty earned by their place in the home and in the world. While some adults fume or seethe when they feel depersonalized, others become depressed, irritable or anxious. Some blow up and rage. These explosions can unleash a fury that is often damaging to the relationship and is sometimes unleashed on the children.

This need we have to feel in control of our lives, although more important in some situations than others, is universally so in our homes. We want to count with our partner and our children and we want home to be our castle. Home is not a place where we want strangers intruding or someone else's kids telling us what to do. We do not want to sleep behind a locked bedroom door because of fear that our partner's children may harm us. Similarly, we do not wish to fear that children may finger or steal our possessions.

Balanced personal power in a home is a stabilizing element; unbridled entitlement between birth parents and their children is not. Partners must grant each other different kinds of entitlement than they grant their birth children. This is a big part of becoming a *we*. Partners stand together as partners and they agree about the rules. Until partners reach this point, problems related to the children drive a wedge between them, and two separate and distinct families occupy the household.

In any new-family where fear, anger, possessiveness, grief, exhaustion, feelings of powerlessness and jealousy exist, chaos and disorder will thrive. These conditions create the volatile chemistry necessary for huge explosions. Think of each emotion as a balance weight on an invisible mobile. In small winds of conflict, the mobile dances and bobs but holds its balance. One heavy argument, or one excessive gust of emotion, however, and it is thrown completely out of kilter. Then all hell breaks loose. The fallout hurts every member of the family—fear and grief are reinforced and defenses tightened. Individuals become less congenial and less open to the possibility of positive exchange. Eventually, family members disengage and shut down.

Another time when entitlement can lead to jealousy is when the children of one partner arrive for a visit. The other partner may feel as if their life goes on hold when *those kids* arrive. The kids are the center of mom or dad's attention while they visit. If this is a primary home for one set of children, tension can also result between the two sets of children. Some conflict occurs because the children who are residents of the home have daily access to the birth parent of the children who visit. The visiting children, who have longstanding entitlements with their birth parent, resent the children who live in the home. One interesting aspect of this jealousy is that it can emerge even when the children who live in the home are not fond of their new-parent.

A circumstance of this nature can be a real *Catch-22* for an adult who is both birth parent and new-parent. When their birth children arrive, the birth parent wants some special closeness with them. If too close, however, there is a risk of sabotaging the bonds with the non-biological children. One way partners can deal with this perplexing situation is to schedule separate time for birth parents to spend with just their children. Mom takes her children and does something while dad takes his and does something else. At some point, they meet and do something as a group. It is important for birth parents and their children to have special private time. Partners should support each other in this effort.

Jealousy also comes up for children when they visit the home where mom or dad has a new life. It can cause them to feel like excess baggage, as if they are just an obligation now, not wanted and in the way. When this occurs they feel sad and powerless. These children need a lot of reassurance that can be provided by making them feel welcome and wanted.

One way we all maintain our identity when it feels threatened is by holding on to that which is familiar. In familiarity we find comfort. Consequently birth parents may become possessive of their children. Jealousy is destructive because it creates competition, leads to blaming, and to overt and covert emotional reactions that create conflict. A big part of recreating family is the clarification of each person's rights and responsibilities. Everyone needs a job description of sorts.

Save Your Marriage:
Get a Role for the New-Parent

Every role has certain rights and responsibilities that define its entitlements and power. For example, a police officer has a right to carry a gun and arrest others for wrongful acts. An attorney has a right to private, confidential communication with a client. A corporate CEO has amenities not granted to the secretaries or the loading-dock personnel. Unique rights and responsibilities, entitlements and power are fixtures of every role. What are the rights of a new-parent? What are their responsibilities? The role of police officer or teacher may be quite similar from one city to the next, but the role of new-parents varies a great deal from one new-family to the next because there is no universally accepted description.

Defining the role of *houseparent* helps everyone orient to one another and, by doing so, it helps stabilize the home. For example, a teacher's job description defines what a teacher's role is and thus, by creating expectations, it empowers the teacher and helps bring order to the classroom. Kids know that teachers have the right to require certain things of them. They also know that teachers have means of recourse if students do not comply. When children know what to expect, daily activity in a classroom flows more smoothly, and the same is true in new-family. New-parents need a well-defined role.

The first step in creating a role for a new-parent is to determine the expectations partners want to implement as a couple: *What do we want in our home?* When partners have competing or unknown expectations, dissatisfaction and troubles reign.

Some of the work needed to define expectations was completed at the end of Chapter Three: **"You Expect Me to What?"** Review the work of that exercise. The critical agreements to be negotiated now are those that create for the new-parent a well-defined houseparent role. Keep in mind that the ways in which the children may limit the role in the beginning may not dictate what it may evolve into over time. Interpersonal relationships strengthen as trust is established and affection garnered.

Clarifying the role of the New-Parent

Each partner should review the work done in Chapter Three that dealt with expectations. Review what you expect of yourself and your partner as biological parents and as new-parents. Revise your work in any way you find necessary. The revisions may require you to renegotiate agreements previously completed.

The Inside

Keep in mind your agreements on expectations, because you will now identify ground rules necessary for the in-home lifestyle you wish to create. Call this set of rules the *inside*. The inside ground rules are the rules a new-family requires for living together. These are the expectations everyone must embrace if there is to be a cooperative home environment.

Inside issues are those that require daily management and partners should parent equally around these issues. If one of the ground rules is, for example, to not leave wet towels on the bathroom floor, it does not matter whose child left the towel. Each parent assumes full responsibility for reminding the child who left the towel. On the *inside* there is no mine and yours; there is only *ours,* and it is in this way partners become equal heads-of-household. Working together they manage a household as equal partners. Their primary responsibility is leadership, and within the home they form a leadership team.

It is within the parenting partnership that partners negotiate their needs and desires, and it is out of those agreements that the new-parent's role gains definition and strength. Within the home new-parents are managers and overseers who are never free of the moral demands of leadership as a mature adult role model. They are guardians of the emotional safety that must prevail if everyone's self-esteem is to be protected and preserved.

Refer to Figure 5-1. It is a diagrammatic representation of the inside and outside.

Once there is agreement between partners about the role that a new-parent will play, it is the responsibility of the birth parent to legitimize and support that role with their children. The birth

Create a Role for the New-Parent

Inside: The Living-Together Issues

Outside: The Birth-Parent Issues

Figure 5-1

parent must say to the children, "These are the house rules; I expect you to cooperate and to follow regardless of who is giving direction." Or, "If (partner) asks you to do something I expect you to do it just as if I had asked you." As has been stated before, a birth parent must to some extent mediate the relationship between his or her children and the new-parent. Dumping a parenting role into the lap of a new-partner by declaring, "You figure it out!" is totally unfair. And it goes the other way, as well. Do not dump a new-parent on the children by declaring, "Here's a new boss, figure it out!" These relationships will more than likely fail. The birth parent has to continually teach and reorient the children to new expectations, and he must continually interact and renegotiate with the new partner.

The Outside

We will call issues that belong to matters outside the home the *outside*. Whereas with *inside* issues both partners parent equally, with outside issues they do not—they parent differentially. Outside issues require the biological parent to take the parenting lead. The new-parent supports the partner but hangs back. This is because outside issues are those where children are most apt to resent intrusion by a new-parent. Consequently, this is where children tend to be most reactive and passively resistant. Outside issues create a great deal of stress because when new-parents become involved, children feel the new-parent is usurping mom or dad's position. Children resent new-parents getting into something regarded by the children as none of their business. Since outside issues are the areas where children's boundaries are most often overlooked, differentiating inside and outside reduces conflict between new-parents and children. It also reduces tension that may exist between new-parents and the biological parent who resides elsewhere.

What are the outside issues? Outside issues vary somewhat from one new-family to the next and are determined by a family's unique situation and by the age and dispositions of the children. The next section presents areas children commonly identify as outside issues. These categories offer a basis for partners to determine what the outside issues are in their new-family.

The extent to which a new-parent may become an *other-mom* or *other-dad* is dependent in part on the non-custodial biological parent's involvement with their birth children. Some new-parents actually become, to the extent it is possible, "the parent" for whom they are substituting. Although significant time is typically required for this to occur, it can and does happen. When it does, the new-parent becomes an intimate other who is then capable of effectively managing outside issues, at least as effectively as the limitations of parenting permit.

Outside Issues

School—Children tend to regard school issues as the purview of their biological parents only. "It is none of their business," is the protest often voiced by children about the intrusion of a new-parent. This is one of those areas where the retort, "You are not my mother (or father)," is apt to come up. Many children, and teenagers in particular, say they do not want their new-parents at school conferences or in any way responsible for overseeing their homework. Asking for help from a new-parent is one thing, having it forced on them quite another.

Seemingly unexplained tension and strife between a new-parent and the partner's children can on occasion be traced to the new-parent's role in homework. When kids either have no options or are incapable of politely saying, "I do not want you involved in this part of my life," they find ways to act out their displeasure.

Some new-parents believe that being excluded from school matters by the children is a decision children have no right to make. Yet, what new-parents must be sensitive to is the reaction they will encounter if the children are coerced into an arrangement they reject. To what extent will the tension create an emotionally unsafe household or erode the partnered relationship? New-parents need to cautiously approach school matters.

School is also an area where birth parents can defer too much responsibility to a new-partner. For example, a man can be so happy to finally have a partner to help with the responsibilities of parenting and homework that he pushes too much authority onto the partner too fast.

There is no easy test for determining whether a child will accept direction on school matters from a new-parent. New-parents need to be watchful, keep their ear to the ground and avoid a power struggle, at all costs. Power struggles between children and new-parents can tear a household apart and destroy a marriage overnight. If it looks as if a struggle is going to ensue, the biological parent should take the lead even if he is disinterested in school matters. A struggle between the birth parent and the children may also be difficult to manage, and may wreak havoc on the household, but is far less apt to destroy the marriage. Children grant their biological parents greater latitude in dealing with them than they do others. We will all hear things from mom or dad that we refuse to hear from others.

Children's performance at school can be a barometer of how well they are faring at home. If a child has always done well and then their performance slips, there is cause for concern. When situational turmoil or stress troubles children, school performance is often the first to be affected. Observing such a decline can tempt new-parents to take charge, but the "take charge" manner can move things backward rather than forward. Remember, the problem is not school performance; school performance is the symptom. The problem is the child's pain and how he or she is dealing with that pain. Address the pain.

Church—Whether children attend church or synagogue should be a decision shared by biological parents, and it is a matter that demands absolute harmony and agreement. Children become extremely distressed when they are pulled in two directions over anything, but religion is one of the more distressing. If ex-partners are already in a tug of war and then the new-parent becomes involved, children's resentment can erect a stone wall between themselves and the new-parent.

On occasion, a birth parent who does not attend church marries someone who attends regularly. In these situations the regular attendee often places pressure on the partner and his or her children to also attend. This can rankle the children's other birth parent and create a possibility for the children to become the rope in a holy tug of war. The solution to the matter is simple to understand but is not always so simple to accomplish. Birth parents must negotiate this matter without interference from the new-parent. Above all, the needs and rights of the children need to be respected.

How old should children be before they can make an informed choice about their religious preference? Probably eight years old—and children do typically have preferences, even if the preference is that it does not matter. What children fear in stating a preference is that the parent who is not pleased by it may punish them. And the unhappy truth is that if religion is a hot issue the children will be punished, even if subtly, by the dissatisfied parent. Therefore, if there are entrenched differences, this matter requires professional assistance. There is great temptation for birth parents, and new-parents as well, to push their religious interests at the expense of the children.

If it truly makes no difference to former partners which church their children attend, then the children can choose. Parents might say something like, "Mom goes to this church, Dad goes to that church. If it didn't make any difference to either Mom or Dad where would you like to go?" If we ask the question, we must honor the answer. What if the children say they want to do some of both? What if they each have different preferences? What if none of them want to attend at all? One has to be prepared to address the unexpected. When given a choice, children often choose to go where their best friends attend. Children are typically more loyal to their peers than to religious doctrine at this point in their lives.

Friends outside the home—The children's friends outside the home are an outside issue; the friends they bring home an inside one. Children's friends are sacred to them and tampering with those friendships requires great caution. Children's friendships are, however, a window into their world. If a birth parent realizes their child is associating with kids who obviously use drugs or are a bad influence in other ways, she has to carefully consider what to do. Any intervention requires thorough consideration because even an inquiry can spark a reaction that only makes matters worse.

When it comes to friendships, it cannot be stressed enough that new-parents should avoid direct involvement. Children are hyper-sensitive to birth parent intrusion and this sensitivity increases when new-parents intrude. These intrusions lead to confrontations that can become volatile, tempting both child and new-parent into verbal or physical confrontation. These scenes are tragic when they occur, and the fallout is devastating. They leave the family divided and partners in serious conflict.

A tip in dealing with these issues is to focus on the children's behavior rather than on their friendships. Discuss with them directly which behaviors are acceptable and which are not. Work with the behavior. Let them know when they please you. Reward the behavior you want repeated but do not ignore the behavior that concerns you, because ignoring it will not cause it to go away. Once a destructive behavior is in place, ignoring it will not extinguish it. The peer group is reinforcing it. It is crucial to stop self-defeating behavior before it becomes self-destructive.

Most children want to please, but the truth is they lose themselves in their pain and the daily shuffle of life. When they do, part of a parent's role is to pull them back. This often requires being firm and frank in a friendly, understanding manner. Firm discipline should be followed with kindness and compassion so that the child does not come to fear their parent or regard them as an enemy. New-parents, especially, should remember this. The purpose of discipline should not be to punish but to prevent and redirect. Consequences should not belittle, or bitter resentment will result. Firmness coupled with fair consequences offer an opportunity for insight, improved judgment and internalized self-control.

Clothing worn outside the home—What kids wear at school and socially is an outside issue for most of them. Mary, a new mother, became increasingly agitated with her partner's teenage daughter,

Beth, because of the way Beth dressed for school and social occasions. Mary and Beth were constantly fighting over Beth's outfits and it kept the home in constant turmoil. Finally, after Beth disappeared for two days, Mary and her husband Richard sought consultation. It was immediately obvious that Richard was unconcerned about Beth's style of dress. He said, "Kids are kids, they have to go through this; don't make an issue of it." He believed it was Mary's issue. She was too strict and making much about little. He felt, therefore, that she was responsible for the conflict.

Mary, on the other hand, thought Beth's manner of dress was an indication that things were not well in Beth's life. She took it as an indication that Beth and her friends were without appropriate limits for children their age, but she could not get Richard to see her point or to admit that there might be something to it. So, instead, Mary was browbeating Beth, trying to rein her in.

Mary definitely had a problem, but her problem was not with Beth. It was with Richard, with the agreements between the two of them and with the way in which they communicated. How Beth dresses when she leaves the home is an outside issue. If Mary and Richard could agree that there is a problem, then Richard would need to assume the leadership position with Beth. He would need to define what is acceptable and clarify what he, her birth parent, expects. He would no doubt have a battle on his hands, but it would be a different kind of battle than the one occurring between Mary and Beth. Beth may or may not take direction from her father, but she is not going to take it from Mary. If Mary cannot convince Richard, she will remain powerless and will then have to deal with managing the emotional side effects of feeling powerless.

Curfew—Curfew is another area where kids tend to have difficulty taking direction from a new-parent. Curfews are an issue where inside and outside cross. The time children must be home is an inside issue, so there needs to be agreement between partners about what's permissible and acceptable. When there are problems, the biological parent should take the lead with the new-parent remaining in the background.

Grounding—Grounding is a form of discipline that can be effective when used appropriately and for limited periods. The problem with grounding in new-family is that it requires varying degrees of policing, and whenever new-parents assume an authoritarian role, the potential for conflict is high. If there is trouble, the fallout ends up, as most conflict does, in the middle of the partnered relationship.

What items children may or may not take to the other home—Here is another tricky matter (aren't they all?); the clothing and toys that disappear into the black hole of the other home. School things and playthings intended for the children may accompany them on a visit to the other home and be lost forever. This can become such a problem for couples that they begin to limit what the children may take with them. New-parents are often more sensitive about the black hole than the children's birth parent because the new-parent has different boundaries with the partner's ex.

Children are sensitive and have a sense of ownership about their things. As one teenager expressed it, "What's mine is mine and I should be able to do with it as I please." It is an understandable point and hard to contest. Yet, it is also unreasonable to be constantly replacing what never comes home. Given the sensitivity of this issue it is best if birth parents define for the children what they may or may not take with them. Here are some leads from others who have been in this situation:

- I don't want you to take your new jacket because you might forget it and you're going to need it next week for school.

- I don't want you to take your new Game Boy with you this weekend. You could lose it or forget it, and if you forget it your brothers will use it. Remember what happened to your Power Ranger.

- Remember you'll need your good tennies for school next week. You hate to wear those old ones, but if you forget the new ones, what choice will you have?

This predicament with things leaving and never returning is reminiscent of a story told by a father upset because his support money was not paying for better clothing for his children. At least he had surmised that this was the case because the children arrived with only old, rather tattered clothing. When he complained to his ex, he learned that the children brought only old things because what they brought seldom returned home. After forgetting their good things the children would become angry because they were without them. Mom felt trapped. The only way she could manage the problem was to keep the good school clothing at home.

Bedtime—Some young children are very sensitive about who tucks them in bed. They want it to be their birth parent. It may be okay if their new-parent participates, but they want their birth parent to be in charge. Many young children find this comforting and a particularly wonderful time to have a special visit. It is comforting to be read a story or to have the monsters chased from under the bed. How pleasant to fall asleep knowing that mom or dad banished all those things that go bump in the night. Bedtime is an intimate time. The familiarity and comfort of a birth parent makes the world seem safe.

Demonstrative Affection—Some children are uncomfortable being hugged or kissed by a new-parent before they develop affectionate feelings themselves. Being demonstrative with affection is another area where a new-parent can benefit by going slowly. In nonverbal ways children let adults know if intimate affection is acceptable. Take subtle clues seriously. It is also a wise plan to not force young children to circle the room kissing everyone goodnight.

Is it Inside or Outside?

The only way couples can determine which issues are truly *inside* or *outside* is to watch and listen. Children indicate where they draw the line, but they will also attempt to turn inside issues into outside issues to keep the new-parent from gaining power. So, when a new-parent meets this challenge, "You can't tell me to do this; you're not my mother," it is time to re-evaluate whether the issue is *inside* or *outside*. If it is clearly an inside matter then the birth parent must remind the children that within the household the new-parent is a full-fledged parent.

Children need to know that the adults have agreements about house rules. When children understand this, the new-parent has an appropriate response to their challenge: "You're right! I am not your mother/father, *but* I am a parent in this home and there are house rules with which you are expected to cooperate." It is important for a new-parent to resist being coerced or bamboozled out of their housemother, or housefather, role. It is equally important to avoid any emotional fray. If a new-parent takes the children's challenges personally, rather than as just kids rebelling against changing authority, he will respond with hurt or too much power. Be neutral but emphatic, and don't be put off by the moaning and groaning. Kids love to moan and groan about life—it is a part of the teen job description.

A challenge for all new-parents is to remain open to change as the relationship with the children develops and unfolds. Be prepared to modify expectations as relationships take on added meaning. As positive relationships develop, children permit a new-parent much greater influence and control. They may even ask a new-parent for advice. If, however, relationships become more distant and less intimate, as can also happen, children allow the new-parent little influence or control. There are many variables that account for the unique relationships that develop between new-parents and the children. New-parents need to hold to a long-term view about who it is they want to become to their partner's children. Overwhelming the children with discipline and control will keep them distant and may even alienate them completely. Being unnecessarily permissive and friendly can frighten them as well. Whenever possible, and especially in the beginning, come to the middle of the seesaw. If you want to have a positive future influence in their lives, enter slowly. Be as emotionally neutral as possible, be above the fray, be a leader, lead toward cooperation and harmony. Be firm, fair, frank, friendly, flexible and, above all, have faith in the children's goodness.

One factor that complicates the ability of new-parents to create relationships with the partner's children is the extent to which the partner is willing to share her children. The biological parent's willingness to share and change is a big factor here. If the birth parent wants the children strictly on his or her terms, then the new-parent will not be permitted a parenting role even on the inside. Jealousy keeps some birth parents from sharing the children with anyone. Following are some of the fears birth parents express:

- What if they get to liking you better than me! Then what?

- What if this relationship doesn't work out; then where will those kids be if they lose another parent?

- I don't like what he's teaching the children. Those things are contrary to my views.

- If my ex has a piece and then my partner takes a piece what's left for me?

The answer to the question above is this: What is left is the whole pie. Love is not like money that once spent is gone. Love is renewable—there *can* be a never-ending supply. Because the children love others does not mean they love you less. Power and the desire to possess motivate a jealous birth parent. Children should have every opportunity to love and be loved, and this means being permitted to develop as close a relationship with a new-parent as they may desire.

New-Parents: Drawing on the Power of the Birth Parent

One skill a new-parent can learn is to use the authority of the birth parent. Here is an example: Johnny, who is thirteen, is watching television. It is five-thirty p.m. and his mother instructs him to shut off the TV and do his homework. She reminds him at six and six-thirty but he continues to watch television. Johnny's new-parent, Glen, has been reading the newspaper in another room and has overheard the exchanges between his wife and her son. After she reminds Johnny at six-thirty that it is an hour since she first asked him to shut off the television, Glen steps in to support her. He calmly says to Johnny. *"Your mother* asked you an hour ago to do your homework; now do as *your mother* asks." Johnny moans and groans, but Glen does not make an issue of the moaning. He expects it and knows the resistance is not about him personally. Johnny would rather watch TV than do his homework (so what's new?). Glen goes back to his chair; Johnny continues to grumble, but eventually it stops and he gets to his homework.

The manner in which Glen stayed behind his wife's power is important because school is an *outside* issue for both Johnny and his mother. Neither of them wants Glen involved but his wife does want his support in the manner offered. Glen avoided getting directly involved in the homework. Instead, he supported his wife in moving Johnny toward the unpleasant task of homework.

Glen did not get angry with Johnny and punish him for not being more responsive to his mother, for being disrespectful or lazy. He did not demean him for watching too much TV, or accuse him of showing no interest in his education. He did not get angry, he never raised his voice; he just firmly and frankly, in an emotionally neutral manner, supported his partner.

Glen also did not scold his wife for being an awful parent, for allowing her kids the upper hand, or for giving them indirect permission to walk all over her. He treated her respectfully and as a team member who needed support.

Nevertheless, Glen felt there was a problem in the way his wife parented Johnny. When the children were absent, Glen told his wife that her lack of follow-through was difficult for him to watch. It was hard listening to her constantly nagging rather than being firm and more direct. He did it kindly and in a manner that offered support instead of criticism. Because Glen is also a birth parent he knows how easy it is to fall into ineffective patterns. Glen knows parenting is not easy and that complication after divorce makes it all the more difficult. Glen is a leader who leads with compassion.

Does Glen seem too perfect? Does the scene seem too ideal-istic? If so, is it because Glen did not lose his cool and it remained an emotionally neutral scene? The truth is these scenes play on a daily basis in homes across the country. In Glen's case, he had learned in counseling years before that directing power from his anger only made things worse. Because he had learned to con-trol his anger, he was able to become a reasonable and rational new-parent. Glen understands that a kid might rather watch TV than do homework. He knows, therefore, that Johnny's resistance is not blatant disrespect. He also realizes that his wife's fatigue after a long day hampers her ability to be firm. Glen's age, his divorce and counseling have tempered his emotions. He is more patient than he once was because he knows life is not simple. Glen has grown up.

Feelings can be menacing because we often give them more weight than they deserve and more than we give the rational parts of our mind. There is a popular notion that feelings represent what is true and authentic—"Never go against your feelings," is how the saying goes. Yet feelings are great deceivers. They can be irra-tional and unreasonable. They can also feed intense reactions and a weak, insecure side that needs to conquer and control. People are most successful when they combine feelings with reason. Impulsiveness springs from reactions unmediated by reason. Thinking and feeling need to work together. Slowing one's reac-tion time may mean counting to ten, leaving the room, going for a walk or a drive. This gives the thinking part of the mind time to engage and assess the situation.

Parenting Is a Relationship

An effective parenting role emerges for new-parents when they know the ground rules for the *inside* and are cautious around issues on the *outside*. The role is reinforced as partners work together and address difficulties from the partnership.

Expecting children to respond to a new-parent as if the new-parent holds the status of a birth parent can lead to constant dis-appointment and feelings of rejection for the new-parent. Children are very reluctant, as has already been pointed out, to grant new-parents full-fledged parental status. New-parents must build a bridge between themselves and their partner's children. This bridge must be built emotional brick by emotional brick. Some new-parents try to jump the chasm between themselves and the children, but the distance is too far and the abyss too deep. Better to build slowly than risk a fall into annihilation.

One contingency for which new-parents should prepare is that their partner's children may eventually want a closer relationship with the non-custodial birth parent. This can be a hard time for a new-parent who is jealous or feels betrayed. If this happens it is good to remember that it is possessing, not loving, that is a win-lose game. New-parents must give freely and unconditionally. The fruit of giving is giving itself. They must rest content in the gift.

The attraction children display for the birth parent they see least occurs for numerous understandable reasons. There are natural blood bonds between children and birth parents. The children seek affection from both birth parents. The children's desire does not necessarily mean they like their new-parent less. Yet it can be hard for a new-parent to not feel jealous of a birth parent who does little but who gets the glory. When a new-parent feels over-looked, or taken for granted, it is difficult to honor the children's love and longing for the absent birth parent. When a new-parent cannot be supportive for any of these reasons, it is best to keep the feelings from the children. If children know, they may be guarded and maintain greater emotional distance. When they hear no criticism of their absent birth parent, the children tend to like the new-parent better and to take direction better.

Parenting is a relationship. By contrast, *mother* and *father* are biological definitions based on the contributions of egg and sperm. We have only one mother and one father but we may have many different parents and caregivers. New-parents can replace a mother or father by giving children the care birth moms and dads typi-cally provide. Nothing should detract from the beauty of relationships between children and non-biological parents. They are a gift, both to the children who receive and to the adults who provide. That gift, however, should not stand in the way of children wanting to know the other fifty percent of their genes. It takes big people—compassionate, understanding adults—to love children irrespective of whom the children love.

Figure 5-2 represents the unique and important role of the new-parent, which is initially a role on the inside. As the connection and bond between new-parents and the partners' children deepens, the breadth of that role expands.

The Ongoing Challenge:
To Not Become Overly Powerful

Because new-family creates complicated circumstances, there are ongoing interactions that cause new-parents to feel powerless. It is downright irritating to feel powerless in one's home; thus understandable that some new-parents turn to their power for support. By taking control in an aggressive manner they gain a sense of authority that can help them hang on to their identity. Power in these instances helps one feel alive and important. It is very normal for new-parents to want to feel significant and that their presence matters.

When a new-parent is coming from a sense of powerlessness, there is always the potential to be unnecessarily authoritarian or officious. In new-family, power can easily become an issue because the new-parent's authority is not immediately established, and it is continually tested by the children. If a new-parent does not have the support of the partner she will not be able to discipline with authority. Thus, to create a response, she must become louder and more forceful. A vicious cycle becomes established because every excessively powerful command weakens her position, thereby creating the necessity for more power to mobilize a response.

It is not surprising, therefore, that the best way to hold power is by not using it in powerful ways. This is one reason a new-parent should, wherever and whenever possible, draw on the authority of the birth parent. It is also why birth parents need to continually

NEW-PARENT:
A Role on the Inside

Co-Head
of
Household

Figure 5-2

legitimize the role of new-parents. The birth parent's validation reinforces the new-parent's status and reduces the number of occasions when the new-parent might employ excessive power.

Many problems involving power arise when a new-partner becomes angry with the children because of how the children address their birth parent. The new-parent wants to protect his partner. These interventions often lead to punitive exchanges with the children and to a breakdown in understanding between partners. The breakdown occurs because the children's birth parent considers the intervention intrusive. Although the new-partner must be cautious about intervening, he does have a right to ask for consideration in his home. The manner in which birth parents and their children fight within the home is an *inside* issue. Consequently, partners must have their signals straight on this issue. They have to know each other's expectations. Unresolved problems in the partnership lead to conflict and to the inappropriate use of power.

The ability to express caring through compassion is the greatest power parents can hold. This power refuses to strike out, harm, demean, belittle, abuse, reject, or shun. Anyone can get angry; anyone can express anger angrily. There is no skill required. The skill, however, to manager anger, to turn its energy away from power that can harm and toward compassion, reconciliation, and healing, is the nobility inherent in acting from one's Greater Self. It is a manifestation of God within.

• • •

Ennobling one's self as a parent
Is a gift to Self,
Parenting with compassion
Is a gift to God.
Establish....

6. SOLIDIFY:

"If I'm So Happy, Why Am I Sad?"

Solidify

Introduction:
Children Resist Becoming New-Family

How *close* can members in new-family become and how close is close enough? The meaning of *close* is the extent to which individuals within the family experience it as an integrated expression of *we (We are family!)* When asked to state a preference about how close they would like their new-family to become, children state a lower preference than adults. On a scale of one to ten where ten is high and one is low, adults typically desire an eight or higher. Children typically state a preference of five or lower. In new-family where a gap of this nature exists, it is almost impossible for couples to achieve their desires given what the children are willing to give them. Consequently, new-family may look like a family but not feel like one.

The children's history in their biological family and their loyalty ties to blood relatives can render them resistant to bonding into new-family community. Because of this, hopes for a family-like closeness can be unrealistic, and if partners push unrealistic expectations on the children, the demand becomes a barrier to meaningful interpersonal connections. The definition of family that a new-family creates for itself is dependent on the unspoken, collective agreement of the group. The collective agreement is invisible inasmuch as it is mostly unrecognized and rarely written down or discussed; it is not a conscious consideration of each family member. This silent agreement controls, and until it changes, the glue of closeness will become no stronger.

The strength of loyalty ties between children and their birth parent and siblings outside the new-family unit determines how loose children want ties to remain—remember that the children may be a part of two new-families. The children's reluctance to

bond makes perfect sense, especially if their birth parents are warring or vying for a favored position with them. Because children
have to negotiate the emotional terrain of two households, they
attempt to keep life as simple as possible. That can mean not
becoming too deeply attached in either place. Their detachment
is a way of insulating themselves from painful feelings. It is a survival tactic that helps them endure a very difficult time in their
lives. Living with detachment has consequences that may require
attention later in life. Yet, if they did not detach they would be
constantly torn apart. Life is so painful for some children that the
best and wisest thing they can do is insulate and hang on.

If a couple's dream is to recreate the sense of family lost with
divorce or separation, re-framing that dream will not be easy. The
realization that the dream will never be reality can settle with great
impact. Men whose children live with the former partner can especially suffer in this regard. When they remarry, they look forward
to having their children in their home and having that feeling of
family again. When it does not develop, the disappointment can
be devastating. Letting go of dreams, or re-framing them, is an
emotional task we cannot just will ourselves to do. (You have,
perhaps, heard the admonition, "Well, *just* let go." Obviously, he
or she who repeats it has never had to do it. It would be nice if
it were *just* that simple and *just* that easy. It isn't!)

Our heart seems to have a mind of its own and we must work
with both heart and head. Successful detachment and reorienta-
tion require time coupled with an intention to change. Someone
who smokes and wants to quit, for instance, can have the intention but not the genuine desire to do so. All growth requires desire.
Desire must implement good intentions. When the power of desire
is moving one forward, one can step from one good intention to
the next.

Joy and fulfillment often lurk in places we least expect to find
them. The beautiful natural pearl grows inside an unattractive mol-
lusk called the oyster. Pearls form when a grain of sand, or some
other tiny irritant, finds its way inside. The oyster attempts to

protect itself from the irritating intruder by excreting a substance that surrounds and engulfs it. Over time this secreted substance builds up and hardens into a gem—a beautiful pearl.

What do pearls have to do with new-family? Hidden inside almost every new-family is the potential to create a pearl. The oyster turns an invasion into an opportunity; it creates something of beauty. And so it can be for partners in new-family; their problems can empower their transformation.

We know what a grain of sand looks like after it becomes a pearl, but what do the remnants of two first families look like after they become new-family? Do they look like a biological family? Superficially they might, but at the core they are different. They are a bonded, connected group of individuals who have learned to *do* life together. There is tolerance and an acceptance of different values. There is more cooperation than conflict, and there are periods of real harmony. They are a family community.

There is still a dance, but it is a different dance. A line dance or circle dance replaces the death spiral dance previously discussed. In these new dances, family members participate in a synchronization of steps and movement. Their joining is sustained by common understanding and reciprocal respect, their bonding by invisible cords of emotional connection.

Before family community can be realized, partners must decide whether they can back away from a forceful pursuit of their definition of family. Although couples may not discuss directly their definition of family, they nevertheless unconsciously settle the matter within the silent agreement of their expectations. That agreement plays out in the demands they place on each other and members of the household.

What leads to trouble for couples is the frustration and anger that result when they cannot compel their vision of how family should be. Because they cannot achieve the demand inherent in the *should,* they judge their effort a failure. If this sense of failure then sets up a vicious cycle of blaming, it can turn partners against each other. Following is one way in which it happens:

When one partner believes their lack of success is due to the other partner's behavior toward the children who are not his or her offspring, blaming begins. The birth parent who harbors this belief will blame the other and be unable to see his or her own contribution to the problems: "If you weren't so hard on my kids, the kids would like it here and we'd be a family." Once a finger of blame is pointed, the blamer locks into a perception to protect his position and the blamee locks into a defense to protect hers. Partners are then stuck on a moving merry-go-round and the merry-go-round takes them nowhere except on an up-and-down ride.

If couples can take a step back from their demands (or, as the kids might say, "chill out!"), everyone can sigh in relief. The comfort that comes from not having pressure and stress can be the very thing that gets the couples off the merry-go-round. Building solidarity is one effort where going forward with a wait-and-see approach is helpful. Adults in these situations, however, have problems with patience. They want what they want and they want it now. In the process they become demanding and controlling, and the outcome is resistance from the children. A new-family collective cannot be compelled or forced into closeness. Closeness must be a safe, attractive and rewarding destination. Children reach for homemade cookies but not for the bottle of Mr. Yuk.

The admonition voiced by couples who have struggled in this area is, *don't force closeness.* Affectionate feelings require time and the right chemistry in order to develop. Every family member does not have to like every other family member. It is not a realistic expectation even in biologically related families. Yet, in new-family, not meeting the ideal makes it seem as if something is wrong. This, however, is not the case; normal is not wrong.

Adults can live with children who are not their offspring and have very civil and courteous relationships without having to be best of buddies. Courteous behavior is a critical building block in an emotionally safe environment. In this regard, new-family offers a wonderful opportunity for everyone to learn courtesy and respect for others' possessions and feelings. Since the number one rule is cooperation, the number two rule must be courtesy. New-parents, especially, must be careful when they demand respect, to keep the demand respectful. We cannot garner respect by compelling it in non-respectful ways.

Embracing a stop-pushing approach does not mean a couple's disappointment about surrendering their vision will immediately disappear. It does not. But stopping the push will help create a mental attitude that relieves stress. It does not mean throwing in the towel or just giving up. This is an instance where backing up actually means going forward. The ongoing task is to nurture and massage the family collective toward its most potential level of integration or *we-ness*. Creating an emotionally safe environment wherein close relationships can develop does this.

The Problem:
Grief Follows Loss of the Dream

Creating a life together with a new love is a happy time that brings its own special joy. Nevertheless, difficult change accompanies one into new-life. While on one hand it can feel good to be moving on, on the other it can be sad to be distancing from a past that accounts for many years of one's life. "If I'm so happy, why am I sad?" This is the consternation experienced by many new-partners. Beginnings are always linked to endings, and inherent in endings is a distancing from the good times of the past. As we pull up roots on an old life, a melancholy can set in that intrudes on the enchanting spell of new-life. Grief is a calling inward to embrace emotional closures yet unfinished, and grief will have its day.

Experiencing joyful anticipation and sadness simultaneously can cause much inner turmoil. If on top of this turmoil, there is then the painful realization that the new-family is not what one hoped for, grief spelled with a capital G descends on partners. Now, added to the uncertainty of moving forward, is the grief of detaching from the past. Grief can then become mourning, and mourning can mislead one into believing they have made a mistake: "Look at what I've gone and done now!" It can feel overwhelming and, in the wake of it, partners begin to feel helpless and sometimes hopeless. Hopelessness becomes despair.

Thank goodness the picture painted above does not include all new-family couples. Some degree of grief does, however, affect most every new-family member. Partners who do not bring children often find their grief born amidst the disorder and noise that ensues in family living. They are unfamiliar with the bustle and sometimes chaotic nature of an active household. These partners have exchanged quiet living for home life with children who are not only noisy, but who seem to also want to dominate the scene and run the show. They discover that children are sometimes rude, intrusive and insensitive to boundaries. The children take the new-parent's things, their tools or jewelry. The kids do not handle the stereo, the CDs, or the VCR with tender love and care. This is not how the childless partner thought it would be.

Grief does not spare children either. They often experience mom or dad's gain, a new-partner, as their loss. They do not say, "This is a loss," but what they do say is, "I hate this." In these instances it means the same. Children also experience loss when their moms and dads surrender parental control to new-partners. It causes them to feel betrayed and left out. It is only reasonable and normal that children experience grief in these circumstances. Their birth parent's life is changing by choice; their life is changing by default. They have few, if any, choices; they must go along. This coercive force of change need not foreshadow tragedy or emotional breakdowns, but it does cause grief. How birth parents handle the children's grief makes a huge difference for the children emotionally.

But of all the grief endured in new-family, that carried by birth parents may be the heaviest. It can seem for them as though grief is their lot in life. Just being a parent offers a natural dose of grief, and it doubles when parents feel responsible for the children's pain—and most do. Then, too, grief born of the dance saddles birth parents. Being caught between the demands of a new-partner and the constraints inherent in a long-term relationship with one's children is painful. Stopping the dance can be a lonely, challenging endeavor that provides all the ingredients necessary for a triple shot of grief.

Grief is the major emotion in a new household and, in spite of being normal, it is a menace. It underlies mood swings, sadness, anger and instability. Grief is not solidifying; it is not a friend to new-family. Defusing its negative effects is not easy because doing so requires that it be acknowledged and accepted. Grief is an emotion we tend to not talk about; in truth, it can be an emotion that is hard to recognize. Understandably, new-partners are reluctant to tell each other they are hurting, frightened or in pain. It can be enormously unsettling to learn that one's partner is sad or struggling, which is why there is so little permission for either partner to acknowledge grief. A partner's grief can be haunting.

- What does the sadness mean?
- Why is this happening?
- Have I done something to cause this?
- If my partner is disappointed, does it mean they no longer love me?
- Does this mean my partner will turn away?
- Why, if you're happy about being with me, are you also disappointed?
- If you really loved me, wouldn't you be happy?

One thing couples must remember is that a partner's grief may have absolutely nothing to do with feelings of love. Loving someone deeply is one thing, weathering change without grief is quite another. Grief is a natural consequence of change, even desirable change. Yet, because we know our grief can hurt our partner, we may protect them and ourselves by not telling the truth about our feelings. We hide our feelings and mask our grief.

Grief is a compelling emotion that makes its presence known. It can affect our mood and our ability to flow with the natural ups and downs of life. It can affect our physical well being. It can make us depressed, anxious or numb. It can make us sick. One of the best things anyone can do when they experience grief is acknowledge it: "I am feeling sad." Welcome grief as a wise teacher because it always has something to teach us about ourselves. Sit down with it; listen to it. Let it be okay to feel sad, hurt, lonely, or whatever. Cry if need be. Grief opens us to parts of *me* that are begging for attention and care. Ask yourself, what do I need right now? Maybe what one needs is to just feel, however painful that may be, or perhaps one needs to just be. Stuffing and denying can plunge us into despair. If grief becomes so unrelenting that it is unbearably painful, or in some way disabling, then one should seek outside help. Find a professional to talk with about it.

Grief that is not being recognized or reconciled is an enemy of new-family. It is an enormous barrier to bonding. When partners recognize their grief it helps make the children's grief more understandable. Compassion is a wonderful antidote for grief. Minister to grief with loving kindness. Allow it to be acceptable. Don't force anyone to put on a happy face. Say, "There are times when we are going to feel sad; it is okay, this is a hard transition."

Other ways to minister to grief are by joining a support group, doing family or individual counseling, reading a book on the subject and sharing it with other family members, or listening to an audio tape. The healing process demands patience because even in a supportive environment it takes time for grief to pass. The wisdom of grief emerges slowly.

Save Your Marriage:
How to Solidify

Informal family gatherings and occasions for non-intimate recreation centered around eating and relaxing can be effective means for fostering solidarity. Solidarity is a sense of *we-ness;* it is the rubber cement of family community, but rubber cement is not superglue. Solidarity is what gives new-family a sense of identity or form without turning it into a colony of glued-together drones. There is a sense of wholeness, yet individual personalities remain intact. This whole is like a building supported by columns; the columns support the wholeness but remain separate.

New-family gatherings are also an opportune time for couples to observe developing relationships and potential or existing inter-personal trouble spots. But family gatherings take a lot of energy, and they can challenge a new-parent's desire to be self-sacrificing. This is especially so if the new-parent has been hurt by the part-ner's children or the partner's ex. It can be enormously difficult while carrying such hurt to behave in a benevolent manner.

The hue and cry from new-parents is one that goes something like this: "These kids are driving me crazy and now, in addition to everything else, I'm supposed to entertain them? Give me a break!" Planning, providing, encouraging, cheerleading, and just having to be the *adult,* can strain even the best of dispositions. This is especially so when a part of being the adult means tuck-ing one's anger under to spend time with children who are annoy-ing. Sometimes being a parent of any ilk, whether it is birth or otherwise, can seem unbearable.

Children expect to receive certain emotional and material things and, to an extent, they should. Healthy development and emo-tional well being require a certain amount of unconditional *receiv-ing.* Nevertheless, kids can learn to acknowledge the goodness and caring that comes their way. They can learn to express appre-ciation for things given them. It is acceptable for new-parents to place that expectation on children. We must realize as we do, how-ever, that it takes time for habits to develop. Until saying thank you becomes a habit, they may need to be reminded and gen-erously reinforced with praise when they do remember.

One gift new-parents can offer their non-offspring children is the lesson of appreciation taught by example. The children of the other family may not be expected to voice appreciation, therefore they may not know how. If a new-parent shows appreciation to the children for the things they do, then the behavior offers a model for expressing appreciation. Also, if the children seldom saw warmth and kindness pass between their warring birth parents, seeing loving appreciation expressed in mom or dad's new relationship opens healthy options and possibilities for them. Birth parents tend not to expect demonstrative acts of appreciation because giving and receiving are part of the flow in biological families. Appreciation expresses itself in subtle ways—by gestures, body language, and by other expressions not yet understood in new-family settings. It is unwise to expect one's new-partner to understand these subtle acknowledgments that pass between birth children and birth parent.

In new-family the kids that grace the couches, put their feet on the coffee table, slouch at the table, chew with their mouths open, take things that are not theirs, never return things they are given permission to use, cross boundaries they do not understand, and who never do their assigned chores, are, simply, *kids*. Yes, kids can be kids, and that is not an excuse for bad behavior or a case for accepting it. It is just an explanation. Children, and other people's children especially, can behave as though they have no clue about the courtesies of social or family life. Human nature makes it easier to accept clueless behavior from our birth children than from someone else's. We can forgive bad manners and slights in our children, but when it is the partner's kids it grates on our nerves, and the feelings that result affect a new-parent's willingness and ability to give.

All kids have needs. Since we adults know this, why is it so hard to be self-sacrificing? When we resist, are we behaving like children ourselves? Are we selfish, immature grownups when we cannot put ourselves out for ungrateful kids? The answer to the last two questions is, not necessarily. For starters, it is difficult to keep giving in the face of rejection, rebuff and the absence of appreciation. Not only do our partner's children not acknowledge new-parent's efforts, but sometimes partners expect unconditional giving that demands no reward. In other words, it is the new-parent's job to give. The false logic inherent in such a belief is that expecting appreciation is absurd, if not selfish, and having painful feelings about the absence of appreciation is not behaving as an adult. This is not an acceptable expectation to have for a new-parent, and new-parents should not buy into a guilt trip based on such false logic.

When new-parents feel they give, give, give, with no return, they can become extremely angry with *"those kids,"* angry with their partner because of *"those kids,"* and angry with the partner's ex who seems to be the biggest user of all. When new-parents get to this point it is almost impossible to just shelve the anger long enough to have a nice afternoon or outing. They may then find themselves feeling selfish and small, but it is not helpful to be ashamed of the feelings. These feelings are normal fare in new-family. It is when they are left to smolder that problems arise, because the fallout causes irreparable damage. One must do something about one's feelings.

Birth parents who seldom see their children can also become disenchanted when their continual efforts on behalf of their partner's children go unacknowledged and unappreciated. "Why," they ask, "should my partner's kids get the benefit of extras because I live here, when my own children don't get them because they don't?"

One strategy that can solve many problems resulting from the children's lack of appreciative expression is this: never, never, never expect appreciation from a partner's children. Respectfully ask for it, teach it, model it, but never expect it. Expect instead that appreciation will rain from your partner like dew from heaven, that he or she will acknowledge all you do for his or her children. Not only can children be clueless about appreciation, but sometimes one's partner is unaware as well. They either never say *thank you for all you do for my kids,* or they do not say it often enough. For those individuals who have children in the home, it is a good exercise to read this statement aloud: *Thank you for all you do for my children. Thank you for all you do for my children.*

New-parents: expect this appreciation from your partner, demand it, ask for it and see that you get it. Then, when you receive it, an appropriate response is, *"Thank you for noticing."* *"Thanks for expressing your appreciation."*

Strategies for Building Family Community

Feed'em

Some couples have discovered that one basic ingredient in the formula for promoting unity is food. Most children have favorite foods: fast food, non-nutritious food and even some nutritious food, although it may not be appealing to the adults. The food part of the formula for helping to build unity goes like this: Whatever the children's favorite food is, within reason, get it, fix it, cook it, bake it, take it out of the freezer, or whatever, but serve it. Forget the spinach and broccoli for these special occasions if veggies are an issue. (We have all eaten our pound of goodies not made from scratch or all natural ingredients.) Food is a great social lubricant, and that aspect of it is advantageous in these settings.

The problem that can arise around food is when partners believe that the children are not eating nutritiously at the other household: "They're on their own too much; they only eat what they want to eat; they drink too much pop." Concerns of this nature can get partners committed to providing just the opposite while the children are with them, and then eating becomes a serious matter as partners assume a policing vigilance: "You will eat your vegetables and enjoy them!" If the children experience this approach as punishing, they will hate being in the home because it is unpleasant. In a household where eating is stressful and painful, there is little comfort.

It is true that some children are not properly fed at the other household and that their nutritional needs may be neglected. It is also true that mealtime in some new families is a punitive event. There are extremes in both directions, but since in this instance we are addressing typical situations, it is assumed that nutrition in the other household is adequate, even if not stellar.

Another important part of the food equation is to eat in comfortable settings—whether it is around a table, in the family room, buffet style, picnic style or whatever. Keep it simple and easygoing. Many new-family explosions occur during meals because new-parents' expectations differ from those to which the children are accustomed. These expectations make everyone tense. The children fear they will not do it right; their birth parent is certain they will not, and the new-parent is determined to see that the children do it correctly. Therein lies a prescription for disaster, and even more so if partners disagree. These problems often arise when expectations are not realistic. In other words, when the children cannot give what the new-parent wants at a particular point in time.

The recommendation to keep meals simple and relaxed does not rule out ever eating formally. Formality has its place, but it is best if, in the beginning, formality is the exception rather than the rule. New-families that eat in relaxed congenial settings do find it easier to keep fragile relationships intact.

There are some households where family members find it impossible to eat together because it is too tense and traumatic. Partners must then ask if it is necessary to eat together. What other arrangements are possible? Could they serve buffet style or serve the children first? When options are difficult to imagine, it can be because partners believe there is only one acceptable way to have a meal. When this is the case there is a controlling *should*. Try abolishing the word *should* and substituting the word *could*— "How could we do it?" "What could we change?" "What changes would keep us out of conflict and hold us together?"

Whether it is daily dinner or occasional holiday feasting, one of the wonderful things about the American way of life is its acceptance of diversity in the ways people gather and eat. Settings can be as formal or as casual as we wish them to be, and special occasions for eating are perfect events around which to build new traditions. Take a chance—lighten up and do something different. Stretch the parameters in whatever way possible to keep it simple and pleasant. Remember that the goal is to keep the partnership intact while at the same time preserving one's relationship with one's children.

Fun'em

Another ingredient in the equation for building we-ness is coming together as a household for recreational activity that the children enjoy. If the children are going to resist attending the opera, it is best to forget it—this should not be taken to mean that children should never be exposed to things about which they are not enthusiastic. However, in the beginning it is best to engage the children's enthusiasm. Tune in to what they like and what might be possible for the family as a whole. Once there is a recognizable degree of unity, introduce things the children might not otherwise choose.

Avoid activity that is highly intense or competitive. If there is already tension, it is wise to sidestep creating more. Certain games or activities can set up anxiety. Promote events that require some interaction and that have the potential for creating laughter and good feelings. Whenever possible, combine eating and activity. Here again, it is important to loosen up, stretch those emotions, put the anger aside and work at having fun with the kids. (Yes, we are back to that part about how being the adult can be a pain in the neck, or lower.)

The first condition necessary for influencing children's lives is that they be emotionally present and in a receptive frame of mind. Then the children listen to what we want them to hear. Learning is always occurring. If we want children to learn what we want to teach them, then life in the household must be comfortable. If it is tedious and uncomfortable, the children close down and parents find that attempts to connect lead to a stone wall. The first step in opening children up is to make them feel welcome. When the children know they are welcome, they develop a sense of comfort and acceptance. It permits them to let their defenses down a bit. Once this occurs they are more open to those teaching moments parents create.

Set aside time each week to gather for family activity. Following are some prepared excuses for not making a weekly gathering happen:

- The kids will not want to participate.
- Everybody is too busy.
- There is no time when everyone can get together.
- I'm sick of these kids.
- If I get some free time I want it to myself.

Yet we all know that if spending time together is a priority, we will find the time. Children will participate if it is enjoyable, and everyone will schedule time if attendance is required. Just do not be put off by a little grumbling—kids grumble. Nevertheless, they also like to feel they belong and are wanted. Sometimes kids have to push against parental authority because it is part of differentiating and defining their unique identity. There is a sense of security that develops when pushing does not topple the wall of parental stability. Much of what it takes to make family activity happen is in the attitude that the adults bring to it. If parents are enthusiastic it sparks enthusiasm in the children.

One way to deal with children who do not want to participate is to require only their attendance, not their participation. Allow them to be as they are, provided they are not destructive to the situation. Let them mope, but go on with the activity. In the absence of pressure most children do eventually join in. An important consideration is to not allow two *mopers* to sit out together—separate them. If everyone is moping it is time to reassess the activity. Once children decide to become part of the activity, even if it takes a few weeks, allow them to do so without losing face in the group. It is important not to punish them for being unable to join in immediately, or make an issue of their presence when they do. It is equally important to reward them for taking part, but do this in private, which helps keep children from losing face or feeling patronized. Tell them how nice it was to have them involved.

Movies can be an acceptable activity at times, but it is better to engage in activity where family members interact. Non-inter-active activity is the opposite end of the scale from competitive activity that is too intense. Here are some ideas for weekly fam-ily activity:

- miniature golf played in a non-competitive way
- a concert
- a sporting event or other spectator activity
- a picnic
- a trip to the zoo
- cross-country skiing or downhill skiing
- hiking
- fishing
- a walk in some interesting place, like an arboretum, or on a special hiking path
- a boat ride
- swimming
- a parade
- a fair
- a museum
- a weekend camping trip
- a church event
- snowmobiling
- water skiing
- attending a presentation at a children's theater
- an ice cream outing
- an amusement park
- a water slide
- a playground

- inline skating

- beach volleyball

- a play made up and presented by the children. Follow it up with popcorn and conversation.

Those who live in or close to cities have access to many free and interesting events. In most cities the newspaper prints a schedule of local and area events every Friday, many of which are free. This can be a prime source for locating interesting and entertaining things to do as a family.

Watch'em

Another opportunity for building relationships with children is by taking an interest in their school activities and performances, as well as the community or church events in which they participate. Kids love it when mom and dad attend their games and performances. As new-parents and children form attachments, the children are usually glad to also have them attend, although the children may have to hide being pleased. Their fear is that showing pleasure or acceptance may meet with the disapproval of a birth parent. New-parents should be aware of this and not expect too much from the children in these settings. Allow your presence to be a silent gift to the child.

When children resist having new-parents at events, it is often because the presence of both families causes tension. The adults need to be sensitive to the children's feelings. Birth parents, especially, should make a special effort to keep the children out of the middle of any tension. It can be all too easy to force one's parental rights with the child in ways that can cause pain for the child. Birth parents have to recognize that after divorce their relationship with the children is going to change, and that they must be cautious and reasonable in their demands at public occasions when the children are tense.

It is wonderful when both families can be undaunted by one another's presence so they can mutually share in the joy of the children's events. But when it is impossible, there needs to be a way to amicably decide which family will attend which activity. On occasion, new-parents may need to step back and not attend some particular event so that just birth parents can attend.

When new-parents attend events, they should be particularly sensitive to how their presence affects the occasion. They, too, can become possessive in demanding an acknowledgment from the children. Given the new-parent's role, this is understandable, but not acceptable. There are times when the best way to love a partner's children is by stepping back and not demanding a front row seat. When new-parents can do this without feeling hurt, they are above the fray; they are being noble on behalf of the children.

A mother can find it very difficult to not resent the "other mother" who is developing a special relationship with her child. The lioness mother in women has its positive and negative sides. Mom will take life-threatening risks to save her children, but she can also become unnecessarily protective and selfishly possessive. Birth mothers need to be especially aware, when the other family is present, that they can best serve the children by not making an issue of their powerful mother role. The goal is for the child to be comfortable with the behavior of all the family spectators.

These events are a time to show support for the child who is performing. They are not appropriate occasions for discussing a late support payment, why a new pair of jeans never came back from visitation, why the children were not brought home from visitation on time, why the support money is not providing the children with new tennies, and so on. When ex-partners are on anything less than agreeable terms, they should only acknowledge each other if the occasion arises. This should occur in a discreet manner that keeps the children as comfortable as possible.

Organize'em

Some couples achieve success with recreational activities by having the children assume a portion of the responsibility. Some partners go as far as giving the children a budget and guidelines, and then letting them develop the plans for weekly outings. The extent to which this is realistic depends on the age of the children and their interest in taking charge. What they choose for an activity has to ultimately meet with parental approval, but if parents proceed in this manner, then they commit to being involved. Following are some reactions from partners to this idea:

- Good grief—who wants to do what these kids will want to do!

- I can't bear to watch the movies they pick or the music they listen to, and now I should take part in activities they like —gimme a break!

- I find even the thought of them having that much power very frightening.

- No way!

- I think I could if we maintain final approval.

- I think it's interesting and worth a try.

It can be hard to imagine that such a plan could work or that one could actually go along and have fun. Yet this strategy has been very helpful for those who have a willingness to create involvement, and it can be a tremendous boost to building a sense of togetherness. If partners are willing to go with the flow and can maintain a sense of humor, the creativity of children can be quite amusing.

Some partners who have experimented with this approach report that when they became followers they found themselves becoming resistant to taking part. Yet when they were in the lead, they expected the children to get on the bandwagon. These partners were able to see that it was easy to demand what they were not willing to give. If we are truly committed to creating a cooperative community, then we have to give so we can get. There are many opportunities for parents to extend sensitivity and cooperation.

One thing to not do in new-family, at least in the early going, is to hold family meetings. They are a disaster for birth parents. Meetings of this nature only intensify the heat in the emotional hot box they are trying to avoid. If they support their mate the children are angry; if they support their children their partner is angry. Have partner meetings and use the suggestions previously suggested for getting opinions from the children.

Holidazzle'em

The holidays present a unique challenge to partners because they generate more intense emotions than most other occasions. A certain festiveness becomes associated with the enjoyment we anticipate repeating from year to year. We look forward to these special celebrations, so when divorce or death brings the end of first-family, children and adults alike find the loss especially painful. How can a holiday really be enjoyable if not celebrated in the way it acquired its special meaning? That it will not be the same, however, does not mean a holiday cannot be transformed into something truly enjoyable.

Given every family member's attachment to expectations, many differing needs exist, and partners can use these needs as the foundation for new traditions. But before doing so, partners must know who it is with whom traditions should be built. In other words, which children will be included? Which children are in the home for any particular holiday and for how long are they there? This unknown aspect of the holidays, with its potential for being repeated on a yearly basis, can be a major complication. It can drive both adults and children bonkers. Partners find it impossible to create consistency when the children are there one year and gone the next. Traditions require continuity and replication.

Another complication is that if there are two sets of children, they may not be present at the same time. Some partners cheer that arrangement, feeling it is easier to have each set of children at a separate time. Others, however, find it taxing because it can leave them with too little time for themselves or each other. The holiday becomes a two-ring circus.

One difficulty that children report is that visitation often takes them away from their primary home during the holidays. They spend the overwhelming majority of their time in one home, and then travel many miles to be with their other parent for the holidays. It creates a double bind for them. On the one hand they want to see their other birth parent and they look forward to that aspect of their journey. On the other hand they leave what is familiar at a most important time. Because of this, many children do not look forward to holiday visitation; they have a non-holiday relationship with the primary family and a holiday relationship with the family they see the least. And it is the case in many situations that there is just no way to avoid such arrangements. It is, nevertheless, disconcerting for the children, and ex-partners should do what they can to minimize its negative aspects.

Things can be done to reap the best advantage possible from the holidays. First, have a predictable visitation schedule. This schedule should define when the children are in each home and for how long. If, for example, both of the children's families celebrate the Christian holiday, and the children spend Christmas Eve in one home and Christmas Day in the other, the visitation agreement should state this. If the children rotate holidays, the agreement should explain the rotation. Visitation agreements should be very clear and leave no room for misunderstandings. Children should know at least one year in advance where they will be for each holiday and for how long. Partners also need this lead time.

Following are some things families have done to reframe holiday traditions.

- We had everyone list something about the holiday they would like to have included in our plans. Since a lot of the requests were similar, we were able to satisfy almost everyone.

- We talked to the children about doing something entirely new. We asked them what they had never done on the holiday that they would like to do. This time, they had all kinds of ideas.

- Since the holidays are stressful enough without adding complications, and since we would have both sets of children, we decided not to entertain either of our extended families.

We stayed home, rented movies the children asked for and had a lot of good food. Amidst all that I found time to sit in the living room and read.

- We added an out-of-the-house activity. Our city has a big parade every evening during Christmas so we took the children to the parade. We came home to popcorn and hot cider. Getting out in the cold and burning up some energy was good. We tend to sit around too much during the holidays and everyone gets restless.

- What was hardest for me was all the management required to keep everyone else happy. I'd get irritable or angry because my own needs went unmet, and then I'd start taking it out on the children or Bob. So last year I thought about what it was I needed the most. Then I figured out how I could take care of myself as well as everything else that needed to be done. For once I did not neglect myself.

- I can do anything for a while, but I need some alone time with my wife to rejuvenate myself. At first I couldn't figure out how to do that because my children (4, 7 and 9) are with us for most of every holiday. Joan really gets the brunt of it because she's a teacher and is usually off at the same time as the children. I go off to work every morning. I decided, in spite of my guilt, that I had to hire a babysitter to come in for a full day so Joan and I could get away together. It worked so well that I hired the same person to come in and help with the children three days a week. This gave Joan an opportunity to get out, and if she stayed home, to not have to be so preoccupied with the children. I think the arrangement has saved our marriage.

- Our children don't like each other very much and there is quite an age difference. The first couple of years we thought it would really be fun to get everyone together at the same time. Well, it wasn't. It was just awful. We have now redone the visitation schedules with our exes so that the children are, for the most part, not there at the same time. Sometimes there is a little overlap but we try to prevent it. What enormous differences that change has made. One other important aspect of this is that it made it possible for each of us to be more giving with each other's children. When the kids are together they compete and they monitor us like hawks.

Many tricky dilemmas can come up around the holidays, especially Christmas because it involves gift giving. Who should give gifts to whom and how much should they spend? Should new grandparents give gifts to the children of their son or daughter's new-partner? What if they do not want to? And if they do, must they spend the same amount on each child? What if they want to give their biological grandchildren expensive presents?

One of the important aspects of these matters is that what grandparents do affects the feelings of the children's birth parent—one of whom is their adult son or daughter. The birth parent's hurt feelings end up in the middle of the partnered relationship and become a source of conflict. This is a good time to be reminded that blood is thicker than water. We typically feel more enamored of those we are biologically related to than those we are not. New-parents and new in-laws in particular should not take these natural differences personally. Being a non-biological outsider feels different than when one is a biologically related insider, and no amount of planning may be able to counter those feelings. Every situation requires utmost sensitivity. Create settings that allow for diversity without amplifying differences between insiders and outsiders and, when this cannot be done, avoid settings that exacerbate negativity.

Partners should discuss and clarify their expectations about gift giving and receiving. Then they should each talk with their parents. They should help grandma and grandpa understand the complications in the situation. Develop a plan with the grandparents that allows their needs to find expression without creating divisions in the new home. Partners should also talk with the children and prepare them for what they can expect. Be sensitive to the children's feelings and keep them from situations where favoritism could be harmful.

A grandparent dilemma that can be troublesome is the relationship between children and the grandparents on the ex-partner's side of the family. This is especially so if a divorce has made those grandparents antagonistic toward their ex-son-in-law or daughter-in-law. One of the better ways to deal with issues of this nature is to maintain distance. Have each birth parent be responsible for seeing to the relationship the children have with grandma and grandpa. This avoids the potential for clashes between ex-in-laws. But it does not avoid the difficulties that arise in situations where an ex-partner is deceased. Then the remaining birth parent is forced to interact directly with the grandparents, and they should do so in as forthright and yet sensitive manner as possible.

A recommendation that could serve grandparents well is to never say or do anything that would turn your grandchildren against the new-parent who is in your son or daughter's place. In the long run it may come back to haunt you. It may alienate the very children with whom you wish to remain close.

Ennoble'em

One excellent means of promoting cohesion is by participating in some endeavor with a spiritual or charitable aspect to it. There are plenty of opportunities for volunteering, and a by-product of charitable service is that it bolsters everyone's self-esteem. This boost lifts spirits and, when spirits are up, doors open to positive ways of connecting. Many communities have an office that maintains a list of activities and organizations that need volunteers. Call your city hall or county courthouse and ask the person answering to direct you. Churches and synagogues are also potential sources of information, as are newspapers. Some papers print a list of organizations seeking assistance.

Following is a list of ways some partners met the goal of *ennobling*:

- Adopted a highway (road-side cleaning projects offered in some states).

- Served holiday (and weekend) meals at a center for the poor and homeless.

- Volunteered in a nursing home (helped serve meals and ferry wheelchair residents to and from the dining room).

- Assisted an older couple in the neighborhood with yard work and other chores.

- Gave a weekend of work to Habitat for Humanity (good for older kids).

- Assisted with clean-up and other projects at a nature center.

- Helped the Department of Natural Resources with a bird count.

- Invaded a local park once a week with pooper-scoopers and picked up dog droppings others had left behind.

- Baked cookies each week for two battered women's shelters.

- Did babysitting for single mothers (volunteered through a single-mother organization).

- Adopted an elderly person as a family friend and surrogate grandparent.

- Worked at a local charity that collects and distributes food.

- Volunteered time to a charity (try Goodwill, Salvation Army, Red Cross).

- Attended church together regularly.

After a service project, stop for a treat or go out to eat. Talk about what you did. What did everyone enjoy? Was anything scary? Did anything unexpected occur? What did you learn? What about next time?

Say to the children, "You did a good thing, kids." Children tend to translate such statements into, "I am a good person." This belief is the foundation of self-esteem. Therefore, if a child's self-image is low, praise for giving service can help them frame an image of their goodness.

The key to all ennobling is that it must be fun and elevating for the adults as well. If it is a drag, forget it, because the children

—the masters at reading vibes—will pick up on it. If you cannot make it fun, at least make it rewarding. It can be done.

Harmonize'em

There are so many things happening at once in new-family that it requires partners to function like orchestra conductors. They must bring individual parts together in collective harmony. Have you ever listened to the discordant sound made by an orchestra warming up? Each player is practicing without regard for what the other musicians are playing. The outcome is not melodious. One reason orchestras have conductors is because someone must synchronize the playing of the notes and the timing of separate parts. Otherwise, there is noise instead of music.

Each family member is like an orchestra musician who has his or her unique part to play. Partners must assume the conductor's role and mount the podium of leadership. They must harmonize those individual parts and personalities. They do this, first, by being in tune with each other. From this place of solidarity they lead with purpose, with intent and with direction. When the partnership has the baton there is a symphony of sound rather than the discordant banging of angry notes—no leadership, no melody; no partnership, no family. New-families are noisy, out of tune places when partners are not on the podium together and are not simultaneously waving the baton of leadership.

Figure 6-1 shows some of the available categories of activities that can be drawn on to help integrate a new family and solidify its center.

The Ongoing Challenge:
To Accept Differing Needs for Closeness

No approach to building we-ness works one hundred percent of the time, but when repeated efforts fail there are typically a couple of reasons. First, failure occurs when one or both partners are very angry with each other's children; or second, when one or both partners are angry with their partner's ex. Here, again, is the menacing and undermining effect of anger impairing efforts to recreate family.

SOLIDIFY:

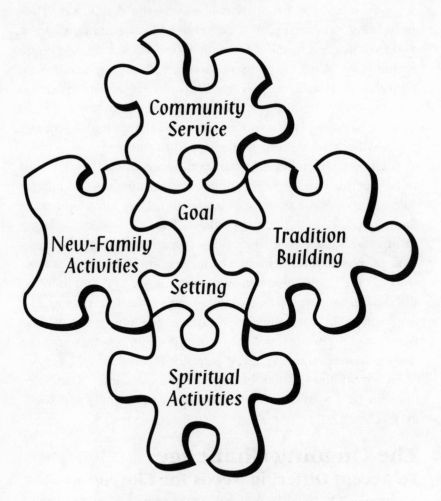

Get It Together

Figure 6-1

Metaphorically speaking, anger is a soul-eating dragon every person stables. If this dragon breaks loose and takes over, it can refuse to sleep, and it will feed on any morsel of contention it can find. We have to harness it, manage it and tame it. Anger destroys one's ability to love, to give and to extend understanding and compassion.

Children's anger can also impose itself on partners' efforts to build solidarity. It is helpful to see the children's anger as a symptom of unhappiness and emotional pain, and to consider what emotional balm comforts grief and relieves anger. In the early stages of new-family, the children's angst is often the result of issues in their first family. Perhaps they remain in grief about their birth parents' bad marriage. Maybe they are grieving the divorce. Possibly they are trapped in painful divided loyalties. Maybe they have left friends behind. It is important to become a part of the solution to their problems by recognizing the pain as real and legitimate. Try not to personalize it, and provide help in the best way possible.

If forward movement stalls, couples may wish to try these strategies. First, ask the children directly what activities they would enjoy, although they may need to be reminded that they cannot be flown to the moon. For example, "What could we plan that you would enjoy?" Or, "What would you like to do if you had a choice?" Avoid beginning the question with *if;* asking *what* usually elicits a different response than if. When you get an answer like, "I don't know," try this as a follow-up question: "What would you say if you did know?" Listen carefully and be frank, friendly and fair with the children. Sometimes we have to loosen our resistance to work out something acceptable.

Second, in a friendly but firm manner (birth parents in the lead) tell the children that an occasion is being planned. They can have a voice in planning or say nothing and just come along. Remind them again in a firm and friendly way that they will be included and that this is their chance to have a voice. Be sure to stress that you want them to be a part of the planning, but only say it if you mean it. Do all this in sincerity and honesty and without anger. Remember that at the heart of kids' resistance is pain.

If, after a whole-hearted effort, the children remain highly resistant or angry, some problem is being overlooked. Does the problem involve all the children, or is one child influencing the others? One sibling can hold great power because of the loyalty among siblings. Work directly with the children or child having the most trouble.

Couples do give up, but it is unfortunate when it happens. A family community needs events and special occasions around which to connect and rally. Here, as in so many things, timing is everything, and the keeper of the clock is the partnership. When couples can work together without anger to create opportunities for family gatherings, they can move slowly forward accumulating small measures of solidarity. When partners have a desire and willingness to provide leadership, when they are willing to bide their time in meeting their expectations, activity can be a path to new-family community.

Partners are working with the invisible, collective, unconscious agreements previously mentioned, and they must, therefore, make coming together convenient and comfortable. When it is comfortable, children let their defenses down. Partners have to gently beckon children to join as one beckons a reluctant cat from its special hiding place with a favorite treat.

It is worth mentioning that teenagers usually handle their resistance to joining differently than young children. What is apt to happen with teens is that they come along but they act out by being flippant, sulky or surly. If this occurs, partners need to prevent the behavior from becoming disrespectful or abusive. Sulking can be ignored, but mean or demeaning behavior cannot. It is easy to react in these situations, but reacting only further provokes the children's resistance. It gives them an excuse and it enables their bad behavior. Do not take it on; do not take it personally. To do so will only make you angrier. Remain rational and above the emotion of the moment.

If disruptive behavior does not moderate, or if it feels beyond control, it is best to obtain professional guidance. However, in some new-family situations it is difficult to get appropriate help for children. This can occur when a birth parent who holds joint legal custody uses his or her power to sabotage the children's inclusion in counseling. If this happens, one possible way around it is to initiate counseling for the new-family as a group. There is hardly a judge in the land who would prevent a new-family from taking positive action to improve the quality of their living environment. Apprise the therapist of the problem and let the therapist offer guidance about how to proceed. A therapist who understands the family's specific issues can be a great ally in helping reduce conflict.

What children often report as a source of resistance to signing-on is an expectation that they must be happy and satisfied. Yet, from their standpoint, the living situation is one where they do not feel accepted or welcome. Since kids find it hard to appear happy and satisfied when they are not, they use provocation as a means of subverting cooperation. If partners insist that everything be on their terms, and that the needs of the children have no place, they face a painful journey. There are times when partners need to broaden the range of acceptable possibilities—to go easy, to lighten up or slow down a bit.

Having a family room where rules of formality do not apply is a real asset. If you have available space, create a room where adults and children can mingle, watch television, play games, sprawl, slouch, drink pop and eat. Children and teens need engaged adults in their lives. Get the kids out of the basement resort, or their television and video game caves. Be involved with them. Talk with them; laugh with them.

Nothing works if adults cling to unachievable goals. We have to redesign our proposed picture, and therein lies a challenge. What will it take to move us away from a particular mind-set or attitude that keeps reproducing failure? New-family does not have to be the way we may think family should be in order for it to be okay, or good enough. How can we expect children to adjust and change if we cannot? We must ask ourselves at times, "What's right about this family? What's working?" It is easy to become lost in our negative tunnel vision and to not see all that is good, right and working.

The following example illustrates negative tunnel vision. Nancy complained repeatedly about her partner's children. They were irresponsible slackers—too laid back and, hence, irresponsible. They were resistant to doing chores and to accepting direction, especially from her. Yet when she was queried about the specifics of the children's lives, quite a different picture emerged. They were all honor roll students who participated in various extra-curricular activities at school. One of the boys had received special honors for citizenship and for helping his fellow students. Another of the boys was on his way to becoming an Eagle Scout. The teenage girl, who was a cheerleader, also worked twenty hours a week at a fast-food restaurant. They obeyed curfew and none of them used drugs or alcohol. The list of positive qualities went on.

Why was Nancy so negative? Her eventual insight was that her negativity resulted from the belief that the children's birth mother was a slacker. Nancy felt she did all the dirty work but the absent mom got all the glory. Once Nancy could see her misdirected anger, she was able to reframe her relationship with the children.

The children genuinely liked Nancy, in spite of her nagging, but she was neither the birth mother they missed nor the birth mother for whom they longed. In counseling, the children's eventual insight was that they dumped their disappointment about their birth mother on Nancy. As everyone redefined their role in the new-family, they also redefined what it was they wanted to be as a new-family community. In addition, they developed some strategies for dealing with the grief everyone felt about the children's absent mother. At the end of the chapter are some of the exercises that helped Nancy and her partner.

Always remember that building new-family is one of the hardest things in the world to do—there is hardly a task more difficult than creating family community. The second thing to remember is that one of the wonderful things about achieving family community is that it opens the door to love. Love develops in the presence of emotional safety and after a sense of belonging has been established. In new-families, family members grow to love one another, but that growth may require years. Partners must be patient.

Caring can, however, exist in family community even when love does not. There are many new-parents who do not find their partner's children especially appealing but who do care deeply about them. New-family really challenges us to reach for our highest, best self, and for the nobility in our being. Since negative feelings can be intense, we must reach up for the spiritual part of our *me* that lives above our sometimes petty feelings, that part wherein resides our compassion and loving-kindness.

● ● ●

Grief is an inescapable consequence
Of life.
Grief is assuaged by hearts
Open to the goodness
Of each moment
Solidify . . .

Exercise:
Define New-Family

1. What is your new-family about?
Write a paragraph describing what your new-family is about. Understand the word *about* as it is used in the following sentences. "This is what that's all about." "What's Tracy's snit all about?" "John's big birthday celebration was really about his promotion at work." "Nancy's dissatisfaction with the children was really about her anger at the children's mother."

Make sure that what you write characterizes your family at this time and is not a characterization of what you hope it will become. New-families are usually about many things, some positive and some negative. Each partner should do this task in private and not share until they have finished all three parts of the exercise.

Following are excerpts from paragraphs others have written:

- Right now our family is about fighting and anger. Everyone seems angry with everyone else, and it's very unpleasant.

- Our family is about accomplishing the things of daily life: everybody getting where they are supposed to be and home again.

- It's about a lot of drudgery and hard work.

- My family is about my partner's kids and all the things they constantly need. If it's not one thing it's another. They seem to rule our life.

- Our family seems to be about my husband's relationship with his ex-wife and how she influences everything we do. The court case, his anger and her constant intrusions and demands make it impossible for us to get on with our partnership.

- Our family seems to be about kids coming and going between our place and their other parent's place. It is hard to tell who is supposed to be where, when. So our life is about constantly trying to manage all the comings and goings.

- My new-family seems to be about my oldest son's anger because he tries to control everyone with it. His father has been dead for four years and my son didn't want me to remarry. I guess my son thought he was the man of the house. He hates my new husband and he lets him know it.

- My family seems like it is about nothing, but it must be about something. We are all just plodding along. Maybe it is about depression; everyone seems depressed.

- Chaos and anger.

- Trying to deal with the problems of four teenagers: drugs, pregnancy, truancy and, well, you name it, we seem to be dealing with it.

2. What would you like this new-family to be about?

Write a paragraph about what you would like this family to be about. This is the wish list. In this paragraph include all those things you wish the family could become if it were willing. Again, each partner should do this in private.

Following are excerpts from paragraphs others have written:

- I would like my new-family to be about cooperation and sharing. I'd like it to feel like a family. I want us to be able to do things together and have fun.

- I want everyone in my new-family to feel comfortable in our home. I want the kids to feel like they can talk to us about things that are bothering them. I want us to have fun together.

- Right now I don't know. I am just too angry to be able to figure it out.

- I know this is unrealistic, but I want it to be just like it would have been if each of us hadn't been through a divorce. You know, I want it to be like "our family." I know it can't be, but I'd like it to be better than it is; and I know for that to happen I, most of all, have to change my attitude. I have never really welcomed Pete's kids. I don't like them very much.

- I want peace and happiness, no conflict, and for everybody to do their chores without ever having to be told more than once.

- I'd like us to all be able to get along, to be able to talk together around the table and to not feel like enemies. I'd like us to be able to laugh sometimes. I'd like the children to respect us for trying to make a nice home for them.

- I'd like my wife's ex-husband to fall off the edge of the Earth and to take his attorney with him. Then we would have a chance to be something better than what we are right now. I'd just like some peace.

- I'd like some routine and consistency. Our place is like a hotel, and there is no private space where I can go to get away from it. We need quiet hours.

- I'd like it to be about living together in a very respectful way. I'd like it to be a place of security and comfort for everyone. I wish I knew how to make that happen.

3. Given what you believe your family is about at this time, what do you believe you could realistically become?

Write a paragraph about what you believe your family could become given its present strengths and weaknesses. This statement should consider where you are presently and where you would like to be. It should become something of a compromise between the two. As you do this, remember this is not a final statement. You may revise it a month from now or a year from now. Consider the needs of the children and the extent to which you perceive them as able to be vested in two households. What's fair to ask of them? Again, each partner should do this in private.

Following are excerpts from paragraphs others have written:

- I realize that my expectations have not been realistic, and that my desire for us to be the family we would have been if these were our children is out of the question. I would now like us all to grow toward being friends in the ways members of a family can also be friends. I want us to like each other better than we do now. I want us to cooperate and be kind, and when we can't be kind, be civil. I want us to make it as easy as possible for the children to go back and forth, and I don't want either of us to fight with our exes any more.

- I don't care anymore if Jim's girls don't think I'm the greatest. I see that I have been trying to replace their mother by being a better mother than she is—as though there was some contest to win, and the girls' affection is the prize. I want to be a good wife. I want to support my husband as a father, and I want him to support me as a mother. My boys do like him though, and I admit there are times when I find that hard because I'm not sure I want to share them. A lot of trouble in our new-family has been because of my selfishness, and

I want to try very hard to be less selfish and less possessive. I want us to be a bunch. I know that sounds dumb, but what I mean is like a bunch of bananas—kinda hang together. We don't have to hang that close, but I'd like us to just accept each other for who we are and quit putting each other down. Oh yes, and some of what I want to be isn't a family, but a couple. I really love my husband, and I want to spend time just with him without the kids.

4. What do you have to do to achieve what you wrote in 3 above? Consider where you are with what it is you would realistically like to achieve. What will you have to do to get there? These are the baby steps that will add up to success. Again, do this separately and try to be as honest as possible about the things you personally will have to change in order to have your new vision come true.

Following are some excerpts from the work of others:

- Plan time for the whole family every week. Be willing to take responsibility for seeing that it happens (I can, I know I can, I know I can. I'll keep saying it!).

- Get son John some counseling for his anger.

- Quit bad-mouthing the children's mother. I know Jim does not see how much it upsets his daughters when he is so angry toward her in front of them.

- Give up trying to keep bedrooms as clean as I want them to be. I have to learn to shut up and close the doors. I have to be less bossy and rigid.

- Paula and I have got to come to a better agreement about what my kids are supposed to do when they visit. I think she is too demanding, and I feel sorry for the kids so I just fade into the background. I think the kids feel abandoned by me in my home.

- To get some marital counseling, get our stuff together and stop fighting in front of the kids. We have to learn to work

together as a couple. We have to find someone who can help
us learn that.

- Make our number one goal to get everyone to stop talking
at each other in a loud, shouting way. Let's start there and
then see if we can get just one person talking at a time. You
talk, I listen; then I talk, you listen. Our house has been chaotic.

Exercise:
Define New-Family Expectations

It is time for partners to compare notes. Some partners are able
to do this without the help of a third party; others are not. Partners
have to decide what will work best for them. When partners have
remarkable differences, discussion is best led by a neutral third
party. Working with a therapist, minister, rabbi, spiritual advisor
or consultant helps each partner clarify his or her needs and wants.
The outsider will also help partners hear one another. There can
be differences between what one hopes for and what one's partner is capable of giving. Therefore, discussion requires honesty,
and compromises must be negotiated.

What We Want to Be

Whether you work alone or with a third party, create from your
separate work a joint statement that defines what you as partners
want your new-family to become.

- Make a list of at least ten tasks that will help you get to your
goal. Make sure these tasks are actually doable.

- Each month focus on just one or two things you want to
change. Many small efforts eventually add up to big changes.

- When feeling discouraged, spend time together doing something that refreshes and recharges your batteries.

Life in new-family cannot be restructured overnight. Baby steps
are the key. Partners need to give each other time to reframe
expectations.

7. SUPPORT:

"I Feel Like Giving Up."

Support

Introduction:
New-family Life Doesn't Have to be Hell

To state that the demands of new-family overwhelm couples is to understate the case. The demands are enormous and the energy expenditure ends up taking a toll on the intimate relationship. Partners go to bed exhausted and irritable, and neither wants to be affectionate. One woman expressed it in these words: "I didn't want him to touch me. I was mad at his kids and mad at him for not doing something about his kids. Because the kids overwhelmed me, I would get crabby and irritable." When the partnership struggles, the *lovership* suffers.

Recall the image of the rowboat on rough water presented in Chapter One. As you do, recall that the journey on which those partners embarked was to take them through rough water to a safe harbor on the distant shore. Now imagine that this boat has been sailing day and night for a long time and that shore is not yet in sight. Exhausted and weakened, the couple can no longer keep the boat on course. The waves batter them. The boat is tossed to and fro. As partners row, they are unaware of their direction. Eventually, because of fatigue and disorientation, they relinquish the rowing and orienting responsibilities to the children. The children are eager to take control but have no idea to where they should row. Since partners are too weary to care, the children navigate on their own.

The children feel both triumphant and disappointed. They know they are in charge. Eventually they also tire, and they give up. With no one at the helm, the boat drifts. Partners, now angry with each other, are sitting at different ends of the boat. The children inflate life rafts and bail out.

Now what? The answer to that question for approximately sixty percent of couples, is divorce. They want to leave the boat. But is it necessary? Is there some way partners can navigate rough water and howling winds? Is there a way that, once control is lost, partners can revive themselves and get back on course? Is there a way to make the journey less painful and exhausting? Navigational skills can be learned. There are ways to hold on and stay at the helm. There are ways to prevent mutiny.

There are no Loch Ness type monsters lurking in deep water waiting to swallow a new-family boat. The journey to safe harbor has only one enemy, and that enemy is the partnership itself—when couples meet the enemy, they are it. Those who have not bonded and cannot cooperate, cannot lead. A partnership that cannot resolve its own internal conflict can never achieve family community. A couple that wants to beat the sixty-percent odds has to build a solid parenting partnership. This must manage the demands of new-family life or the demands will destroy it.

Demands in new-family can be likened to the waves in the imaginary picture above. At some level and intensity the waves are always there and, in real life, those waves are demands that must be met. Ignoring them opens the door to chaos, and when chaos takes over, fatigue is crippling and crushing. A new-family must be managed, and it is always a demanding, energy-expending task.

The demands of partnership in new-family can be likened to those of dairy farmers a generation or two ago. If you know something about cows, you know they require milking twice a day: morning and night. No matter how those farmers might have wished to spend any particular day, there were always the cows. The cows had to be milked and fed. The barn and the milk house had to be cleaned. The critical element, however, was the demand inherent in caring for those cows! What if the farmer was not feeling well, or if he or she was unable to work? Then what? What if the farmer said, "To hell with it, I'm not dealing with those cows today!"

Many people, both city and country folk alike, are simplifying by eliminating the *cows* in their lives. But in new-family, it is an impossible task. In a manner of speaking, the new-family is a *cow* itself. As one gentleman stated it, "This family is not a horse, it's a cow." What he meant is that you cannot turn a milk cow out to pasture in the same way you can a horse. Cows require attention that shapes the daily life of those who tend them.

The leadership and management function in new-family cannot be turned out to pasture either. New-family requires time-consuming management, and weary partners need respite and free time. It is the case that as partners' management abilities improve, they gain greater freedom; but the problems they face are usually complicated and seldom lend themselves to being solved overnight.

Partners must ask themselves, "What needs to be done today, this week, this month?" There are so many pressing demands—

- We need time to talk!

- You need to talk to your kids.

- The car isn't running correctly.

- We need to get some new clothes for your kids. No, I'm not getting new clothes for the kids, that's my ex's job.

- The dishes aren't getting done. Your daughter was supposed to do the dishes. Will you please talk to her?

- Your kids always duck out on their chores.

- You have to attend school conferences this week.

- I'll be home late from work tomorrow.

- Your ex called and needs you to return the call. The kids all have colds.

- Our kids are fighting.

- Your daughter talked back to me.

- Why are you shouting at me?

- We need to plan some family activity.

- We haven't been on a date for weeks.

- Why do we have this huge telephone bill? Who is calling this 900 number?

- The kids' rooms are beginning to look like an annex of the local dump.
- Why does the house smell like pot when we come home?
- Your grades are falling; why is that?
- I have a doctor appointment tomorrow.
- I'm feeling depressed.
- Who's driving Jane to her piano lesson on Thursday?
- Your mother called. Your father is real sick; they need you to come by.
- The garbage disposal is plugged again.
- One of your kids had friends home after school without permission.
- Will you please tell your son he does not have permission to take my tools.
- Please don't dump your school bags on the floor inside the door.
- What do you mean your mother doesn't like the way we do it here?
- No, you may not go to your father's this weekend; it is not his weekend.
- Why can't your ex get the kids home on time on Sunday night?
- If I have to go to one more meeting with your ex, I am going to pack my bags.
- No, I am not taking the MMPI test for county social services; these are not my kids; I'm not on trial.
- Please tell your daughter the pizza person may not come to the door at 2:00 a.m.
- Does your ex have to call me at work?
- Your daughter is running our life.
- No, your father may not buy you a car if you're living here.
- I don't care if my kids don't go to bed at 10 p.m. I figure bedtime is their problem.

- What kind of a parent are you anyway?

- Why is the house a mess?

- I do not want you to bring your mother into our house when she picks you up; she can just wait in the car for you.

- I think one of your kids is stealing our booze and giving it to their father.

- You're always thinking the worst of my kids.

- Well, when it comes to your kids, you can't see the forest for the trees.

- Do you think your kids have ever once in their life uttered the words "thank you"?

- I don't want the kids in our bathroom, and don't give them permission to use the Jacuzzi.

- Who in the hell ate all the cherries?

- No, I am not putting up with that snake in my house!

- All right, which one of you told your mother I got a big raise? You are not to tell stuff at the other house that belongs to this family.

- Your kids have the worst table manners I have ever encountered in my life.

Round and round it goes and where it stops nobody knows. Remember that lament? Well, don't believe it! It will end when the partnership decides it will end. The partnership cannot be a victim of anything except itself. Partners can decide when to end the demanding disarray of chaos. It is up to them, because if they don't end it, it will end them—it is that simple.

In part, the partnership is done in by fatigue. Living in chaos takes us down like almost no other stress. It depresses our spirit, lowers our resistance to illness and pushes us into overwhelm. We become incapacitated. Gone is the presence of mind and body required to face or tackle a challenge—from there it is not far to clinical depression and despair.

The Problem:
Fatigue Leads to Despair

I can't do this anymore is what partners say when fatigue overwhelms their ability to hang on in the relationship. When waves of contention and turmoil pound intensely, the glue holding partners together begins to wash away. The loss makes it difficult to find comfort and solace in the relationship. Partners feel alone, lonely, distressed and spent. They find it impossible to renew their zest and desire to work through the complexities.

When intimate relationships break down, partners can feel as though they are coming apart at the seams. Women who have reached this point often begin a first counseling session by saying, "I think I'm going crazy!" They feel this way because their identity is no longer clear. When asked, "Who are you in the household?" the typical response is, "I don't know," or "I guess I'm the maid (the doormat, the nanny)." When we are no longer clear about who we are, or feel trapped in a painful role not of our making, it is "crazy making." We feel as though we are losing it.

Some of the loss of grounding experienced by the women above results from laboring in energy-draining situations where the lovership has been lost. The lovership is always a casualty of chaos and, once it is gone, there is no longer a mirror in which partners can reinforce their image in the household. Therefore, partners lose their identity as a parent to their partner's children. Lost identity, exhaustion and isolation combine to disorient them. Eventually, they experience that feeling of coming unglued. Without their relationship as a source of comfort, there is no means of recharging their batteries.

By contrast, men tend to deal with the exhaustion by becoming irritable or by pulling out emotionally. They avoid the issues by spending more time at work, organizing the garage, doing mechanical tasks, or they go off into another room and surf the Internet or TV channels. Men's identities are typically less threatened by chaos in the household, and they tend to deal with emotional difficulties in the home differently than women. This does not mean that the pain is any less for men, but merely that they cope with it differently.

When partners arrive at a point of utter exhaustion, they usually also feel trapped, depleted and demoralized. And interestingly, partners often experience their exhaustion physically just as things are beginning to mellow out. This happens because as stress lessens, so does muscle tension; the body, in other words, exhales. As it does, the individual feels the exhaustion she or he has been numbing out. It is similar to the phenomenon those who live close to airports can experience. They become deaf to the constant noise until for some reason the planes stop; then they hear the silence.

It is also at the point of depleted energy that couples begin to accuse each other of having grown cold. When fatigue takes over, partners emotionally shut down and then both experience a loss of affection. If one of them is a *pursuer,* inasmuch as she seeks out the other for connection, while the other is a *distancer,* inasmuch as he needs space, a vicious cycle of pursuit and flight can become established. If a *pursuer* pushes too hard, and a *distancer* demands too much, partners are driven further and further apart. The ultimate outcome is anger and exasperation.

Physical and emotional fatigue require monitoring on a daily basis. The more accurate the picture that partners have of their physical and emotional status, the better they will fare. Impatience, irritability and the proclivity to strike out often ride on top of fatigue. Many people become reactive when tired or stressed. It is no wonder that when partners are spent, young energetic teens are able to take control of a household. Partners need adequate rest, proper nutrition, some exercise and time for themselves. They need to be their own best caretakers. They need to know what will recharge their emotional and physical batteries.

Save Your Marriage:
How to Support

In the course of busy lives, it is a challenge to stay in tune with one's emotional and physical needs. The tempo of comings and goings, coupled with life's constant demands, leaves little time for personal fulfillment that can feed body and soul. If an already heavy load multiplies because of an out-of-control home environment, it can throw internal switches that activate defenses necessary for self-protection. These defenses insulate you emotionally, and they thereby shield you from the impact of your emotions. This is what has happened when a partner says, "I feel dead." Or, "I can't respond anymore." Although this numbness is protective, it renders your experience of life as being rather hollow.

What are your needs beyond such things as food, sleep, protective clothing and tending to the elimination of body wastes? What are the more difficult to identify emotional, social and spiritual needs? To not know what you need renders you incapable of really moving toward fulfillment in life. To not have a clue of your longings is a prescription for living with an insatiable yearning for something—but what?

If you find yourself perplexed by what your needs are, use your checkbook or credit card bills as a source of information. Assess where your money goes; on what items do you spend money? How you spend money is a good indication of where your values lie and, hence, your needs and wants. Another good source to evaluate is how and where you spend your time and why. The insight gained from these sources can be very helpful. Refer to the **Identifying and Meeting Personal Needs** exercise at the end of the chapter.

A third question that can bring up interesting information is, *What regularly makes you angry at home?* Anger often results from frustrated needs. Are you angry because you need less stress, fewer financial demands and fewer intrusions from the ex? Do you need fewer hassles at work or fewer struggles about sex? Do you need more peacefulness, more quiet time and more opportunities for relaxation? Do you need more time with children, more affection and more sex?

Partners' incompatibilities around sex and money are often a source of negative undertow in a relationship. It is extremely important to come to some appropriate reconciliation of needs for sexual intimacy. If one partner feels deprived and the other feels hounded, this dissatisfaction is ever-present, and it tends to indirectly influence conversations about other matters. When a couple is sexually and financially compatible (a rare occurrence, by the way), most other issues are easier to air and resolve. Therefore, include sex and money issues when completing the needs and wants exercise.

It is probably impossible to meet all your needs to the degree you would like. Nevertheless, when you see that forty, fifty or eighty percent of them go begging, you have found a source of emotional pain. Everyone's needs differ: introverts want solitude and quiet, extroverts like action and interaction. Universally, however, the needs we tend to overlook are those for rest, good nutrition, affection, peacefulness, and time for doing whatever.

Complete the exercise at the end of the chapter and keep it forever (*forever* is not a misprint). Fold it up and put it in your billfold, purse, inside suit-coat pocket, or someplace where you will always have it with you. The next time you have to wait for the doctor, the oil change or your therapist (heaven forbid), take it out and review it. Ask yourself how you are doing. Many of our needs and wants are not static. Some may no longer be relevant, while others emerge and need to be added. From time to time some will change sides. Make the necessary changes and then put the list back where you keep it. And, yes, on occasion you may need to recopy it.

Some partners lose track of their personal needs amid the hurry-scurry of meeting everyone else's. Most parents, for instance, meet some of their needs by taking good care of their children. Being parents always means there are sacrifices. There is just no way around it. Inherent in all love, and in all parenting, is some measure of devotion and responsibility. This is normal, appropriate and honorable. However, self-sacrifice is one thing, self-denial quite another. Adults have needs that will not be met by taking care of children. No one can get exercise for us. No one can attend that painting class we want to take, spend an afternoon fishing or learning the two-step for us. We must not feel selfish in scheduling time for things that renew us.

Can you satisfy your needs without being selfish? Yes you can. To be selfish is to gain something at someone else's expense. By equalizing the time and resources necessary for meeting needs, no one is left at a disadvantage. However, a man who is never home because of his need to achieve in his profession takes advantage of the children who need some of his time. On the other hand, a man who knows when to quit because the children have needs, honors both himself and the children.

A woman who devotes all her time to her children and never takes time for her partner takes advantage of her partner. She honors her relationship when she balances her roles as mother and partner. Partners who avoid working together to find a sexual comfort level are insensitive to the need for give and take in a relationship. Those who honor each other know that they have to compromise.

One reason it is difficult to satisfy our needs and honor those of others is that we sometimes spread ourselves too thin and become overwhelmed. How many irons can one comfortably have in the fire? How much can one reasonably accomplish? Where does one draw the line? We must consider what we value and decide what is important. How can we honor others and ourselves? These are questions individuals can only answer for themselves.

Using Every Resource Possible

Books

It is surprising how much information is available about creating functional living-together arrangements if one is willing to explore. One of the best places to start an exploration is at a public library. If you are already a library buff, you have some search and find skills at your disposal. If you do not have these skills, find the reference librarian. There is hardly anyone in life more helpful than a reference librarian. What information reference librarians do not carry in their heads they know how to find elsewhere.

In the card catalog, whether on cards or in computer files, you will find many books listed. Once you locate them on the shelves you will find that some are more adequate for your needs than others. Check the table of contents, and then scan it to see if the book covers topics of interest to you. Check the bibliography of each book for clues to other titles that may interest you. In the **Suggested Readings** section at the back of this book, a number of books are listed that have been useful to clients. No book, including this one, says it all, so select a few that offer insights into areas of particular interest or concern.

Another way to find books is to ask your therapist or friends who are also in new-family. Another is to call the Department of Continuing Education at a college near you. They may have someone on their staff or adjunct faculty who teaches classes on the subject and who could make recommendations.

Educational Classes

Taking classes is another means of acquiring information about new-family. Community organizations usually sponsor these classes. On occasion a college or university may offer something appropriate through their continuing education department. Local churches are also good places to make inquiries.

Ask a librarian, a minister or your children's teacher where you might find educational resources related to new-family. Nationwide there are Early Childhood and Family Education programs that offer varied classes. Call the local school district and ask if they have such a program or something similar.

In St. Paul, Minnesota, the school district sponsors a downtown education resource center for adults who work in the downtown area. This center offers classes over the lunch hour and in the late afternoon. Perhaps there is something similar in your area and, again, the way to find out is to call the school district headquarters and question the person who answers the phone. Like reference librarians, those who answer main phone lines are an invaluable resource. They direct many calls each day.

Explain what you are seeking, and they will direct you to someone in the know.

Church Sponsored Programs

Churches also sponsor classes and other programs for new-family, and you can check with the program director even if you are not a member. If the particular church you contact has nothing, ask if they know who does. In some areas local chapters of the Stepfamily Association meet at a local church, but that information may not be readily available to the public. There might be a similar situation in your city.

In the Minneapolis-St. Paul area, the Diocese of the Catholic Church, through its various departments, offers support groups and classes for new-family. If, in your search, you find nothing at the parish level, call the next higher organizational level.

Day Care Services

Not enough good things can be said about the value of having one's young children in the home of a benevolent day care provider or in a kind and competent institutional day care setting. In these settings children find support, warmth and caring. These providers can offer stability and consistency, that because of a custody arrangement, birth parents may be unable to provide.

The fear some parents express is that the children will become more attached to the day care provider than to them. This is always a possibility, but it can be viewed as a benefit rather than a threat. We may, over the course of our lives, have many substitute Moms and Dads, so if such a relationship bridges troubled waters for children, then the parents are the benefactors.

The World Wide Web

The World Wide Web needs no introduction for those already using the Internet. The Web is a network of computers that creates the information super-highway. If you have a computer in your home with access to the Internet, you are ready to go. If not, there are many public sites through which you can acquire access, along with the help of trained personnel. The best place to start an inquiry is with your local or regional library. In rural areas another source can be the county extension agent if your county maintains such a program.

Once you have accessed the Web, you will want to use a search engine to locate information. A search engine is a program maintained by a particular server that can search for information. At the time of this writing the following are a few that are available: Yahoo, Altavista, Excite, Infoseek, Lycos, Hotbot and MSN Web Search. The key words for starting your search are "recreating family." Visit those sites that appear of interest. You will find that almost every site has links to other sites with a similar informational orientation. Once you turn to the Web for assistance, you will likely find more information than it is possible to manage.

Following is the information necessary to contact the national stepfamily associations on the Web.

- **Stepfamily Association of America, Inc.**
  650 J Street, Suite 205
  Lincoln, NE 68508
  Telephone—(402) 477-7837
  Web Site—http://www.stepfam.org/who.htm

- **Stepfamily in Formation**
  P.O. Box 3124.
  Oak Park, IL 60303
  Telephone—(708) 848-0909
  Web Site—http://www.stepfamilyinfo.org/resources.htm

- **Stepfamily Foundation**
  333 West End Ave.
  New York, New York 10023
  Telephone—(212)-877-3244
  Web Site—http://www.stepfamily.org/content.htm

Psychologists, Social Workers and their Associations
Therapists are now being trained to work with new-family and to view it as a unique type of family. It remains true, however, that many therapists do not understand important differences

between new-family and biological family. It is very important, therefore, to inquire about the knowledge base of a therapist before committing to work with them. If a misguided therapist attempts to guide the new-family into working like a traditional family, the stability a new-family has developed can rapidly deteriorate. Your first question of a therapist might be, "Have you ever been in a new-family or stepfamily?" Or, "What specific training do you have for working with new-family?" None of us would take our car to the dentist for a tuneup—right? The distinctions between dentists and auto mechanics are rather obvious. The distinctions between various types of therapists are not. It is a mistake (trust me) to believe that every therapist is a "jack of all trades." They are not, and if they practice with inadequate preparation, they do more harm than good.

There are a number of ways to begin a search for a therapist. First, the State Board of Psychology, the State Board of Social Workers and the State Board of Licensed Marriage and Family Therapists in the state in which you live are excellent starting points. They can provide the names of therapists who have met the criteria of licensure in their particular discipline. There is not always a difference in the way psychologists, social workers and marriage and family therapists conduct therapy. In the long run, their training coupled with their experience is what really counts in the new-family area. Most licensed therapists offer a high level of competence in their particular areas of expertise. It is wise to see a licensed therapist since they must meet certain prescribed educational and ethical standards. Most states also require continuing education for maintaining licensure. Using a licensed therapist is not foolproof protection, but it is an initial step in protecting yourself as a consumer.

The state boards mentioned above will be able to provide you with the addresses and phone numbers of professional organizations. Often these organizations maintain lists of the specialties of their members. Whether you are close to a large city or in a rural setting, a state association will know of competent therapists in your area.

Be generally cautious of those who call themselves psy-
chotherapists but who are not licensed by any regulatory agency.
In some states, state law does not regulate the title psychothera-
pist. Although many states have tightened laws regarding who
may provide mental health services, it is still possible for inade-
quately trained individuals to masquerade behind titles that look
good. This is not to suggest that everyone who practices outside
state licensure is incompetent. They are not, but licensure is, in
part, an attempt to protect the consumer.

Support Groups

Support groups can be enormously helpful, but they can also
be hard to find. An inquiry can begin at any of the groups mentioned above. In Minnesota, for example, the Minnesota
Women's Psychologists Association maintains a list of support
groups and therapy groups offered by its members. Ask each
group you speak with what they know about support groups,
and whether some organization in your area maintains a list of
ongoing groups.

If you cannot find an appropriate support group, start one.
You do not need a professional to conduct a group of partners
or new-parents who want to talk about the ups and downs of
life in new-family. A support group does not need to be large.
It needs a few people who are in need of the guidance and
reassurance that can come from others who are suffering similar distress.

Corporations and Other Businesses

Many corporations and businesses offer noon-hour lectures and
seminars for their employees. Contact the education department
or the department that sponsors these classes and ask about
their programs. Suggest ideas for what you need and would like.
How do you find the department that sponsors such gatherings? Ask the person who answers the main phone line at your
company.

Other Health Care Professionals and Hospitals

Another source of information is your physician, chiropractor or massage therapist. Ask for a reference; most health care professionals know others who specialize in various fields.

Hospitals also have social service or education departments that sponsor programs. Check with them.

Health Maintenance Organizations

When working within an HMO you may have to become your own best advocate, although the type of care you can receive, in any health insurance organization, depends on the limits of care within your policy. It is important to understand your benefits and how they can be used to best meet your needs.

County Social Services

County Social Services is usually a valuable source of information, and they may have resources available even for those who are not eligible for any of their programs.

Crisis Lines and Crisis Centers

In the Minneapolis/St. Paul area there is a non-profit organization called "First Call For Help." It is sponsored by United Way, and it maintains a list of organizations that can offer immediate assistance. Many counties also have a crisis line. This is an important number to have in your possession in case you need it.

One of the resources available in the Twin Cities, for example, is the Walk In Counseling Center (WICC). WICC is a non-profit organization whose therapists are volunteers from the professional health services community. At centers like WICC you can receive quick, competent, short-term help. Your community may have something similar. Call the United Way office in your area and ask what is available.

Invited Speakers

If you belong to an organization that can sponsor speakers or seminars, this is an excellent opportunity to hear from talented people. If you read a book you like and want to contact the author for information and availability, write to that person in care of the publisher.

Gay and Lesbian Families

Gay and lesbian partners may wish to find therapists and other assistance through an organization specifically oriented to helping same-sex couples. It is important to remember, however, that many therapists who are not gay themselves are very gay-sensitive and affirming. Always ask a potential therapist if he or she can work without prejudice with a gay family. If the therapist says no, move on. If you belong to a mental health system such as an HMO, make it clear that you need to work with a therapist who can work without prejudice. Do not settle for anything less.

If you are close to a large city, look in the yellow pages under the heading, **Gay Lesbian Organizations.** If a counseling center is not listed, a church may be. The pastor at this church may be able to direct you to appropriate resources. Another source of information is Parents and Friends of Lesbians and Gays (P-FLAG). Whoever answers their phone will be able to send you in the appropriate direction.

If you are in a rural area, ask a social worker at the county social services department, or inquire at the closest mental health center. It is very important in rural areas to make sure that the therapist is capable of working with a gay family. It can be difficult in rural environs to find therapists because there is usually less diversity in rural areas.

The Power of Support

Taking advantage of available resources helps build a scaffolding of support underneath a couple. It shores them up. See Figure 7-1.

Becoming Experts

After all is said and done, partners must become the experts. It is important to learn as much as possible from others, but equally important to remember that there are no gurus in this field. Every

Figure 7-1

writer and speaker has a particular perspective. Take from each only what works for your situation because your situation is unique. You must adapt what is useful, and that is how you become the experts in your situation.

If this book suggests doing something differently than you presently do it, and what you do works for you, do not change it. In other words, "If it ain't broke, don't fix it."

Read, listen, assess, evaluate, and when necessary, experiment. Most of the strategies in this book evolved from the trial and error of partners like you. Little is carved in stone. Set a course and if it doesn't take you where you want to go, change it. Kids understand midstream shifts if you are honest with them. Do not become locked in by rigid goals or shoulds. Because building a new-family is a complicated endeavor, most partners have to make it up as they go along. It is important to stay loose and flexible. And therein lies the challenge.

The Ongoing Challenge:
To Keep Learning, Adjusting and Renewing

Learning to manage a new-family can be a little like learning a new dance step. No matter how accomplished partners are as solo dancers, they have to learn to synchronize their steps, or they step on each other's toes. What they need are basic instructions in dancing together as a pair. After that they can develop their own style, because each has learned to anticipate the next move of the other. As their form improves, so does the quality of the experience.

As it is in learning to dance, so it is in learning to be co-heads of household. Partners can learn to synchronize their efforts in co-leadership by acquiring some basic instruction. When trouble strikes, many couples turn to therapists for help. This is all well and good, as therapy is a valuable resource, but therapy is not typically instruction-oriented. Partners can often gain more hands-on management skills and basic strategies from a class that teaches them how to co-lead and co-parent.

Partners are in this endeavor together. They function as equals working together for the benefit of their long-term relationship and the psychological and emotional welfare of the children. In order to accomplish this, individuals must constantly renew themselves by meeting their unique needs—and each partner must support the other in taking time to do so. If one partner gets four hours for some enjoyable activity, then the other gets four hours, also.

A truly loving and egalitarian partnership emerges from negotiation borne in compassion, and with an abiding desire to share leadership and responsibility. Flowing together, partners create the harmonious beauty of emotional union. When good dancers are on the floor, one is unaware of who is leading and who is following. It makes no difference, the pair moves as one, each stepping in the right direction at the right time. They glide rhythmically to the unique music of their personalities, bonded and in union. This is relationship's dance at its best.

These partners still fight on occasion and they do step on each other's toes at times. But this faltering does not call the relationship itself into question. These moments of resentment are not taken as indications that the relationship is not working. "Resentment," write Stephen and Ondrea Levine, " . . . is only an invitation to the work that is to be done."*

Learn, adjust, renew and support each other whenever and however possible. When you cannot support your partner, say why honestly and kindly. Talk about it and get help if necessary, but work it through. Remember that the children are going to grow up and move away—where blending must occur is between partners. In order to be old together you have to hang in during the young times, the rough times. Do not call the relationship into question every time your partner's kids or one of the ex-partners becomes unbearable. They are going to be unbearable at times.

Have you signed-on? Are you in the boat? Are you rowing together? Partners have to be willing to dive as the crew of a

---

* Stephen Levine and Ondrea Levine, *Embracing the Beloved: Relationship as a Path of Awakening* (New York: Doubleday, 1995), 152.

submarine dives. They must be as willing as a space shuttle crew to strap themselves in for the ride to space. Partners must be willing to work together to navigate treacherous waters and dangerous shoals, willing to loosen emotional ties with their children and to teach the children a new way of life. They must be willing to end wars with their exes and ensure that their children have stable homes. Partners must be willing to back off each other's kids and not attempt to recreate the kids in the partner's own image. Partners must swallow their pride and assume an adult leadership role—a self-sacrificing role that keeps them from taking personally what the kids dish out.

Partners need to look deeply into the children, deeply enough to understand that they behave as they do because they are in pain. Partners must look deeply enough inside themselves to see that what keeps them from being sensitive, understanding and forgiving is *their* pain, *their* jealousy, *their* possessiveness, *their* insecurity or *their* need for control. Partners must dig deeply to find their compassion so they can be gentle with the children and themselves as well. They must find the courage and greatness of soul to lift themselves into the role of teacher, caregiver, parent and leader. There is something noble in each of us, and where better to start manifesting it than at the dinner table with the partner's kids. *Be your Greater Self.*

The prize is to dance the dance of life with one who is deeply loved. The prize is a wonderful partner, a loving relationship, a home and the future. It is the sweetness of union, for there is no joy on earth that equals it. The gift is to be together in spirit so that on those days when there is no poetry, no music, no rhythm and no dance, one can still say, "I love you—you're the best; you complete me."

You Can Do It!

Exercise:
Identifying and Meeting Personal Needs

The following exercise can help one identify and, subsequently, stay tuned to her or his needs. On a letter size piece of paper draw a line down the middle as shown in the diagram on the next page. Label the left half "Needs" and the right half "Wants." On the needs side, list those things you *must* have to be a satisfied, relatively happy human being. Include those needs you are presently meeting as well as those you are not. Be sure to include the basics such as food, sleep and exercise.

On the wants side, list those things you would like to have but that are not necessary for your emotional, physical and spiritual well-being. *Needs are the necessities and wants the niceties.* Some examples of needs and wants are shown in the diagram. This exercise may take days, a month, a lifetime, because our needs are ever emerging and changing.

Needs	Wants
Three small meals and two snacks each day	A live-in maid !!!!! To lose 10 pounds
To eat more fresh fruits and vegetables	
Eight hours of sleep	A new mattress
A safe place to sleep	A lock on the bedroom door
To walk at least 2 miles five times a week	An electric treadmill
An hour of quiet before bed-time. Connect with Jim during this time	A vacation at a beach, just the two of us
A date a week with Jim	A date on Fri. or Sat. eve
To set aside Sundays for family time	To get to know Jim's kids better
Time with my friends; lunch once a week with someone	To resolve impasse with Jane
To call mom once a week	To have an honest talk with mom about what I can give
A weekly massage after aerobics class	
Reliable transportation	A new car
To figure out how to spend less time in the kitchen and still get everyone fed	To ASK for help and ASK Jim to help more when his children visit
To overcome my fear of asking for help and of being parental with Jim's children	To learn more about how to do that
A more stable job	To make more money
More sex	A lock on the bedroom door
To find the spiritual part of my life	To find a meditation class

APPENDICES

Appendix A

Managing Money
Dollar, Dollar Who's Got the Dollar?

Another important aspect of creating new-family is working out the *how* of handling money. How much does each partner earn? How much support money is received and how much is paid out? How many children in the home belong to each partner, and what proportion of a month are they there? How will equity be achieved? Who will oversee finances? Can partners spend money on their birth children without the other's permission? Many issues require negotiation and each is a potential source of conflict.

Money, like sex, *always* matters because it ties to feelings of power and autonomy, or powerlessness and dependency. This is why money fights are not always about money. They are about the desire for control, about feelings of powerlessness, loss of control or jealousy. There are three barometers of the functional compatibility of partners in new-family. One is the extent to which they can agree about household ground rules and support each other in managing them. The other two are sexual fulfillment and satisfying money arrangements. Dissatisfaction in any one of these areas can destroy the stability existing in the others.

In a first marriage, one merged and shared money pot can work quite well. In new families, however, it seldom does, and there are numerous reasons for this. Most women arrive in new partnerships after having singularly managed a household. They are now unwilling to be without discretionary funds and quite unwilling to be dependent and controlled by their partner. They have been on their own, and they have become empowered where money is concerned. They have learned to budget and manage, now they are averse to asking permission and to being punished because of how they spend household money. The haggles that arise over money, haggles these women have been free of, become irritating and irksome in the relationship.

Men, conversely, are less willing in this age of feminism to be the sole wage earner in a household. Most men expect their partner to share household expenses. Many also feel, and rightly so, that it is not their responsibility to fully support their partner's children. It is true, however, that a large percentage of men provide generous financial assistance to these children, far beyond any obligation. Although they do not wish to feel like an ATM machine, many are exceedingly giving, and remarkably unappreciated for being so.

Another reason for strife is that both partners want to spend money on their children without having to ask the other's permission. Most partners resent being harangued because they buy things for their children that the partner believes the ex should buy with support money. New-parents do have a tendency to resent money being spent on a partner's birth children, especially when they are not residents of the home. If partners settle these matters before conflict begins, it averts a great deal of turmoil.

The goal of any plan is for partners to feel it is an equitable arrangement. It is also imperative that the plan be judged fair. Therefore, in formulating a plan, partners must not mask their true feelings. If they hedge or lie, the underlying reality of what they feel will sabotage compatibility. The fallout will land in the middle of the lovership, and it will push partners away from each other.

The section that follows presents a strategy that has worked for many partners. By using its basic structure and formulas, couples can create and fashion a workable plan for their situation.

As the diagram shows, the calculations are as follows:

1) Create three separate money pots. Typically, these are checking accounts, but they could also be envelopes. The examples that follow assume that both partners earn money, although they do not earn a similar amount.

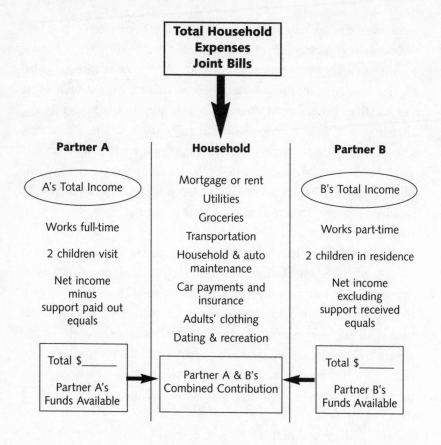

2) Each partner should figure the total amount of available income (the amount after taxes). Partners who pay support should deduct that amount from the total since it is not available. Partners who receive support should not add it into their total at this point. These figures represent each partner's total available monthly resource.

3) The total household budget is calculated next. How much money does the household require each month? Include all joint expenses and joint bills. Partners must determine what items to include and which to exclude. Automobile payments and auto insurance, for example: are these household expenses or will each partner assume his or her payments?

Answer this question: living where we live, in this home, what does it cost for the two of us? Do not at this point introduce any differential for the children's presence in the home.

4) Calculate the ratio of the higher income to the lower. If partner A's available income is $3,000 each month, and partner B's is $1,500, the ratio is 2:1. The math for computing this is as follows: divide the larger amount by the smaller. Since there are two $1,500s in $3,000 the ratio is 2:1. This math is the same regardless of how large A's amount is, or how small B's.

5) If the total, shared household expenses are $3,000 each month and the available resources ratio is 2:1, then partner A assumes $2,000 of those expenses and partner B assumes $1,000.

6) Now figure the cost of the children: both partner A and partner B have two children under the age of 13. Figure the cost of maintaining a child that age at $10 a day (or some other figure you choose to use). Partner A's children are in the home six days a month, partner B's 24 days. This means that A's contribution must increase by $120 ($10 a day times 6 days equals $60, times 2 children equals $120) and partner B's by $480.

7) Since partner B receives $600 each month in support, B has $120 remaining to spend on the children's clothing and other expenses. In addition, note that B has $500 remaining from net income after household expenses. Therefore, B ends up with $620 of discretionary income each month. Partner A, the higher wage earner has $880. Remember, too, that partner A has sent a portion of net income to an ex-partner for child support.

The figure of $10 a day for the children, in the example above, is arbitrary. It seemed like a reasonable amount, but that is a point for negotiation between partners. Teenagers and young adults certainly cost more to maintain than young children (excluding day

care), if only the cost of hot water, electricity and the extra telephone line are considered. Therefore, a higher daily figure would
be appropriate for teens. Besides utilities, the daily figure should
include a room and board amount. Groceries are easy enough
to figure, but what percentage of the mortgage or rent is attrib-
utable to the children is more difficult to determine.

Here is how one couple got technical. They divided the total
of their monthly mortgage and utility bills by the number of rooms
in the home. The mortgage was $1,500 and the utilities $200. They
had 10 rooms; therefore, the cost per room was $170 a month.
$170 divided by 30 days made the approximate cost of each room
$6 per day. These partners assumed that because of the children,
they had 3 extra bedrooms. The three additional rooms costs $18
a day, $540 a month. Since two children were there six days per
month and two were there twenty-four days per month, the cost
to each partner was assessed as follows: The partner whose children were there twenty-four days paid $432 ($18 for each day
times 24 days) and the partner whose children were there six days
paid $108 ($18 for each day times 6 days). The remaining $960
of the mortgage and utilities was divided equally between the partners: $480 each.

Although it seems like a lot of trivial figuring, the importance
of the outcome is immeasurable if it leads to a conclusion on which
partners can agree. Then neither of them comes away from the
efforts feeling as if they got the short end of the stick. It is enormously important to arrive at a point of mutual satisfaction in any
agreement. If either partner allows hurt feelings to smolder, the
embers will eventually catch on fire and burn down other positive accomplishments.

One caution: do not use partner B's discretionary income to
pay a portion of A's support. Some partners do this, but it can
become a terrible trap for partner B and the first step on the path
to divorce court for both. Why is this? First, partner B surrenders
money required for meeting the needs of her or his children; this
is not the expectation of the ex sending support. Therefore, Partner

B ends up feeling poor and powerless and will begin to resent the partner and the partner's ex, who is the recipient of support money. This anger will eventually stifle loving feelings for the partner. Moreover, partner B's resentment of partner A's ex will eventually affect B's ability to parent A's children.

Partner A must accept that his or her financial lifestyle is affected by the amount of support sent to his or her ex. This is a cost of divorce not always obvious until the first bill comes due. It is unfair to expect partner B to assist in paying partner A's support. Also, partner B must accept that A's available income, reduced by a support payment, affects her or his financial lifestyle. It is hard to have it all.

The above example is very simple and straightforward, but what happens when partner A earns a great deal more money than B? Suppose, for example, that Partner A's available income is $10,000 a month and Partner B's is $1,500. Again, divide the largest by the smallest. The quotient is 6.66. Round this figure to 7. The ratio is 7 to 1. Partner A will pay 7 times more than partner B.

One reason for doing these calculations is that the partner with the higher income typically drives the lifestyle of the household. If one knows coming into a relationship they will be partner A; that is, they will earn a lot more money than their partner, they must consider whether they can be satisfied married to a partner B (one who does not earn nearly as much). Can they accept the disparity without lauding it over B, without using money as power to punish or control B? Those who are a "Partner A" need to be clear about whether money is a means of acquiring material things and future security, or a power through which they control the lives of others. These are fundamental issues that high income partner A's should address before they commit. And within these issues are fundamental questions to which partner B's should request answers. These matters need to be discussed and agreements reached.

Some partner A's who are either high wage earners, or who come to a new relationship with many assets, request a prenuptial agreement. These agreements have their good and bad sides.

If partner B links A's desire to retain control of premarital assets with partner A's love for B, there is going to be long term hurt and resentment. Is it unreasonable for A to want a prenuptial agreement to protect certain assets? The logical answer is, of course not. However, partner B's inner voice may say, "If A loves me, then what belongs to A also belongs to me." The hurt feelings associated with the prenuptial will underlie long-term resentment. Again, we see the need to address and resolve these issues before a union is completed, and a part of that encounter must be to examine one's feelings and get them out in the open.

Before A and B join, they should consider which assets they wish to protect for their children. This is the time to settle that matter. The settlement affects the extended new-family because it influences the attitudes of the children toward their birth parent's new-partner. This is an issue usually on the minds of birth children when their middle-aged or senior citizen parents join a new-partner. The kids want to know who has how much and who is going to get it—"What's going to happen to my inheritance?"

Another thing partners must accept about each other is that each has a relationship history. In other words, there were other relationships and there are, perhaps, children from those relationships. All that history is going to color what happens now. A second or third marriage is not a first, and that statement has nothing to do with love. Marriages after the first may be filled with a love never present in the first, but marriages after the first are also a package deal. The package is the history and the progeny that each partner brings. We are never free of our history. Every event in our lives, every decision is like that butterfly on the other side of the world that flaps its wings and affects our weather. Every moment in our life is a flap of our wings; yet when we are doing our flapping, we seldom think about it in that way.

Throughout this book the recommendation has been that when the going gets tough, help is in order. Today in every city and village, professionals can be found who assist couples in the

mechanics of hands on money management. These are not invest-
ment advisors, but professionals who help couples set up budg-
ets and negotiate each partner's commitment to a budget. These
are the people to turn to for help in this area. The feelings that
surface can be processed with a therapist, but never trust your
therapist to be a financial advisor (*never*).

One of the most important mathematical equations to remember when setting up money distribution in a new-family is that
one plus one equals three. That is not a misprint, 1+1=3: your
money, my money, household money.

Appendix B

Exercises for Those Still Undecided
(Continued from Chapter One)

Should I Do This or Not?
Clarifying Fear:

When we ask the question, "Should I do this or not?" we are acknowledging uncertainty. Our inquiry is often a sign we are in dangerous territory. The head is pulling in one direction and the heart in another. The travesty is that we ignore red flags waved by our rational mind when emotions control behavior. Many of us have successfully traversed emotional mine fields to win relationships we ultimately did not want. When we finally wake up and look back, we wonder how we overlooked and denied the obvious. That realization can be mind-boggling.

The juicy delirium that leads us blindly into our love nests does not belong to the rational part of the mind but to its unconscious part. We call that stage of falling in love, *limerence.** Limerence is that time when one obsesses over their new love. Nothing will get this person off one's mind. This is not an abnormal state; most people have limerent experiences. Nevertheless, it is a menacing time because it creates dangerous possibilities.

The positive aspect of limerence is that the delicious stuff in early love pulls us toward relationship, and that is not necessarily a bad thing. What is dangerous is that the obsession creates an idealization—a distorted impression of who the other person really is. We are in love with someone we have, in part, created in our mind. How much of the other person is our creation is an enormously important question. Will we be happy when we awaken from our love stupor? Will we like the human being we

---

* Dorothy Tennove, *Love and Limerence: The Experience of Being in Love* (Stein and Day Publishers, 1979; Chelsea, MI: Scarborough House Publishers, 1989), 23.

then find on the other side of the bed? Will he or she still garner our affection and devotion?

We are captives of our longing and our desires. Longing tempts us to create a daydream to, distort the object of our love. When longing is banished in favor of well-grounded affection and liking, the truth of the other manifests itself.

Information Gathering

One way to begin breaking an illusion is to confront ourselves with some general considerations. Start this task by reviewing each of the considerations listed below. Make every effort to be as honest as possible. There is no one with whom it is more difficult to be honest than with one's self. Notice as you read these considerations which ones cause internal tension, which ones cause a bit of anxiety making the belly muscles tighten. One of the goals of the exercise is to engage the rational thinking mind. By putting on our "thinking cap" we can sometimes slow a pounding heart.

Writing the answers makes this exercise a more powerful experience. Begin each of the following items with the following clause:

I am making an effort at breaking through illusion:

1) By not making a decision too quickly; this is far too important a decision to be made in haste. (How long have we known each other? Am I moving too quickly?)

2) By not joining someone who does not respect the children. (Does he or she respect my children?)

3) By not joining someone who has not spent a lot of time with the children. (Have we spent enough time together for him or her to know what my children are really like?)

4) By not joining someone when I care more about their children than I do about my prospective partner. (Do I like the children better than him or her?)

5) By not joining someone if I am jealous of one or more of his or her children. (Do I feel competitive with any of his or her children?)

6) By not joining someone whose parenting style I dislike or believe is harmful. (How do I feel about how he or she parents? How will I feel if he or she parents my children in the same way?)

7) By not joining someone who is into push-pull. (Does he or she pull me in and then push me away?)

8) By not joining someone primarily because they will be a good source of financial support. (Will I be financially dependent in this relationship?)

9) By not joining someone primarily because they seem like a good parent when I am uncertain about them as an intimate partner. (Am I looking for a parent for my children more than a mate for myself?)

10) By not joining someone the children are begging me to marry if I am uncertain about him or her as an intimate partner. (Do I like this person as much as my children do?)

11) By not believing that I will make a life-saving difference in the troubled lives of his or her children. (Do I want to protect his or her children from his or her ex-partner?)

12) By not believing that his or her children, whom I do not like, but who do not live with us, will never be permanent residents in our home. (Could I live with his or her children?)

13) By realizing that if my prospective partner's ex is a meddler that he or she may never change. (How will I handle his or her ex's meddling once it affects our home?)

14) By not turning his or her ex into the "bad one" or the "crazy one" who is responsible for all the children's problems. (Can I accept that my prospective partner played a role in the children becoming who they are? Can I accept that life can turn out to be much more complicated than we ever imagined and that bad things happen to very good people?)

After answering these questions, you might wonder why anyone would become involved in a situation where there are so many potential complications. Every situation presents challenges, but we must remember that every situation is also different. Some situations are less complicated than others. If you find yourself concerned about one or more of the areas mentioned, write your thoughts and feelings out on a separate sheet of paper. Remember that this effort is just for you. No one else has to see it, so be as honest as possible.

In addition to the exercise above, also complete exercises in Chapter One that are relevant. Your efforts will create a great deal of information, and although it may not be new information, it can now be addressed in a step by step fashion. *Do not throw these pages away.* Also, do not hide these pages in some secret spot and then forget them until accidentally discovered some years from now, when you will emotionally whip yourself for not having paid attention. Now is the time to do something about everything that concerns you.

What does one do with all this information? If there are only minor concerns, one may wish to address them directly with his or her partner. Arrange a time to talk and then review your concerns with your prospective partner. Continue to work together until you feel you have resolved the issues to your mutual satisfaction. Each partner has to make tradeoffs and compromises. In a committed relationship neither partner gets to have everything her or his way. There has to be give and take on both sides.

If there are big concerns, major ones, there is only one alternative. Get the help of a trained professional to assist in sorting it out and developing strategies for addressing the issues.

What can one do to be sure of making the right decision? That is an impossible question to answer. Whether a decision turns out to be right or wrong is a Monday morning quarterback question. When we make any choice, it is based on the information available at the time. If we look back to call any particular decision into question, we can only say, "I did what seemed right at the time." It is impossible to know what lies ahead. Life can be as unpredictable as the Minnesota weather. No decision comes with a guarantee. At some point one has to take a leap of faith.

After making the efforts suggested above, you can certainly feel satisfied about having done your homework. You have considered your feelings and the pluses and minuses of the other person and the situation. The time comes when one has to decide whether to get in the boat or not.

Appendix C

Custody and Visitation Alternatives

1) Legal custody—shared equally
Physical custody—shared equally

In this arrangement, parents have equal legal claim in determining how the children are raised, and they share financial support equally. The children move regularly between the two households. Schedules for how often the children move vary, but the agreements are typically for an equal time-share. The positive aspect of this arrangement is that it keeps both parents involved in parenting and in financially supporting their children. As the following list shows, however, the minuses are many:

a) The more often children move, the more vulnerable they are to transitional syndrome, a condition described in Chapter Four.

b) Two houses don't always equal two homes for the children.

c) The children are continually presented with competing ideas and values.

d) The high degree of coordination required can keep ex-partners emotionally married and this confuses children—there is a family, but there isn't. This makes it difficult for everyone to psychologically move on.

e) Only the court or negotiators can settle issues when ex-partners reach an impasse.

f) Kids are often shifting between two neighborhoods and this can destroy their ability to bond with friendship groups and best friends.

g) This arrangement provides many opportunities for warring parents to menace one another.

Typically, this arrangement works better for parents than for children because it is based more on the needs of the adults than on the needs of the children. After living in this arrangement for a number of years, an eight-year-old said, "I felt like a human yo-yo." When this alternative is the only option, ex-partners must be mindful of its many pitfalls.

2. Legal custody—shared equally
Physical custody—to one birth parent
(custodial parent)
Visitation—with the non-custodial birth parent

In this arrangement, parents continue to have equal legal claim to decisions regarding the children, but the children spend the majority of their time in the home of one parent (custodial parent). The other parent (non-custodial parent) helps provide financial and, it is hoped, emotional support. He or she sees the children according to a court sanctioned visitation schedule.

The positive aspect of this is that it provides a primary home for the children. It provides them with greater opportunity for being re-rooted and for maintaining neighborhood friends. They also tend to be less conflicted by the competing ideas and values of their parents.

One negative aspect is that parents still have equal legal claim and must, therefore, appeal to an outside authority if there is an impasse. Another is that parents who do not have physical custody can become angry about financially supporting the children. They often feel they do not see the children enough and that they have little influence in their lives. Their anger can then cause them to withdraw their love from the children.

Another negative aspect is that birth parents with physical custody can end up feeling resentful because they do most of the gofer work associated with parenting. They see the non-custodial parent as having a good deal because he or she does less parenting and less disciplining. Therefore, the non-custodial parent seems to end up getting all the glory. They tend to be viewed as the Santa Claus parent and not taken seriously.

3. Legal custody—to one birth parent
Physical custody—to same birth parent
(custodial parent)
Visitation—with the non-custodial birth parent

This arrangement grants full legal custody and physical custody to one parent. The non-custodial parent provides financial and emotional support and has regular visitation. It has the same pros and cons as arrangement 2, but it has the advantage of keeping children out of the middle of birth parent disagreements about their care. Since one parent has legal control, there is a parent with power to say where the "buck stops" without involving mediators or the courts. The downside is that it increases the probability of the non-custodial parent becoming even more absent. It is hard for some adults to follow through with their children if they have little or no control. Love and support often become tied to control: "If I don't have power in your life, I'm not going to love you," is a sad outcome in some of these arrangements.

4. A variation of Number 3 above

Another option, which is a variation of 3, is to have the children live in the home of their mother while they are young and shift to their dad's home when they are eight or nine. This option can provide the children with the stability of a home base and, yet, give them opportunities to know each of their parents. Fathers who initially surrender their children into the custody of their ex-wife find this option difficult; women who send the children to Dad's when they are eight or nine find this arrangement tormenting. Women can greatly overlook the pain of the children's non-custodial father until they become non-custodial mothers.

The children carry the burden of lost family into the remainder of their lives. Their loss is permanent. Their birth parents can turn back to their original family for support or move on to new partners. They can change their lives, start a new life or begin new families. Yes, they too have lost and the changes are not easy, but they can recoup. It is much harder for children still at home because they are dependent and, consequently, powerless when it comes to determining the future.

Readings

Suggestions for Further Reading

*Personal Growth, and Strategies for Managing Anger
and Cultivating Compassion*

Chopra, Deepak. *The Seven Spiritual Laws of Success: A Practical Guide to the Fulfillment of Your Dreams*. San Rafael, CA: Amber-Allen Publishing and New World Library, 1993.

Goleman, Daniel. *Emotional Intelligence*. New York: Bantam Books, 1995.

Kabat-Zinn, Jon. *Wherever You Go There You Are, Mindfulness Meditation in Everyday Life*. New York: Hyperion, 1994.

Levine, Stephen. *A Gradual Awakening*. New York: Bantam Doubleday Dell Publishing Group, 1989.

Hanh, Thich Nhat. *Being Peace*. Berkeley: Parallax Press, 1987.

———. *The Blooming of a Lotus: Guided Meditation Exercises for Healing and Transformation*. Boston: Beacon Press, 1993.

———. *Peace Is Every Step: The Path of Mindfulness in Everyday Life*. New York: Bantam Books, 1991.

———. *Teachings on Love*. Berkeley: Parallax Press, 1997. (Couples may wish to refer to the peace treaty suggested and found on page 119.)

———. *Touching Peace: Practicing the Art of Mindful Living*. Berkeley: Parallax Press, 1992.

Kasl, Charlotte, Ph.D. *If the Budda Dated: A Handbook for Finding Love on a Spiritual Path*. New York: Penguin Arkana, 1999.

Thondup, Tulku. *The Healing Power of Mind: Simple Meditation Exercises for Health, Well-Being, and Enlightenment*. Boston: Shambala Publications, Inc., 1996.

Warren, Neil Clark. *Make Anger Your Ally: Harnessing Our Most Baffling Emotion*. Garden City, New York: Doubleday & Co., 1983.

Wolinsky, Stephen. *The Dark Side of the Inner Child, The Next Step*. Norfolk, CT: Bramble Books, 1993.

Wolinsky, Stephen, with Margaret O. Ryan. *Trances People Live: Healing Approaches in Quantum Psychology.* Norfolk, CT: Bramble Books, 1991.

Moore, Thomas. *Care of the Soul: A Guide for Cultivating Depth and Sacredness in Everyday Life,* New York: HarperCollins Publishers, Inc., 1992.

Relationships

Campbell, Joseph, with Bill Moyers; Betty Sue Flower, ed. *The Power of Myth.* New York: Doubleday, 1988.

De Angelis, Barbara. *Are You the One for Me? Knowing Who's Right & Avoiding Who's Wrong.* New York: Delacorte Press, 1992.

De Angelis, Barbara. *Secrets about Life Every Woman Should Know: Ten Principles for Total Emotional and Spiritual Fulfillment.* New York: Hyperion, 1999.

Levine, Stephen, and Ondrea Levine. *Embracing The Beloved: Relationship as a Path of Awakening.* New York: Doubleday, 1995.

Mason, Marilyn J. *Seven Mountains: The Inner Climb to Commitment and Caring.* New York: Dutton, 1997.

Moore, Thomas. *Soul Mates: Honoring the Mysteries of Love and Relationship.* Hingham, MA:Wheeler Pub, 1994.

Osbon, Diane K., ed. *A Joseph Campbell Companion/Reflections on the Art of Living.* New York: Harper Collins Publishers, 1991.

Tannen, Deborah. *That's Not What I Meant: How Conversational Style Makes or Breaks Your Relations with Others.* New York: Morrow, 1986.

———. *You Just Don't Understand: Women and Men in Conversation.* New York: Morrow, 1990.

Tennove, Dorothy. *Love and Limerence: The Experience of Being in Love.* Stein and Day Publishers, 1979. Reprint, Chelsea, MI: Scarborough House Publishers, 1989.

Welwood, John. *Journey of the Heart: The Path of Conscious Love.* New York: Harper Perennial, 1990.

Divorce and Remarriage

Wallerstein, Judith S. and Sandra Blakeslee. *The Good Marriage: How and Why Love Lasts.* Boston: Houghton Mifflin, 1995.

———. *Second Chances: Men, Women and Children a Decade after Divorce.* New York: Ticknor and Fields, 1989.

248

Parenting

de Becker, Gavin. *Protecting the Gift.* New York: The Dial Press, 1999.

Clinton, Hillary Rodham: *It Takes a Village: And Other Lessons Children Teach Us.* New York: Touchstone, 1996.

Marinakis, Maria M. *Parenting Infants and Toddlers without Going Nuts.* Las Vegas, NV: Summit, 2000.

Nelson, Jane, and Lynn Lott. *Positive Discipline for Teenagers.* Rocklin, CA: Prima Publishing, 1994.

Nelson, Jane, Lynn Lott, and H. Stephen Glenn. *Positive Discipline A-Z: 1001 Solutions to Everyday Parenting Problems.* Rocklin, CA: Prima Publishing, 1993.

Pryor, Karen. *Don't Shoot the Dog! The New Art of Teaching and Training.* New York: Bantam Books, 1984.

Finances

Dominguez, Joe and Vicki Robin. *Your Money or Your Life, Transforming Your Relationship with Money and Achieving Financial Independence.* New York: Penguin Books, 1992.

Gillies, Jerry. *Moneylove.* New York: Warner Books, 1978.

Acknowledgments

There are those whose contributions to this work and to my life are significant. In the gift of this space, I wish to thank them. Amongst those deserving of recognition, *and* totally without expectation on his part, is my black Labrador Louie—King of all the labbies. I love you. You have been a source of joy in my life and my "Buddy," during many hours of isolation while I was writing.

I thank those who have been my clients. Your triumphs empowered me; your defeats agonized and humbled me. I thank you for your trust and for allowing me to share your journey. I thank not only those who were enthusiastic about my approach but also those who were not and who had the courage to tell me. All served to change me, to inform my work and to fashion the substance of this book.

Over the years I have seen hundreds of young people ranging in age from four through the teens. I remain in awe of their honesty and ability to endure significant emotional trauma. It is one thing to have the trust of adults who come with some prior knowledge of one's credentials, it is quite another to be granted trust by innocent, vulnerable children who are not there by choice. These children taught me in ways that only innocence can teach. Some shared their most painful agonies, others their deepest secrets. To all of them I say, I was humbled in your presence and inspired by your fortitude—thank you for risking and trusting.

From my father and mother, Fred and Geneva Brandes, both deceased, I received many gifts. My father, a scholar and idealist, challenged me to "climb every mountain and ford every stream." He gave me a vision of the world and a sense of wonder. My mother, a strong-willed pragmatist, tempered my father's challenges by reminding me that it was cold on mountaintops and that fording streams can be dangerous. She admonished me to remember my mittens and to learn to swim. From Mother I gained the perseverance that sustained my efforts with this book.

My younger sister, Annelle Galvin, has always been a cheerleader in my life. She has encouraged me and looked up to me. I have appreciated her support and admiration. She is a bright woman with a tenacious spirit whose will and determination I look up to. My brother-in-law Patrick has been a source of wise counsel and encouragement. Thank you Annelle and Pat.

My older brother, Fred Brandes, is a reference point against which I read my bearings when I feel overwhelmed or lost. He is a bright, loving, kind and gentle man, who has loved me, challenged me, reassured me and affirmed me. Thank you Freddy B.

My mother's second husband, Morey Dearden, was a delightful addition to my life. I grew to love him as a father figure and in the process

I learned a lot about new-family. He was a tender, humorous man who brought many lighthearted moments to our home with his sense of humor and infectious laugh.

I want to also acknowledge two sisters, Marilyn and Betty Jean, who died early in their lives, before I was born. What is important about these sisters was their absence and the effect it had on my family. The vacuum created by their absence has everything to do with who I am, with my career choice and my interest in new-family.

I wish to acknowledge those Professors at the University of Chicago whose contributions to my academic journey helped me formulate the theoretical underpinnings of this pragmatic work. Some of these professors have passed away; my gratitude has not. My Chairman, James S. Coleman, and professors, Bruno Bettelheim, Jack (John C.) Glidewell, Roger Pillet, Herbert Thelen and Jacob Getzels. Jack Glidewell's unique insights and engaging perspective on psychosocial systems has spurred my continued inquiry into elements that differentiate the unitary design of a family (kinship) system from that which I call in this book "new-family": a "non-kinship" system of individuals functioning as family.

Thank you to the Dell Computer Corporation, Intel and Microsoft for the genie in the machinery that assisted in producing revision after revision. Thank you Hewlett Packard for the wonderfully reliable ink-jet that in ten years has never skipped a letter. Thank you to the many trees that sacrificed themselves in the shredder to make room for yet another printing.

Thank you Valerie Hugues for suggestions that strengthened passages that were weak, and gave wings to those with potential to fly. Thank you Gerry Brandes for your editorial assistance, for your objective critiques, and for making suggestions that improved the internal organization. Thank you, Dr. Charlene Follett, Kay Despard, Ann Whittemore, Katy Gray, Melissa Sibley and Susan Breene for reading and assisting with the editorial process.

Thank you Sue Knopf, Carolyn Johnson and Elizabeth Edelman for your talents. Sue designed the interior and is responsible for the typesetting. Carolyn created the cover and the illustrations. Elizabeth polished her lens for the cover photography.

Thank you Margaret McBride for believing in this work. Thank you Laura Skaalrud, Dr. Linda Harness and Maria Marinakis for just everything. Thank you Carolyn Newcomb for all the e-mail that kept me going while I was hidden away in the woods. And thank you for reminding me on occasion of the inspiration to be found in a bowl of sweet cherries capped with a little dark rum.

Thank you Virginia and Carl Leadens, and the Glen Ruis family, for making sure there were lights in my window and smoke coming from the chimney during many bitter-cold days and nights of winter. I was grateful for the love and caring of good neighbors when I was alone and vulnerable—when I was stuck in a snow bank and needed help.

Thank you Dr. Carolyn McGinnis for being a source of loving encouragement and brilliant insight during the early going. Your discursive reasoning and our stimulating, sometimes humorous, conversations left an endearing and indelible impression on some of the ideas presented on these pages.

I am very proud to be a member of two psychologist peer-consultation groups in the Twin Cities, as my fellow group members are the crème de la crème. They have provided me with professional and personal support. They are: Charlene Follett, Ph.D., Corrine Geiger, Ph.D., Sheila Herbert, Ph.D., Abby Dawkins, MSW, Susan Bourgerie, MA, Mary Lou Caskey, MA, LaNay Davis, Ph.D., and Jann Fredrickson, MSW. Thanks you guys! (That's Minnesotan for: Womyn—I love you.)

Thank you Erskine Caperton M.D., Margaret MacRae, M.D., Ignacio Fortuny, M.D., and Ronald Jankowski, M.D. my physicians who have kept me alive and functional through two major illnesses.

Kay and Dale Despard are a sustaining source of unconditional love. They have cared for me and rescued me on more than one occasion when a dinghy would just not do. For all the years this book was in process they encouraged my efforts. They read and commented on drafts, and Kay provided invaluable editorial assistance. Thank you Kay and Dale for always being there for me.

Thank you to K.M. and the goils: my stepfamily. I wouldn't have missed it for the world—karma is . . .

Thank you Dr. Anne Meissner—through you I could hear my voice echoed, and it moved me through uncertainty about this work. One of your gifts is knowing how to tilt the mirror to focus and rebound the projection.

Thank you to my fellow *partners* at Starbucks in Las Vegas, and especially Laurie LeSeney and Sherri Powell for gifts of immeasurable support. May all your shots be perfect and all your froth hold peaks. Starbucks has been my therapy. I consider it an honor to be called *barista*, and to have learned that a perfect shot is, above all, a state of mind. A Grande latte please, and hold those shots at 17.

And lastly and mostly, with ineffable gratitude, Rakeich. Thou art friend, teacher, physician, and healer—I call you a *Buddha*.

It is wonderful to be alive and dancing with life. I hope to always be aware of its wonders and each of its breath-filled moments. Thank you to all who have and are sharing the dance—be it the two-step or the tango.

Annette,
From the woods of Northern Minnesota and the
Desert of the Southwest

Index

A

Abandonment, 63
Abuse
 emotional, 102
 sexual, 102
Acting out, 61
Affection, 158
Agreements, 20
 negotiate, 27
 our style, 71
 renegotiating, 127
 unity, 81
Anger, 36, 193
 acute episodes, 53
 diminishes loving
  kindness, 44
 ex-partners, 126
 first-level reaction, 41
 managing, 42
 meditation, 43, 51
 no skill necessary, 42
 sabotages compassion,
  49
 undermines bonding,
  41
 unresolved, 37, 99

B

Bartering, 73, 75
Bedtime, 158
Birth parent
 entitlement, 143
 fear, 38
 fear of abandonment,
  63
 fears, 160
 in middle, 5, 38
 power, 160
 responsibility, 81
Blaming, 7, 142
Blended family, 4
Blending, 4
 focus of, 4
Blood
 thicker than water, 37
Bonding, 44
 patterns, 84
Books, 216

Boundaries, 62, 138, 144
 between strangers, 139

C

Change
 can I?, 31
 promotes change, 33
Chaos, 60
Children
 anger, 195
 best interest, 102, 114,
  125, 130
 boundaries, 138
 clothing, 155, 157
 do not alienate, 83
 friends outside home,
  154
 in the middle, 103, 105
 lean what they live, 85
 lost family, 121
 needs, 85
 not blameless, 141
 post-divorce adjust-
  ment, 101
 reorienting, 81
 resentment. See New-
  parent:power
 resist new-family, 168
 resistance, 195
 source of resistance,
  197
 too much power, 64
 troubled, 122, 123
Church, 153
Closeness
 differeing needs, 193
Clothing, 156
Co-head of household,
  64, 165
Co-leadership, ix
Commitment, 17, 19
 definition, 20
 emotional, 23
 in the boat, 21
Compassion, 48, 49, 50
Conflict, 5, 7, 63
 drives a wedge, 68
 reducing, 9
 sours love, 7

Cooperation, 3, 58, 65,
  69, 114
 the bridge, 70
Co-parenting, 65
Cow, 208
Create, 118
Curfew, 156
Custody, 99, 118, 244
 arrangements, 110
 renegotiating, 128

D

Dance, the, 64, 170, 173
 eliminating, 40
 not two-step, 37
Dass, Ram, 43
Date night, 46
 goal, 47
De Angelis, Ph.D., 24
Dependency needs, 85
Despair, 212
Disappointment, 6
Distancer, 213
Divided loyalties, 5, 33,
  36
Divorce, 108

E

Emotional safety, 3, 50,
  172
Emotionally safe environ-
  ment, 171, 172
Ennoble'em, 191
Entitlement, 143, 146
 changing, 144
Entitlements, 72
 determining, 178
Escalator, 10
Ex-partners
 communication, 112
 selfish, 134
Expectations, 73
 clarifying, 148
 partners, 148

F

Family
 bonded, xi
 caring, xi

doesn't feel like, 5
  no greater anchor, xi
Family-community, x, 11,
    170, 198
  strategies, 179
Familyless refugees, 98
Father
  the father, 134
Fatigue, 212, 213
Fear, 14, 15
  clarifying, 27, 238
  in control, 64
  like a wave, 25
  managing, 24
  stifles honesty, 26
  stuffing, 17
  three sources, 20
  undermines, 15
  unrecognized, 18
Feedíem, 179
Feelings, 26
  painful, 91
Fights
  his and hers, 78
First-family, 4, 11, 187
Forgiveness, 50
Friedman, Milton, 93
Friends. See Children
Fun'em, 181

G

Gay and lesbian, 223
Ghost
  buster, 23
  living, 111
  of memory, 23
Ghosts, 134
Goal
  this book, 12
Grandchildren, 190
Grandparents, 190, 191
Grief, 112, 172, 174, 175
  a partner's, 174
  Grounding, 157

H

Harmonize'em, 193
Harmony, 65, 66, 170
Heads of household, 7
Holidays, 189, 190
Holidazzle'em, 187
Home, 103, 119, 120
  stable, 118

Honesty
  without anger, 29
Household, 61
Houseparent, 148
Hurt, 15

I

Identity, 143, 144, 147
Illusion, 18, 23
I'm sorry, 50
Inner critic, 78, 79
Innies, 116, 122, 123
Inside, 149, 158, 166
Insider, 11, 59
Interdependence, 3
Intervention
  professional, 29
Intimate relationshps
  breakdown, 212
It, 47, 48

J

Jealousy, 142, 143, 144,
    147

K

Kid power, 62, 63, 64
Kids, xi
  as kids, 177
Kinship, 11

L

Levine
  Stephen, 51
  Stephen and Ondrea,
    225
Lie, the, 78
Limerence, 239
Love, 7, 50
  not solution, 8
Lovership, 44
  analysis, 55
  casualty of chaos, 212
  requirements, 46
Loving kindness, 3
Loyalty
  definition, 9
  ties, 168

M

Marriage
  defined, 36
  true, 36
Maslow, 66, 67

hierarchy of needs, 65,
    68
Master bedroom, 143
Meditation, 51
Money, 82, 214, 215
  managing, 230
Moral goal
  new-parent, 140
Mother, the, 134

N

Needs
  belonging, 66
  personal, 214, 215
Physiological, 66
  safety, 66
New-family, 3, 4, 11, 71,
    170, 198
  closeness, 171
  define expectations,
    205
  define yours, 200
  definition, 2
  demands, 208
  different, 8
  focus on structure, 5
  getting help, 207
  job description, 147
  journey, 26
  package deal, 8
  positive model, 2
New-parent, xii, 134, 141,
    164
  authority, 6
  birth parent power,
    160
  challenge, 159
  co-head of household,
    165
  depersonalization, 141
  feel powerless, 60
  giving, 163, 176
  goal, 140
  power, 138
  role, 139, 140, 148,
    149, 150
  strangers, 140
New-partners
  major task, 40
Noble, 50

O

Old dad, 38

Old mom, 38
Organize'em, 185
Other-father, xii
Other-mother, xii
Outie
  flaming, 122
Outies, 116, 117, 122, 123
Outside, 151, 158
Outsider, 59, 145

P

Pain, 37, 41, 42, 49, 61,
    112, 117, 123, 126,
    153
Parental power
  too little, 62
  too much, 62
Parentership, 208
Parenting
  definition, 162
  requires, 62
Parenting partners, 73
  co-captains, 9
Parenting partnership, 64
Parenting team, 64
Parents
  selfish, 134
Partnership, 44
  where cooperation
    begins, 69
Peaceful coexistence, 3
Pearls, 170
Personal needs
defining, 227
Possessive, 133
Possessiveness, 98
Power, 60
  appropriate, 63
  balanced, 146
  powerfulness, 164
Power struggles, 63, 98
Powerlessness, 58, 60,
    61, 65, 164
Powerlessness., 103
Primary home, 123, 125,
    127
  home base, 124
Privileges. *See*
    Entitlement
Psychologists, 219
Pursuer, 213

R

Real family, 4
Resource
  day care, 218
Resources
  books, 216
  educational classes,
    217
Risky shift, 14
Rowboat, ix, 207
  on stormy sea, 20
  tied to dock, 15
Rules, 149
  house, 80

S

School, 152
Second Chances, 108
Self-destructive acts, 90
Self-esteem, 63, 65
Self-images, 78, 79
Separation, 27
Seven tasks
  spell success, 9
Sex, 214
Sexual intimacy, 215
Shame, 78
Shaming, 141
Shunning, 141
Shuttling, 115, 120
Signing-on
  children's resistance,
    197
Sign-on
  definition, 14
  how to, 19
Social workers, 219
Solidarity, 194
  definition, 175
Stepchild, 4
Stepfamily, 2
  negative roles, 4
Stepfamily Foundation, 3
Stepmonster, 4
Structure, 5, 123
  defines relationships, 5
Submarine, 14
Success
  definition, 9
  escalator, 10
Support
  partner, 164
Support groups, 221

Survive
  definition, 2

T

Teachers
  role models, 142
Temporary enlistment, 27
Tennov
  limerence, 239
Thank you, 178
Thich Nhat Hanh, 51
Those kids, 146, 178
Thrive
  definition, 2
Ties
  loosen, 37
Transition syndrome
    (TS)
  definition, 115
Trust, 72
Trustworthiness, 62, 63
Truth, 43
Tunnel vision, 198

U

Unite
  standing united, 72
United we stand, 73
Us
  at all costs, 20, 22

V

Visitation, 99, 118, 187,
    244
  arrangements, 101
  effect on new-family,
    110
  renegotiating, 128

W

Wallerstein and
    Blakeslee, 108
War, 64
  home divided, 3
Watchíem, 184
We, 146
  defined, 36
  identity, 36
We-ness, 4, 12, 65, 66,
    69, 172, 175
  building, 193
Who am I here:, 143
Wicked stepmother, 4

About the Author
Annette T. Brandes, Ph.D.

Annette T. Brandes holds a Ph.D. from the University of Chicago. She is a Minnesota-licensed psychologist and an educator specializing in work with *new-family*. *New-family* is the family born when a biological parent and his or her children joins another adult, who may or may not have children, in the formation of a family unit. Whether these new families are stepfamilies, gay and lesbian families or domestic partner familes, their commonalities render them unique and dynamically different from biological family.

Annette has extensive experience in various practice settings, and for fifteen years she was in private practice in the Minneapolis/St. Paul area. During her thirty-year career as a counselor and therapist, she has been a featured presenter at workshops, a guest on radio and television, the keynote speaker at numerous conferences, and has provided testimony as an expert witness. In addition to her psychotherapeutic work with new-family, she has also provided psychotherapy, hypnosis and interactive guided imagery for adults and teenagers.

Dr. Brandes is on the adjunct faculty of the Minnesota College System and, in addition, she regularly conducts seminars for couples and for professionals working with new-family. Before attending the University of Chicago, Annette obtained a Master's Degree from the University of Minnesota. She is a member of the American Psychological Association, the Minnesota Society of Clinical Hypnosis and Minnesota Women Psychologists. She holds certification in interactive guided imagery from the Academy for Guided Imagery.

Dr. Brandes and her black Labrador, Louie, live in Las Vegas, Nevada, where she now devotes her time to writing and teaching. She is available for television and radio appearances, workshops, seminars and lectures. She may be contacted through Segue Publishing or via the Internet at www.abrandes.com